The Debt of a Nation

The Debt of a Nation

Land and the Financing of the Canadian Settler State, 1820–73

ANGELA C. TOZER

UBCPress · Vancouver

Printed in Canada on FSC-certified ancient-forest-free paper (100% post-consumer recycled) that is processed chlorine- and acid-free.

UBC Press is a Benetech Global Certified Accessible™ publisher. The epub version of this book meets stringent accessibility standards, ensuring it is available to people with diverse needs.

Library and Archives Canada Cataloguing in Publication

Title: The debt of a nation : land and the financing of the Canadian settler state, 1820–73 / Angela C. Tozer.
Names: Tozer, Angela C., author.
Description: Includes bibliographical references and index.
Identifiers: Canadiana (print) 20250153157 | Canadiana (ebook) 20250153246 | ISBN 9780774871556 (softcover) | ISBN 9780774871570 (EPUB) | ISBN 9780774871563 (PDF)
Subjects: LCSH: Debts, Public—Canada—History—19th century. | LCSH: Settler colonialism—Economic aspects—Canada—History—19th century. | LCSH: Credit—Canada—History—19th century. | LCSH: Loans—Canada—History—19th century. | LCSH: Land tenure—Canada—History—19th century. | LCSH: Colonists—Canada—Economic conditions—19th century. | LCSH: Indigenous peoples—Land tenure—Canada—History—19th century.
Classification: LCC HJ8513.T69 2025 | DDC 336.3/4097109034—dc23

UBC Press gratefully acknowledges the financial support for our publishing program of the Government of Canada, the Canada Council for the Arts, and the British Columbia Arts Council.

This book has been published with the help of a grant from the Canadian Federation for the Humanities and Social Sciences, through the Scholarly Book Awards, using funds provided by the Social Sciences and Humanities Research Council of Canada.

UBC Press is situated on the traditional, ancestral, and unceded territory of the xʷməθkʷəy̓əm (Musqueam) people. This land has always been a place of learning for the xʷməθkʷəy̓əm, who have passed on their culture, history, and traditions for millennia, from one generation to the next.

UBC Press
The University of British Columbia
www.ubcpress.ca

To Matt, always.

Contents

Acknowledgments

Anything that I write in these acknowledgments will fall short of capturing my gratitude for the people who literally saved my life. I know just how razor thin the line was drawn in my life between where I am now and being stuck in that life of my late teens and early twenties: struggling with trauma, struggling with domestic abuse, struggling with housing insecurity, struggling with addictions. So many of us, together. I thank first those who held me during that time but lost their lives along the way. I am so sorry. Thank you to my dad, who passed away in 2018 from his own complications. And thank you to my brother and mom.

When I started the University of Toronto's Academic Bridging Program in 2005, I had many wonderful people around me. Martina Altman's kindness and belief in me stands out during this time. Thank you to Hilly Yeung, Laura Boswell, Lawrose Grant for being wonderful. Thank you to Simona Heath, my first writing collaborator. In the Bridging Program, I had the good fortune to have J. Barbara Rose as my first professor and, as it turns out now that I'm "done" with school, one of the best professors I've ever had. I should have failed that English lit. class, and Professor Rose was one of the first people to give me a chance where it counted.

Once I became a full-time student, I met several people who would deeply influence my academic career and my intellectual life. Ritu Birla – Ritu, thank you. Words cannot express how absolutely excited I was every day attending your classes. Your lectures, the readings, everything. You showed me the language that described so much of my own life experience; your courses were such a bright moment in my life. You are the first person that I thank for deeply influencing my scholarship. This book would not be what it is if I had not known you, had not been in your courses, had not read your work. I cherish the year between my master's and PhD, when I worked as your assistant at the Centre for South Asian Studies. As it goes, I met one of my dearest friends during my undergrad, Kirubhalini Giruparajah. Kiru, your intense belief in healing, care, and love as necessary work – but also as revolutionary work – grounds this book. I am inspired by your courage and your unyielding sense of justice.

I am grateful to the wonderful folks I met at McGill University, to Elizabeth Elbourne, in particular. Elizabeth, you never made me feel like I didn't belong. I cannot convey to people who do not know Elizabeth how absolutely excited she is to engage with students' work, undergraduate and graduate alike. She always approached everyone with an open mind, fairness, and deep consideration. Elizabeth, I was always trying to impress you and do something to make you proud, with the hope that this would somehow thank you for your generosity and support.

I also want to thank both Laura Madokoro and Allan Downey. Both of these fantastic scholars shaped the way I wrote and engaged with scholarship. Laura, your comments about clarification and structure are unmatched and greatly helped the coherence of this book. Allan, thank you for all your support, from employing me as a research assistant to showing me ways to think critically about Canadian history and its relationship to ongoing settler colonialism. Other scholars at McGill – far too many to name here – also provided support for this work, but I want to especially thank Max Hamon, Elsbeth Heamon, Alex Ketchum, Vincenza Mazzeo, Jason Opal, Stephen Pigeon, Chris Reid, Rebecca Robinson, Rammy Saini, Rachel Sandwell, Travis Wysote, and the wonderful Tyler Yank. Subho Basu, thank you for our many conversations about labour and capital that influenced my reflections on the history of capitalism more generally. Subho, you are a kind and generous scholar. Finally, Shiri Pasternak offered insightful comments at a critical time in the evolution of this project and shaped its structure and overall coherence.

The list of people who have supported me since I took up a position with the Department of Historical Studies at the University of New Brunswick is long. When I interviewed for this job in the spring of 2020 – online – I was thrilled to have the opportunity to join a department with a strong history of labour and capitalism tradition that in no small part was thanks to Bill Parenteau. Tragically, Bill passed away in the fall of 2023. He was a kind, cool, punk, generous, and vivacious person. I felt like I knew Bill when I first met him because I had followed his work for nearly a decade, and the welcoming atmosphere he created made me feel at home. I especially want to thank others who asked me to dinners, who helped out with my kids and schooling, who aided me in navigating New Brunswick and the university: Funké Aladejebi, Elder Jean Bartibogue, Rachel Bryant, Gül Çalışkan, Sabine Le Bel, Erin Morton, Mercedes Peters, and Natasha Simon. Wendy Johnson, I am deeply grateful for all your support over the years. I need to say a very special thank you to Auralia Brooke for your kindness and support. And the students – the students at the University of New Brunswick have been next-level. They are kind, compassionate, critical, and open-minded. I want to thank them for making this job something that I look forward to.

The editors and production team at UBC Press have been kind, patient, and diligent. I am grateful to my editor, Randy Schmidt, who invested considerable time in guiding this process. And to my production editor, Katrina Petrik, and copyeditor, Deborah Kerr, whose intensive editing support took this work to the next level. Thank you to John van der Woude for the thoughtful cover design, and to Cheryl Lemmens for skillfully putting together the index. Thank you to the anonymous reviewers who offered helpful and attentive comments and suggestions. Any and all remaining mistakes are my own.

This work has been generously supported by the Canadian Federation for the Humanities and Social Sciences, through the Scholarly Book Awards, which supported print publication as well as Open Access publication; the Social Sciences and Humanities Research Council; the Busteed Publication Fund at the University of New Brunswick; the Department of Historical Studies at the University of New Brunswick; the McGill Institute for the Study of Canada; and the Department of History and Classical Studies at McGill University. I would also like to thank

University of Toronto Press, and McGill-Queen's University Press for permission to include published materials in this book. A special thank you is needed for all the archivists and staff who worked with me during many archival visits, and who made this work easier.

To everyone on Epekwitk (Prince Edward Island) who supported this work in various ways throughout the years, thank you. Jamie Thomas, your support of my work with Lennox Island First Nation allowed me to add a dimension to this book that I couldn't otherwise have achieved. Thank you to the wonderful archivist John Boylan at the Public Archives and Records Office of Prince Edward Island – working at this archive with someone like John is a dream come true for any historian. I am grateful to all the Pendergasts, who have shown me nothing but love and kindness from the day I met them. They welcomed me into their massive family with literal open arms (they are big huggers and talkers). What a privilege and a joy to be part of such a warm and close family. Mary Pendergast, my esteemed mother-in-law, your generosity knows no bounds, you have an inspiring zest for life, and you are the best Nana to my two children I could ever hope for. You have gone above and beyond in your support of me and my work. Thank you. Thank you to Mel Crane, my helpful and steadfast father-in-law – thank you for your support and for being a fantastic Papa to our kids.

And to my little family: Matt, Chellamma, and Fox. To be the mother of Chella and Fox has been my greatest achievement and my greatest joy. I cannot believe how lucky I am to have you both as my children. I would gladly go through everything again if I knew you two waited for me at the end. Matt, it doesn't matter if we find each other again in infinite universes in infinite lifetimes – I will never be able to speak, I will never be able to write out a single thought that could ever capture even the briefest glimmer of how dearly I love you.

Prologue: Debt and Land

It started with a kidnapped schoolgirl, a threat of financial ruin, and an undercurrent of sexual violence. Ellen Turner had just turned fifteen, and as an only child she stood to inherit her father's large fortune, which included lands outside of Manchester. In March of 1826, when the kidnapping plot unfolded, she was attending a boarding school near Liverpool. Posing as a Turner family servant, one of the kidnappers, Edward Thevenot, arrived at the school with the story that Ellen's mother was seriously ill and wished to see her. Believing this lie, the school permitted Ellen to accompany him. He conveyed her to Manchester, telling her that her father awaited her there and would take her home to Shrigley Park. Once in Manchester, however, she was met by the masterminds of the plot, Edward Gibbon Wakefield and his brother William. Their goal: manipulating her into marrying one of them. Together, the Wakefield brothers and Thevenot, their servant, created an atmosphere of fear to ensure that Ellen went along with their scheme.[1] They told her that her father was not in Manchester but had commissioned them to take her to him. Heading north, they stopped at an inn in Carlisle, where two women noticed Ellen's distress and tried to help her but were rebuffed by her abductors. The kidnappers took her to Gretna Green in Scotland, which had notoriously lax marriage requirements and where people could marry underage without parental consent. There, the fifteen-year-old was married to Edward Wakefield just shy of Wakefield's thirtieth birthday.[2] Ellen got into carriages and checked into inns with her kidnappers because they manipulated her reality, making her believe that her father was in terrible financial trouble and that she alone could save him. Spinning a web of lies that made her believe horrible stories about her father, they told her at one of the inns that her father was "concealed in a back room ... surrounded by sheriff's officers' who would arrest him for not paying his personal debts."[3] They told her that the banks her father had money in had failed, and that he had borrowed £60,000 that he could not pay.[4] Fortunately, however, all was not lost. Edward Wakefield told Ellen that if she were to marry him, she would save her father from ruin. William Wakefield claimed that he had spoken briefly with the father, who urged Ellen that if she had "ever loved him," she would not hesitate to "accept Mr. Wakefield as a husband."[5] Ellen consented and the two were married.

This was not Edward Wakefield's first venture into a dubious form of matrimony. Ten years earlier, he had "eloped" with sixteen-year-old Eliza Pattle, who was also an heiress, marrying her in Scotland, but she had died in 1820 giving birth to their third child.[6] Her mother had acknowledged Wakefield as a son-in-law, and he hoped that Ellen Turner's father would be equally compliant. But William Turner refused to cooperate. Instead, he fought the marriage, and Ellen was found and returned home, whereas the Wakefields were arrested and brought to trial.

The spectre of debt permeated this incident, as it weighed heavily on the lives of the kidnappers themselves. In fact, William Wakefield was not initially present at the trial, because he had been arrested in a civil action for debt.[7] Personal debt carried with it the undercurrent of a threat. In explaining why she consented to marriage at Gretna Green, Ellen noted that she had agreed to marry Wakefield due to her "fear, that if I did not, my papa would be ruined."[8] A jury found the Wakefield brothers guilty of kidnapping Ellen, referred to as an "infant" in the parliamentary act that annulled the marriage.[9] In his efforts to force consent from the parents of his brides, Edward Wakefield relied on social convention. Forced consent, an oxymoron, is more aptly phrased as an attempt to steal Ellen's social capital, which was derived from her virginity within the patriarchal society of nineteenth-century England, and to access her father's wealth through the capture of her body. Marriage naturally came with the assumption of consummation, and this jeopardized the possibility of future marriages for the girl, once she had been disentangled from Wakefield. Eliza Pattle's mother had accepted her daughter's "elopement" to shield her from the social ruin that might follow the rumours of pre-marital sex had her marriage to Wakefield been found to be illegitimate. The trial of the Wakefields spent some time on determining whether Edward and Ellen had had sexual intercourse. Staff at an inn where they had stayed were asked if the beds had been slept in by one or two persons and how many beds and rooms had been rented.[10] As Sergeant Cross, the counsel for the prosecution, argued, Wakefield's effort to force William Turner to accept the marriage as a fait accompli relied on "a hope that they had done something irretrievable, and that the family at Shrigley would be obliged to make the best of it" – it relied on the threat of sexual violence.[11] In 1827, an act of Parliament annulled the marriage.[12] England had enacted laws against forced marriage, which was classed as a capital felony. Luckily for the Wakefields, forced marriage no longer warranted the death penalty, after the law had been changed in 1820.[13] But because Edward and Ellen had married in Scotland, which was outside of English jurisdiction, Edward was only found guilty of abduction.[14] The jury sentenced Edward Wakefield to three years in London's Newgate Prison. Unlike his brother, William maintained his innocence and even claimed that he thought he was aiding an elopement, not an abduction. Failing to convince the jury, he, too, was sentenced to three years in jail.[15] Although what became known as the Shrigley Abduction caused a sensation at the time, it occupies a tiny space in the vast literature on Edward Gibbon Wakefield. While in prison, he turned his attention to colonization, evolving a settlement scheme that was so successful that he has been proudly touted as the "founder of New Zealand."[16] While in prison, he anonymously outlined his colonization plan in *A Letter from Sydney*, in which he posed as a wealthy landowner.[17] Once it was published in 1829, it spread like wildfire through the British liberal reformer community. Gabriel

Piterberg and Lorenzo Veracini suggest that Wakefield blamed social circumstances for forcing him to resort to drastic measures and that his "fascination with settler colonization was formed" during his time in Newgate. However, Wakefield's grandmother, Priscilla Wakefield, was a prolific and popular writer on many social "improvement" subjects, including empire and colonization, which had certainly influenced her grandson.[18] From prison, Wakefield began to make a career out of settler colonization.

Taking the Turner kidnapping as a start point for Wakefield's life-long involvement in colonization unravels the complex layers of settler colonialism that are premised on the uttermost disregard for consent and the prioritization of British male individual rights of possession over all else. Though Ellen technically consented to the marriage with Edward, the coercion, fear, and abuse that he and his confederates inflicted on her contextualize that so-called consent. This "ruse of consent" for exploitative purposes would come to ground settler colonialism in its atrocious theft of the territories of Indigenous nations. The "trick of law in settler spaces," Audra Simpson writes, "is to pretend that this in fact was not a theft that all parties consented to this fully."[19] Wakefield's conceit in marrying girls to inherit their wealth through the threat of, and possible, sexual violence, and his work on his colonization plan while imprisoned for tricking a girl into marrying him centred on this pretend consent and white supremacist patriarchal logic that delimited who had rights to their bodily autonomy and self-governance and who could forcibly take from others. When Ellen agreed to marry Edward, she succumbed to the terror and threat of violence, believing that she could save her father with her body. So-called consent in such a white supremacist heteropatriarchal system laid bare Wakefield's conquest ideology – that violent conquerors could legitimize themselves and erase their violence by an invocation of "consent." As if Ellen Turner, who had only just turned fifteen and who lived in an aggressively patriarchal society where she had few political, legal, social, or economic rights, could ever "consent" to a man such as Wakefield, whom the system privileged in so many ways. Tellingly, Ellen's father had to be the one to fight for her freedom.

How, exactly, did a convicted felon manage to enamour so many and thus change the trajectory of settler colonialism?[20] Wakefield was not a political economist, and yet his theories on the settler colonies upended the political economic orthodoxy of Adam Smith.[21] According to Michael Perelman, Wakefield won over every political economist, with the exception of John Ramsay McCulloch. Nassau Senior even praised Wakefield for advancing colonization "in the manner most beneficial to the mother country and to the colony" that "was discovered only twenty-five years ago. The discoverer was Edward Gibbon Wakefield."[22] Despite his tarnished reputation after the Shrigley Abduction, Wakefield travelled to the British North American colonies as an aide to political giant John George Lambton (Lord Durham). He even played a key role in the settler colonial logic that underpinned Lambton's 1839 *Report on the Affairs of British North America*, or the Durham Report, a foundational document of the Canadian settler state. He inspired political economists who were staunchly opposed to settler colonialism to change their minds and was praised by John Stuart Mill and other eminent theorists. Wakefield had succeeded where those before him had failed: He had found a way to pay for settler colonization; he theorized a way to transform land into a liquid asset that worked to increase its value in the colonies, in seeming perpetuity. He suggested that the colonies take out government loans on the security of Indigenous lands and waters as a way to pay for colonization.

Due to the colonial "right" (always underscored by violence) to claim Indigenous land as security for government loans, it could be bought and sold on the London money market via circulating debt instruments. Furthermore, the loans would allow the colonies themselves, not the British government, to finance their own immigration and development, which would contribute to increasing the market value of land. Importantly, Indigenous land provided them with the necessary credit to take out loans. After all, one cannot simply walk into a bank and ask for a loan – one must demonstrate creditworthiness and the ability to pay back the principal, with interest. Much as Ellen's body could secure Wakefield's future prosperity – her body was a mortgage, a debt instrument that gave the thief access to her father's capital – the territories of Indigenous nations secured capital via debt instruments such as debentures.[23] According to Robert Nichols, "dispossession merges commodification (or, perhaps more accurately, 'propertization') and theft into one moment"; Wakefield's colonization plan successfully generated credit through theft.[24] The loans, backed by Indigenous land, paid for intense settler colonialism, helped pay for the creation of the Canadian settler state, and funded Canadian imperialism.[25] Non-consensual, exploitative, and violent relationships coalesced with debt financing and cultivated a new era of colonialism that blossomed into the Canadian settler state.

The Debt of a Nation

Introduction: Racial Capital and Settler Public Credit

> National debts, *i.e.*, the alienation of the state – whether despotic, constitutional or republican – marked with its stamp the capitalistic era. The only part of the so-called national wealth that actually enters into the collective possessions of modern peoples is – their national debt. Hence, as a necessary consequence, the modern doctrine that a nation becomes the richer the more deeply it is in debt. Public credit becomes the *credo* of capital. And with the rise of national debt-making, want of faith in the national debt takes the place of the blasphemy against the Holy Ghost, which may not be forgiven.
>
> – Karl Marx, *Capital*

New Histories of Canadian Imperialism

The Debt of a Nation's central argument is that the territories of Indigenous nations directly and explicitly secured a multitude of low-interest and large-principal loans to pay for the establishment of the white settler state named Canada. Canadian public credit derived from the theft of Indigenous lands and waters. As this book will show, when the British North American governments asked London financiers for a loan, they listed unceded Indigenous homelands as their assets. In calculating how much they were willing to lend, the financiers based that amount on the projected future value of the assets. This calculated value programmed an expansionary mechanism into what became the Canadian settler state, as creating a market for land and pursuing development projects became the primary argument for how loans would be repaid. As Manu Karuka points out, the manoeuvres that emancipated capital in the mid-nineteenth century, including notions of "corporate personhood" and, here, public debts, had "delinked" claims of actual existing assets of corporations and colonial governments and had organized the value of these entities around "future claims."[1]

Edward Gibbon Wakefield created a system of colonial expansion that had the potential to never end, not because it turned out to be a fantastical perpetual motion machine, as envisioned by John Stuart Mill, but precisely because it relied on a white supremacist order that already existed throughout the British Empire and in the United States.[2] Wakefield's suggestion that a settler colony should take out a public debt to pay for itself relied on the fact that its government could do so only because its credit derived from the belief that Europeans had every right to claim the territories of Indigenous nations as assets.[3]

This book traces the unfolding of Canada and concludes that public debt financing in the British North American colonies produced three irreducible and irradicable principles that structured the settler state: the necessity of expansion throughout Indigenous territories to promise future value, the necessity of generating market value for land to access capital, and the necessity for settler colonies to consolidate to maintain good credit – expansion, market value, consolidation. *The Debt of a Nation* casts light on each of these factors by examining the public funding of private development in Upper Canada; how landownership and the ability to speculate saved the Prince Edward Island government from its credit problem; and the role of imperial guarantees in the purchase of Rupert's Land and the construction of the railways.[4] The focus on these regions highlights the importance of expansion, speculation, and consolidation in maintaining settler credit. These three factors gave the British North American colonies, which became Canada, credit to borrow, but that credit seeped from deep within a bedrock of white supremacy. In the colonies, the public debt ushered in a new era that prepared the ground for Confederation and, in fact, for white settler sovereignty.[5]

In 2016, discussing shifts in the academic approach to Canadian history, historian Jerry Bannister wrote that "settler colonialism is where the academic winds are blowing." Publishing a corrective to his essay that same year, Laura Ishiguro reminds us that "these 'academic winds' have not emerged from still air."[6] In recognition of this fact, I note that I wrote part of this book while living on the unceded territory of the Wəlastəkwey Nation, where eighteenth-century settlers expressed imperial power along the banks of the Wolastoq River, as Wəlastəkwey historian Andrea Bear Nicholas has mapped.[7] She frames settler colonialism *as* imperialism, an approach that is central to *The Debt of a Nation*. Heidi Kiiwetinepinesiik Stark's historical inquiry into Canada as a "criminal empire" sees Canada as an imperial power that trespassed on the territories of Indigenous nations and disregarded their laws.[8] In writing this book, I wanted to understand the historical context in which the Canadian nation-state was born, and I conclude that the many threads that stitched Confederation together derived from an imperial wool. As Bear Nicholas and Stark show, the imperial power of Canada is primarily expressed over Indigenous nations.

This book highlights how the early Canadian settler state clutched onto British imperial power, which metastasized settler sovereignty and jurisdiction throughout the territories of Indigenous nations. Shiri Pasternak writes that the settler colonial Canadian imperial project centres on the contest for jurisdictional control of land, life, and resources.[9] *The Debt of a Nation* narrates Confederation as a transfer of imperial power from Britain to Canada and reads foundational documents such as the Durham Report of 1839 and the British North America Act of 1867 through this lens. The mid-nineteenth century witnessed an acceleration of British imperialism's cancerous growth in settler colonies that were premised on the destruction of human and other-than-human lifeworlds for capital, as explored in this book. The advent of public debt financing in the early nineteenth century contributed significantly to the realization of Canada and Canadian imperialism.

The Debt of a Nation pulls together settler colonial studies, Indigenous studies, and studies on racial capital to understand Canada and Canadian historical scholarship in the bright light of critiques from scholars such as Bear Nicholas and Stark. I wrote this book, not from an assumption of Canada as a reified political entity with naturally legitimate claims to Indigenous geographical spaces, but from the perspective of a transfer of British imperial power to Canadian imperial power. In a sense, this view holds Canadian history as a self-contained rendering of the Canadian state, its citizens, its immigrants, and its institutions. How can Canadian history making and makers capture the imperial power dynamic that makes itself felt, albeit in a variety of ways, to every person who lives in this place? And, a question that I've often directed at myself: Can a Canadian historian who (intentionally or not) participates in and benefits from Canada's ongoing imperial conquests write about that history with any sort of clarity? Historians of "new" British imperial history have long understood, sometimes ironically, the acquisition of empire in a "fit of absence of mind," as the oft quoted late nineteenth-century historian John Robert Seeley wrote.[10] Many Canadians probably do not see themselves as part of an imperial project, even when such imperialism permeates the news, our government structure, settler cultural production, and so on. Jim Reynolds, an expert in "Aboriginal" law, notes that there was "no anti-imperialist movement of any size" in Canada; Canadians were "enthusiastic imperialists."[11] As Seeley observed some 140 years ago, much the same was true for Britons and their historians.

In fact, all settler Canadians perpetuate this imperial power, whether they know it or not. This does not mean that individual settlers did not have good intentions, but as the literary historian Rachel Bryant puts it, attempts to spread the "Good Newes" of positive settler intentions have historically worked as "colonial propaganda from this continent that sought to develop and naturalise notions of Western sovereignty and dominion over Indigenous lands and peoples."[12] *The Debt of a Nation* turns away from, and refuses to contribute to, the many historical biographies on settlers, focusing instead on the often invisible structures that trapped individuals in a system that limited their choices.[13] But one does get tired of explaining that the intentions of individual settlers have nothing to do with the power structures that limit their options for "good" choices.[14] Narratives that attempt to rehabilitate the settler sift through historical evidence to present one settler or the other as "one of the good ones" or as a person "who helped," without making any reference to the ample evidence of the role of imperialism, capitalism, and colonialism in shaping their lives as it shapes ours.[15] Not only does this exercise read as an emotionally wrought settler move to innocence, but it completely misses the contours of Canadian imperialism and a truly phenomenal amount of historical and contemporary evidence.[16] For example, this omission is apparent in some historical scholarship that focuses on the development of Canadian business but refer only vaguely to "investment" as the source of capital. Even business histories that centre on the literal colonization of Indigenous territories give the impression that businesses relied on a "service of a capital fallen from heaven" to build Canada.[17] This capital, it needs emphasizing, made colonialism possible.

The colonial governments of British North America acquired capital to develop through debt. Specifically, the technology of a public debt issued as securities on the London Stock Exchange (LSE) fashioned the Canadian settler state in an immensely profound way. It was no coincidence that the rise of public debt financing on the LSE from the 1820s onward coincided with settler colonialism and the emergence of the Canadian settler state. This analysis of Canada's public debt narrates such a history and outlines the structure of Canadian imperialism. It also encourages further research that does not present Canada as a stable, discrete, national entity and hopes that scholars will deploy an analytical lens that can discern imperialism – even when they themselves are implicated in it.

Much of this book reflects on the universalizing logic behind the imperial transfer of power. Liberal universalizing relates all human, other-than-human, and diverse spaces to a capitalist conceptualization of value that renders all things commensurate within the function of markets. I end this study in the 1870s, when the 1872 Dominion Lands Act and the 1876 Indian Act concretized Canada's imperialism in law. The Indian Act, in particular, legally marked all Indigenous nations as a universalized category named "Indian" for the specific purpose of eradicating this legal status, attempting to end nation-to-nations treaties, and freeing up the land to colonize.[18] Under this universalizing liberal logic, the idea of the nation is predicated on sameness for the purpose of imperial expansion over the territories of Indigenous nations that attempted and attempts to sustain only one nation over one territory. It "recognizes" the sovereignty of Indigenous nations, but at the same time it actively denies their right to self-determination and their jurisdiction (particularly legal jurisdiction) because it claims all the land as national territory that is universalized as Canadian. The "nested" sovereignty, as Audra Simpson calls it, is lost in this recognition process because, from the view of the state, it is sovereignty without jurisdiction or self-determination – a hollowed-out sovereignty.[19]

The universalizing of discrete Indigenous nations as "Indian" also facilitates the erasure of Canadian imperialism. After all, how can one perceive imperialism if one only recognizes Indigenous people as individuals who are managed under Canada's "Indian" policy? Canada as an imperialist power continuously attempts to invade the territories of Indigenous nations and to eradicate and assimilate Indigenous individuals, whom it pulls out of their communities to open up space for "just settlement."[20] Casting this imperialism as "internal colonization" does not capture the historical and contemporary fact that it is, and has always been, directed at Indigenous nations for the explicit purpose of gaining access to resources, including grounding the Canadian economy in a real estate market.[21] Shiri Pasternak and Tia Dafnos explain how Indigenous peoples "disrupt" the circuitry of capital and how the Canadian settler state, in turn, violently attempts to "secure" capital.[22] This book also follows the lead of scholars who link Canadian imperialism with mining and banking initiatives that occur outside its claimed borders.[23]

Indigenous Lands as Settler Government Assets

The English word "credit" originates from the Latin *credere:* to believe, to trust. The public credit, Karl Marx laconically commented, was the "*credo* of capital."[24] Public credit made nations. It allowed them to borrow unprecedented amounts to pay for their wars, development, and imperial expansion, but all of this was possible only if lenders saw them as creditworthy – capable of paying off the loans at some point in the future.[25] Settler colonial governments commonly used the public debt to fund private companies to build public works, canals, railways, and a multitude of other projects.[26] Though debts existed in some form in many human societies, and Britain began to incur its own public debt in the 1690s, not until after the formalization of the London Stock Exchange (LSE) in 1801 did every nation have the potential to participate directly in what was then the new credit economy. In the 1820s, public debts issued as securities on the LSE increased exponentially. Britain's early nineteenth-century debt market ballooned – and burst – with the Latin American "loan bubble." Between 1822 and 1825, British investors speculated fervently on Latin American government securities, which eventually led to the collapse of the Latin American debt market.[27] Other national debts as a place for speculation and investment carried on, particularly France's *rentes* (government securities). In Britain, however, being unable to pay one's debts could lead to a stretch in debtors' prison until reformers lobbied to change laws that punished indebted individuals. As the early nineteenth century progressed, debt slowly became an acceptable method of finance across the British Empire.[28]

The gradual social acceptance of a system of credit and debt was accompanied by an explosion of public debts on the LSE. Diverse social interpretations of debt and credit, however, endured from the eighteenth century into the nineteenth. Mary Poovey shows that the emergent credit economy infiltrated many aspects of British society, including fiction writing. For example, Daniel Defoe argued that "the system of public credit" was a "national resource," and he devised the figure of Lady Credit to portray both the instability and the appeal of the credit economy.[29] His use of a female persona tied in with the popular view of credit as irrational, volatile, and susceptible to emotional outbursts but also as highly desirable if treated correctly. Terry Mulcaire contends that these acutely gendered philosophical musings about credit reified it as an object of value. Accessing credit was not seen as a moral failing, but as a rational decision to pursue a valuable object, just as a virtuous man would court a worthy woman.[30]

The canny *Homo economicus* used credit to his advantage and thus displayed both the ability to reason and the attributes of a "civilized" man.[31] From the outset, the credit economy relied on a white supremacist order that naturalized the British debt economy as civilized and became profoundly implicated in colonial expansion. Lance Davis and Robert Huttenback show that the "vast majority" of British capital went to the "colonies of white settlement," arriving in the form of low-interest and large-principal loans to settler governments.[32] Borrowed money became the capital that built the settler colonies.[33] One must be careful, however, not to draw too much of a distinction between white settler colonies and those in places such as India. This distinction is somewhat anachronistic, particularly in the mid- to late nineteenth century. Although liberal reforms took root in Upper Canada and Tamil Nadu in very different ways, the market governance that shaped their colonial governments had the same underlying liberal logic. Ritu Birla shows that the reformer attempts to make India more conducive to capitalist exploitation employed legislation that tried to change "vernacular" practices such as land holding in families. Indeed, this focus on India as a birthplace of the practices of modern capitalism highlights the fundamental importance of British imperialism to the function of a global market economy.[34]

In discussing why so many people chose to emigrate from Britain during the 1830s, James Belich suggests that there are many "missing pieces" in this "Anglo migration jigsaw puzzle" and hints at an unexplained mystery.[35] However, Jack Harrington argues that "to dismiss" settler colonial policy, "as James Belich does, is to fail to integrate settler colonialism into the history of mainstream political thought in a way that individual national histories can only ever do partially."[36] Duncan Bell offers a salient explanation for the 1830s turning point in British emigration when he examines the shifts in political economic concern for settler colonies.[37] *The Debt of a Nation* offers its own deceptively simple explanation for the change: public debts paid for colonization. They solved three interrelated problems in the settler colonies that had hindered mass colonization. To put it simply, they solved the trifecta of how to pay for people, how to pay for things, and how to increase the market value of lands and waters. They would pay for immigrants, who would increase the value of the land through their labour and physical occupation. They would pay for the development projects, such as canals and railways, that were essential to increase land value. They also gave land liquidity, as future value could circulate as debentures, bonds, and other debt instruments on money markets.[38] All three of these elements worked together to give Indigenous land market value as property. As Henry Yu notes, the public debt made real estate "real."[39]

Settler colonies could avail themselves of credit from the security of Indigenous lands because the government debt was underwritten by the Doctrine of Discovery, a set of beliefs that allowed a European nation to claim sovereignty over any newly "discovered" land that was not occupied or governed by Christians and therefore not inhabited by people whom it perceived as civilized. Emerging from the Crusades, it was enshrined in a series of fifteenth- and sixteenth-century papal bulls, which essentially gave designated Christians the legal right to deprive non-Christians of their lands and sovereignty, and even to enslave and murder them.[40] The papal bulls framed a logic of who had the right to possess land, which underpins Canada's current claims to land.[41] Eventually, rights derived from the colonizing and enslaving logic behind the Doctrine of Discovery gave the British Crown title over the territories of Indigenous nations and bestowed it on British colonizers. In addition, Indigenous land could be claimed via the logic of conquest, especially in connection with the War of the Spanish Succession (1701–14) and the War of the Austrian Succession (1740–48), which ended with the 1713 Treaty of Utrecht and the 1748 Treaty of Aix-la-Chapelle, respectively.[42] Each treaty shifted Indigenous land from one European power to another. When Britain defeated France in the Seven Years' War (1756–63), it applied the European conventions of war to claim jurisdiction over the territory that the French had lost. Britain had a "right" to the land by both "the right of conquest" and the "right of cession."[43] In 1763, Britain generated a Royal Proclamation, which established that the British Crown held the highest title in land, or the right of preemption, in the British North American colonies.[44] At best, this system extended British usufructuary rights to Indigenous nations and "recognized" what came to be known as "Aboriginal title" in Canadian law; at worst, it made space for a campaign to remove Indigenous peoples from their homelands. Within a British property system of varied and stratified land titles, settlers could own private property that ultimately belonged to the Crown, where the Crown still had the jurisdiction to expropriate privately owned lands.[45] The 1763 Royal Proclamation also made it so that only the Crown could appropriate Indigenous lands, and that everything west of the Appalachian mountain range would, in theory, be off limits to settlers – that is, until the Crown acquired Indigenous lands. This property system guaranteed the Crown's ownership rights and allowed for westward expansion under imperial sovereignty and territoriality.[46] As John Stuart Mill pointed out, a secure property system could be leveraged to pay for immigration and development, both of which had the potential to raise land value.[47] All of this, however, depended on the credo of whiteness.

To a capitalist, everything was potential capital – land, water, even the eel larvae that emerged from the Sargasso Sea could all become assets to determine credit. Things, places, humans, and other-than-human beings become valuable when they can be exchanged on a market, releasing potential capital. The public debt in settler colonies was the upfront payment to execute these market transactions. At its core, the system of capitalism allows for this exchange to occur through institutions such as stock exchanges, banks, and even national governments that establish legal rights that protect capital.[48] However, before one can access potential capital, one must first claim ownership over a thing that is objectified as potential capital. This was how the system of racialized chattel slavery worked: individuals who were kidnapped from Africa were rendered as capital through a complex global legal and policing system that linked Blackness to property.[49] Property, Aileen Moreton-Robinson observes, is marked as the white possessive that allows for ownership claims centred on the virtue of "civilization."[50] All capital derived from the right to possess property is racialized, including capital drawn from the low wages of labour that ensure capital profits. Racial difference legitimized the possession of people, lands, waters, non-human beings, and everything on Earth and even beyond.[51] Jodi A. Byrd warns us, however, that contemporary discourses on racialization affect critiques of colonialism, and "the structuring logics of dispossession are displaced onto settlers and arrivants who substitute for and as indigenous in order to consolidate control and borders at that site of differentiation."[52] We must remember that a focus on race should never preclude an analysis of settler colonialism. In the case of Canada, the settler colonial project of multiculturalism detaches Indigenous peoples from land and racializes them as part of a "diverse" population in a naturalized Canadian state. Global anti-Blackness and the theft of Indigenous lands were and are a part of the same system.[53]

Throughout this book, I use Cedric Robinson's and Sylvia Wynter's conceptualizations of racial capital developed out of Black South African articulations of capitalism and colonialism.[54] "Racial capital" does not refer to capitalism as a system that produces racism in order to privilege one "race" over another. On the contrary, it refers to a system where all capital is derived from a hierarchical system of exploitation that requires racialization to make that exploitation justifiable. This start point of capitalism does not foreclose the possibility of gender or other social hierarchies. Stephanie Smallwood corrects Marx's "misunderstanding of slavery" and points out that "slave-trading was analogous to the capitalist labour market because it gave birth to the capitalist mode of production."[55] Ableism, sexism, and homophobia make certain people easy to exploit because they fall outside of white heteropatriarchal power structures; however, white supremacy undergirds all of these social relations. Scholars in Indigenous studies and Black radical tradition, and particularly Black feminists, have long connected the advent of colonialism that bonded racialized chattel slavery to the emergence of capitalism.[56] The processes that removed Black people from the category of human originate in the twinned genealogies of labour and property (human and otherwise) that buttress European philosophical and scientific discourses of race.[57] These genealogies iron out the ethical kinks in European colonialism that are at odds with Christian, Enlightenment, and even humanist self-interpretation, establishing a normative regime that dictates who must labour and who must possess. The heritage of the settler state, born out of these interrelated genealogies of labour and property, does more than describe the differences in so-called races. As Patrick Wolfe notes, in the American context, the one-drop rule gave individuals with "any evidence of any African ancestry whatsoever" the legal status of slave; this stands in contrast to the attempts to reduce the number of people legally recognized as Indigenous by the settler state.[58]

Patrick Wolfe interprets race in settler colonies as the progeny of Enlightenment race theory that was tied to the idea of the Great Chain of Being and supported by philosophers such as Immanuel Kant and David Hume.[59] Iyko Day challenges this idea and offers a differing model for the understanding of race in settler colonies, which I have taken as the heart of this book. She dispenses with the Great Chain of Being, which positions humanity as shackled to whiteness and maleness, placing the western European man at the top of the hierarchy and his "natural" foil, the enslaved Black woman, at the bottom – just one link above animality and sometimes not even qualifying for inclusion on the chain.[60] Day presents a triad model of race in the settler colonies – Settler, Native, and Alien – each one a point on the triangle, where land becomes the centre on which race is made legible. In settler colonies, people are racialized in relation to land, or rather in relation to their perceived natural right to possess it.[61] In settler colonies, land possession gives race meaning; however, it needs to be stressed that the right of possession was and is legitimized through anti-Blackness.[62] Settlers attempt to "indigenize" themselves in a variety of ways, including appropriating Indigenous medicines as their own or, in Canada, by singing "Our home and native land!/Terre de nos aïeux!" to legitimize themselves as the true possessors of the land.[63] The settler colonial project racialized Indigenous peoples through various mechanisms, such as the criminalization of treaty rights in order to decouple them from their lands and waters. Joanne Barker notes that "imperialism's capitalism can only expand itself *in perpetuity* by reproducing social relations of gross inequality between the state and Indigenous peoples."[64] Day's category of Alien includes all non-Indigenous racialized peoples in a hierarchy of those who are closest to whiteness and those who are farthest away. They become the source of labour, with no claim to land. We must be careful, however, to make a clear distinction between Black people and other racialized people because the settler-state structure predicated on white supremacy is intelligible only through global anti-Blackness.[65] Capitalism relied on these racialized social relationships mapped onto class stratification to create a world in which certain people deserved "degraded servitude" and the status of "labour."[66]

The settler colonial paradigm of genocide that posits itself as the possessor of everything in the territories of Indigenous nations through displacement and/or assimilation is grounded in racial difference, but the epistemologies and methodologies of race need a site-specific evaluation. The investment of capital, the creation of a public debt for investment, the leveraging of a white tax-paying public as the risk-bearer of loans, and, importantly, the credit derived from Indigenous homelands all built the settler colony – a process replicated *mutatis mutandis* across the British settler colonies.[67] The idea of Indigenous land as a *vacuum domicilium* (empty and unused) that could be redeemed by labour and a transformation into private property presented colonialism as just. Audra Simpson points out that the settler state deploys "self-authorizing techniques and frameworks that sustain dispossession and occupation" that open up an "imagined space of just settlement," which echoed European ideas about the "just war" that fuelled the Crusades.[68]

If the papal bulls legalized racialized chattel slavery and land theft for Europeans to enact on the world, John Locke's liberal philosophy provided a deep moral and even ethical justification for colonialism. Locke suggested that human beings progressed from a "state of nature" and into one of "civilization," applying their labour to land and producing a grain crop for sale in a market – a liberal fantasy sustained through a process of racialization.[69] One would be hard-pressed to find a version of this narrative that did not include a racialized subject to act as a foil for the "civilized" group. Locke's *Two Treatises on Government* outlines colonial possession, but as Lisa Lowe stresses, a society that relied on slavery did not progress to a liberal "free" democracy. Instead, she suggests that liberalism, particularly its mid-nineteenth-century "free" labour and "free" trade iteration, "consisted in the power to adapt and improvise combinations of colonial slavery *with* new forms of migrant labour, monopoly *with* laissez-faire, and an older-style colonial territorial rule *with* new forms of security and governed mobility."[70] In testament to this, even though he supported free trade, John Stuart Mill praised Scottish-born Canadian political economist John Rae in his articulation of protectionist economies for the settler colonies.[71] As this book moves through the history of Canada's own public debt, it does so submerged in the deep waters of discourses on race that surged into capitalism.

The Construction of the White Settler Public

We must ask ourselves why the British North American colonies had to be "white" and not be satisfied with the easy answer that the Fathers of Confederation were "racist" and a "product of their times." This explanation not only attempts to absolve our own position in a system of exploitation, but it gives us nowhere to go. It cannot capture the nuances of how colonizers deployed race for the explicit purpose of turning a profit. Henry Yu comments, "the capture of the state's power in the nineteenth and early twentieth centuries supplied both the means and the ends of implementing white supremacy for the benefit of increasing majorities of European migrant settlers, both men and women. Is it enough to sincerely say that 'we don't believe in that anymore'?"[72] *The Debt of a Nation* shows that if settler colonial governments were to access British money markets, they had to position themselves as white, because a white settler public could be taxed and, as Chapter 5 shows, the men who championed opening up the west had anxieties about how to establish a tax-paying and "civilized" population there. Taxes and the public debt were intertwined. The ability to tax gave the government another layer in its aura of creditworthiness because it assured creditors and investors that payments would not be missed.[73] At the same time, taxpayers themselves were rooted in white possessiveness. "Taxpayer subjects," Kyle Willmott shows, imagine that they have certain rights to spaces because they pay taxes. He explains that they "figure themselves as both legitimate based on a settler tax imaginary that sees tax as a form of white property, and as an officiant of legal sovereignty over Indigenous nations."[74] In many ways, taxes contributed to the regimes of legitimacy that colonial governments needed to "justly" possess Indigenous lands. Although taxes could pay for and sustain colonial ventures, they obviously could not do so if the colony had no population to tax. Taxes and the public debt functioned differently, with the latter generating market value for property in the colonies.[75] Taxes alone could not solve the problem of financing development, and importantly, because they came after claims of territorial possession, they could not raise land value. A colonial government could levy taxes if needed to pay for loans and interest and could use the ability to tax to secure public loans. Taxes themselves were vitally important to the creation of a settler subjectivity that was centred on the right to possess Indigenous land.[76]

As an integral part of "civilization," the white settler body politic had both the knowledge and the ability to contract a loan. Tax and contract shaped and continue to shape the Canadian settler state. All the loans for the public debt had to have specific contracts that described their amounts, number and type of debt securities that could circulate and their price, repayment schedule, interest rate payments, amortization period, and other special circumstances such as a mandate for sinking funds. The contracts were passed in law in colonial and imperial parliaments. David Stasavage convincingly shows the links between the national debt and representative government. He argues that representative government allowed the British government to make credible commitments to borrowing, as forces external to the government held it accountable to debt and interest repayments. Hence, acts of parliament created the loan as a type of contract that outlined, and inscribed in law, the terms of the loan. This was also true of the settler colonies, as the loans the colonial government took out were made legal via a government act.[77] Creditors needed assurance that colonial governments would not default, and that assurance came in the image of a gentlemanly colonist who adhered to the rules of the white patriarchal market society.

The belief in the sound public credit of the white settler colonies determined their creditworthiness. The public debt, or the "alienation of the state," as Marx phrased it, emphasized that the state had to sell itself to investors, literally through debt securities and figuratively when negotiating loans. In settler colonies, a pure-blooded lineage of British settlers sold the creditworthiness of the public to investors. Historically, public credit in Canada depended on a white supremacist order in two fundamental ways: the settler public as white for "good credit" and a violent legal regime that welded together whiteness and rights to possess beings and things that were objectified as property. Manu Karuka's concept of "shareholder whiteness" is helpful here. Karuka notes that "whiteness, as a form of property, can be understood as the capacity to be an owner" and uses W.E.B. Du Bois's formulation of the "dividends of whiteness" that allowed certain peoples to reap the material benefits of "shares" at the expense of those who were racialized as Black and Indigenous.[78] The settler state's proximity to whiteness that eased access to credit might even partially explain why other methods of labour and capital transplantation did not occur in British settler spaces, as they did elsewhere during the same period. For example, racialized indentured labour schemes in a variety of British colonies to enforce low wages were meant to replace the system of racialized chattel slavery after Britain abolished it in 1833–34. "Good credit" floated on whiteness, as Destin Jenkins highlights in his assessment of Standard and Poor's bond ratings in the 1980s.[79] For good credit, the public had to be white.[80] The white settler public acted as both risk-bearer of the loan as a civilized body politic and as the imagined civilized taxpayers who ensured the prompt and sustained payment of interest.[81]

It was important that the settler colonial public be perceived as white and male for public credit. John Stuart Mill, who was so strongly in favour of colonization that he expanded the principles of political economy to include the colonies, believed that public debts could make it work.[82] However, it would succeed only if the colonial governments that contracted the loans behaved in a morally upstanding fashion. On October 15, 1868, three years after the end of the American Civil War, he lambasted the United States government for failing to live up to this standard. The war had increased the national debt from $65.0 million to $2.7 billion.[83] In 1862, desperately attempting to avoid bankruptcy and the possibility of losing the war due to a lack of funds, Congress had passed the controversial Legal Tender Act and authorized the issue of non-specie-backed "greenbacks." In other words, dollar bills became little more than printed paper and were no longer a representation of gold that actually existed. The government also instituted a complex national banking system that created a myriad of problems, making it vulnerable to financial panics.[84]

Once the war ended, the government debt become controversial. Washington wanted to resume specie payments of paper money. This meant that it moved to reduce the number of greenbacks to increase their value, as their post-war worth stood at $35.09 to $100.00 of gold.[85] The depreciation in the value of paper currency raised serious concerns among British investors who held American bonds.[86] Legally, the interest for the national debt had to be paid in gold, not bills, though it was unclear if the principal had to be paid in gold as well. In the United States, the greenbackers, or "soft money" side, insisted that paper money could be used to pay both the principal and the interest for the national debt. They were opposed by the "hard money," or bullionist, faction, which favoured gold.[87]

Mill disagreed with the proponents of soft money. Arguing that the debt must be repaid in gold, he pointed to the moral obligation of honouring the terms of the original contract. His rejection of the soft money alternative shows that those who approved of the national debt for financing government expenditure still tread through morally murky waters. Dramatically, he stated that changing the terms of the contract would be "one of the heaviest blows that could be given to the reputation of popular governments, and to the morality and civilization of the human race."[88] The familiar civilized/uncivilized tropes informed his ideas about the responsibility of the people to the government and the government to the people. The public debt bound the public to the government, but it also bound governments to their creditors in contract. If Washington opted to pay the debt in greenbacks, it would break the contract that obligated it to British bondholders. At the same time, the nature of public debt financing made American taxpayers responsible for their government's debt.

Mill argued that specific bonds had contracts for their interest to be paid with "a promise made by a whole people through their authorised agents." Although Mill referred to "a whole people," by which he meant the public, he was actually defending the private interests of the wealthy. He added that though the citizens "of European countries have sometimes been told that they are not bound to pay their national debts, because the money was borrowed by kings and aristocracies who did not represent the people ... none of these lame excuses can be alleged by the American repudiators."[89] The issue was not that the United States intended to default on its debt, but that it wanted to change the terms of the contract in its favour. This would be achieved by manipulating the value of American money and through a suggested tax on bonds. Mill's comments regarding United States monetary policy reveal the complicated relationship between the national debt and the shades of difference between representative and responsible government.[90] In other words, even if governments contracted debts and the money from those debts paid for development and wars, the people were morally bound to the good standing of the national debt. Rhetorically, the "people" could merge easily with the interests of the colonial government because they were bound together through whiteness. The morality of national debts became an issue only when a government threatened to break the contract.

Of course, Indigenous nations were not party to the settler public debt. If the debt were to grow, both they and their territories had to shrink. A loan as a method of capital investment carried with it the multifaceted violence of displacement, isolation on reserves, incarceration of Indigenous children, land theft, and criminalization of treaty rights. In constructing the settler public as white, Wakefield argued that "the land is held by the Government as a trustee for the people," characterizing the settler colonial process itself as democratic and conducted for the benefit of the people. He added that "extinction of Native Title was the indispensable first step in the work of laying open land for appropriation and use by the industrious settlers."[91] Technically, of course, "the people" could include Indigenous peoples, as was the case in Lower Canada, where they could possess the rights of citizens.[92] Importantly, however, this never extended to recognizing their sovereignty or jurisdiction over land. By the mid-nineteenth century, colonial reformers and settler colonial governments alike saw the advantages of taking out a public debt to both raise the market value of land in the colonies and to fund British settlers who relocated to them. Philip Girard argues that under eighteenth-century debtor-credit law, land could be alienated from titleholders in the case of unpaid debt. Mortgages were "more creditor oriented procedures for realizing on land given as security." Settler colonial law changed the laws of primogeniture and made the state of land titles publicly known, which enabled buying and selling land as a commodity.[93] At the end of this process, "land," Girard writes, "is security."[94]

Writing in the midst of the COVID-19 pandemic, Robyn Maynard shows the ways in which "Black peoples are continuously outside the register of the 'public' within common framings of public safety and health."[95] This exclusion of Black people as "alien" has a long history in Canada. For example, during the 1860s, a scheme formed that some "60,000 people of colour now in Canada" would "all [be] taken to Jamaica," where they were expected to enter into three-year indentured labour contracts upon arrival. The Jamaican government engaged in this project with the sanction of "Her Majesty's Ministers and the concurrence of the Canadian Ministers." Although the governor of Jamaica noted that such schemes proved largely unsuccessful, he urged the Africa Aid Society to help it along.[96] Racialized as labour in the transatlantic slave trade, the Black settlers were segregated by the settler state, classed as alien and lacking any claim to land. Their removal would do its part in ensuring that Canada remained a white colony and highlights the fissures in the meanings of race in a settler state. Settler efforts to control Indigenous peoples concentrated on assimilation, with the idea that their territories would be assimilated into the state as well, which led to the attempted termination of their treaty rights.[97] The settler state, therefore, deployed methods of both segregation and assimilation, with the aim of achieving a white body politic.[98] Whiteness is both "the very thing that constitutes the state" and "the very thing that is forgotten."[99] As Katherine McKittrick puts it, Black peoples, knowledges, and history "are not 'Canada,' are not supposed to be Canada, and contradict Canada; they are surprises, unexpected and concealed."[100] The red herring of diversity and inclusion as a path toward justice obfuscates the fact that settler states originated in the attempts to destroy Black and Indigenous lives, knowledge systems, and kinship networks.

A Note on My Approach

As I wrote this book, I hoped to make complex and often opaque accounting and stock exchange information accessible to general and academic readers who may be unfamiliar with economics. Elsbeth Heaman frankly remarks that tax "historians work with the most boring documents imaginable, and they focus on the kind of evidence that makes other historians' eyes glaze over when they stumble across it."[101] Regrettably, my own experience confirms this. One day, I was at the Guildhall Library in London, looking through London Stock Exchange documents when a record of securities listings caught my eye. Digging deeper, I found other documents of the same type, all in massive leather-bound, frayed, and decaying nineteenth-century books. Being a public library, Guildhall had all sorts of people reading and using the computers. Drawn by the interesting-looking books on my desk, a few people asked me what they were. However, when I showed them the pages, with their lists and lists of nothing but numbers, they just nodded and drifted away. Unlike, for example, a journal from the nineteenth century or old photographs, the records themselves, reams of numbers relieved by little else, are far from interesting. So, how do you write an engaging historical narrative about the "most boring documents imaginable"? Trawling through the records to track any changes in monetary amounts or number of securities is one thing, but trying to show other people why you think these documents are important is quite another.

I decided not to focus my analysis solely on numbers – though quantitative analysis can be found throughout these pages. My goal was to find the right balance between narrative and quantitative data in looking at the origins of a complex economic system of credit and debt. There are places throughout the work where I suggest avenues for further research, but much of it deals with how the public debt was raised and with the structures that made it possible. I do not linger on minutiae, such as what loans versus taxes paid for in settler colonial development. I do offer one caveat: the financial records are neither straightforward nor necessarily reliable. I return to this issue in Chapter 5, when I discuss contemporary disagreement about Canada's financial accounts and what was considered debt.

In Chapter 4, I also include oral history evidence from Mi'kmaw Elders and members of the Mi'kmaw community on Lennox Island, Epekwitk/Prince Edward Island. This chapter highlights the specifics of "on the ground" land appropriation. I wanted to stress the histories of the people who had their land stolen, so I chose to centre oral histories in this particular narrative. No other chapter explicitly focuses on the creation of First Nations' reserves, and I wanted to present this history in a way that could include Mi'kmaw evidence. Unsurprisingly, oral histories from Mi'kmaw Elders challenge settler history making.

Chapter Outline

The Debt of a Nation is divided into two parts. Part 1 begins with Britain and the London Stock Exchange, discussing various changes that facilitated the emergence of Canada's public debt. Chapter 1 examines how the public debt idea arose in Britain and explores shifts in political economy, as well as the colonial reform movement launched by Edward Gibbon Wakefield, which concentrated on financing settler colonialism through debt. Chapter 2 looks at the appropriation of Indigenous territories as assets for colonial public credit on the London Stock Exchange.

Part 2 shifts the focus to Canada itself and its public debts. The first Canadian public debt to be issued as securities on the London Stock Exchange, the subject of Chapter 3, was that of Upper Canada. The Upper Canadian government used public debt financing to pay for development, with the hope that this would raise the market value of land. A part of this process involved land reforms, specifically of the clergy reserves, land set aside for use by the Protestant clergy, to access potential capital and highlights the mechanics of expansion behind public debt financing. Chapter 4 turns to the public debt of Prince Edward Island. Unlike the Province of Canada, the island had virtually no Crown land, which meant that most of it was privately owned, typically by absentee British landlords. Using the island as an example, the chapter concentrates on the government's struggle to overturn this system, which would enable a climate of speculation and access to credit. Finally, Chapter 5 explores three significant imperial loan guarantees that paid for Confederation: the Intercolonial Railway loan, the Rupert's Land loan, and the Canadian Railway loan. The guarantees enabled Canada to borrow at a lower interest rate. This cheap money was made possible only via a white supremacist economic ordering that prioritized white nations. The Conclusion of *The Debt of a Nation* discusses what the history of Canada's public debt tells us about the possibility of short-circuiting ongoing Canadian imperialism.

PART I
Public Debt and Colonialism

Colonial Reform: Political Economy, Labour, and Land Value

1

> The working of the scheme will be as follows. A sum of money, say 100,000*l*., is raised on the security of the sale of lands. With this sum a great supply of labour is taken out; this *certain* supply of labour induces capitalists to emigrate (many have already expressed that intention); these capitalists will purchase lands, and the proceeds of the sale, after paying the interest of the loan, will be employed in carrying out more labour. This, again, leads to further purchases of land, and the price is applied to further emigration; and so the stream of emigration is perennially kept up, without any advance of money beyond the original one.
>
> – John Stuart Mill, "The New Colony" (2), 1834

To Secure and to Liquidate Indigenous Lands

Market value radiated from the public debt and sparked life into the machine of settler colonialism. The "scheme" mentioned by John Stuart Mill in the passage above – the colonization of South Australia – supposed that the "security of the sale of lands" would enable a public loan to the colony. Mill's support of the idea that a colony should use its government debt to fund its population and development illuminates a mid-nineteenth-century ideology regarding the naturalness of capitalism: that it simply needed the right conditions to spontaneously occur and would then self-regulate and self-replicate.[1] Mill's scheme about the free circulation of labour, capital, and the easy liquidity of land, however, entailed more than just the natural expansion of capitalism as an economic system.[2] It assumed that the settler colonial governments could use Indigenous lands as security for public loans because they had a right to them. In the British North American colonies, as the following chapters will show, this was far from the case, as nation-to-nation treaties and various colonial proclamations confirmed that the lands were Indigenous spaces. Dreams that the colonies would one day become fully fledged capitalist societies, complete with social stratification, had a long genealogy in British political economy. Adam Smith wrote about the potential of the colonies, but they had a dearth of capital and labourers.[3] For the most part, political economists did not believe that the benefits of settler colonies outweighed the consequences until Edward Gibbon Wakefield's colonial reform movement prescribed the use of debt instruments to direct British capital into them, thus releasing the British government of financial responsibility for colonization.

This chapter argues that political economists who lobbied for colonial reform wanted to remake Indigenous territories as liquid assets in order to raise their market value in settler colonies. Simply taking possession of land by brute force could make one richer only if that land had value in a market. Although colonial reformers made many claims about the good outcomes of colonization as a civilizing mission, a desperate desire for Indigenous land underlay such narratives. The centuries-long intensification in European production of technologies to justify occupation shifted from the colonizers' first principle of land theft and toward the good of civilization.[4]

Wakefield explained why simply holding colonial-claimed land did not give it market value. In *A Letter from Sydney,* which he wrote and published while still in jail for the Turner kidnapping, he pretended to be a colonist who had emigrated to Australia, where he bought twenty thousand acres at a bargain price. He improved his property in various ways, but when he attempted to sell it, he narrated himself as trapped in a conundrum:

> I tried to sell it; but I could not find a purchaser, without submitting to lose great part of what I had expended in improvements. Yet there

> are persons continually reaching the colony on purpose to invest money in the purchase of land; but when I have made overtures to them, they have grumbled at my price, saying that they could obtain a grant from the Crown for less than six-pence per acre ... *In short, my domain has no market value.* It is a noble property to look at; and "20,000 acres in a ring fence" sounds very well in England; but here, such a property *possesses no exchangeable value.* The reason is plain: there are millions upon millions of acres, as fertile as mine, to be had for nothing; and, what is more, there are not people to take them.[5]

Wakefield's "art of colonization" needed capitalists to emigrate to colonies, where they would purchase land to stimulate the real estate market for the explicit purpose of raising land value through commodity exchange. His "systematic colonization" plan, which homed in on how to raise the market value of the land, proposed an expansion of London-based credit and debt systems to give it liquidity and therefore increase exchange value. This chapter begins with Wakefield's proposal on how to increase land value and then examines why certain political economists took up his call to action for colonial reform.

Acting like a conduit, a public debt streamed wealth derived from Indigenous territories into the London money markets. When London financiers and colonial governments determined the amounts of loans, they based their calculations on the presumed future value of Indigenous territories. Colonial governments promised their creditors that after development occurred, land value would outpace the principal and interest of the initial loan. If trade of commodities could increase value, then the public debt made "real" the fictitious commodity of land in the colonies because it gave land liquidity.[6] If land were not liquid, it could not physically move around a market at a distance like other commodities, and therefore made it more difficult to be bought and sold at market. Without such mobility, it could not be traded easily, and without trade, its value could not rapidly increase. The credit (the promise of future value after proposed development) from Indigenous territories imbued the securities (debt instruments such as debentures) with speculative value, and the mobility of the debentures allowed them to circulate freely through the London money market (and later the global one). The public debt literally transferred the wealth from Indigenous territories into the hands of financiers.

After 1815, having been sunk deeper into debt by the costly American Revolutionary War (1775–83) and the Napoleonic Wars (1799–1815), Britain sought to diminish its colonial expenditures. Reformer MPs argued in favour of this and proposed the solution of colonial independence. For example, Joseph Hume suggested that the government should give the colonies "what they ask – let them have an Executive Council of their own choice ... They will maintain not only their own civil establishment, but also the whole of their military establishment ... They will not cost England one shilling."[7]

When Wakefield finished his prison sentence, he co-founded the National Colonization Society in 1830, which lobbied Parliament for what became known as colonial reform.[8] The primary mouthpiece for this movement, Wakefield published many works on the subject and was aided by famous "Wakefieldians" such as MP Charles Buller, John George Lambton (Lord Durham), William Molesworth, and Robert Torrens, whose son Robert Richard Torrens would later implement the Torrens title system that revolutionized land title around the world and is still in use today. Development and emigration became the double nuclei at the heart of Wakefield's colonization model.[9]

Far from inventing the pillars of his systematic colonization theory, Wakefield came to understand North America through his grandmother Priscilla Wakefield's *Excursions in North America* (1806) and then through Fanny Trollope's *Domestic Manners of the Americans* (1832). Robert Gourlay's *Statistical Account of Upper Canada* (1822) deeply influenced him as well.[10] Gourlay's concern about the settlers in Upper Canada, who had an abundance of land, was reflected in the writings of Scottish-born political economist John Rae, which caught the attention of John Stuart Mill, particularly his thoughts on protectionism for nascent nations such as the settler colonies.[11] Such writers problematized the territories of Indigenous nations as *too much* – too much land, with the result that at least some of it would go to waste. Rae noted that a farmer should give "more activity to his capital" in order to lessen "dead stock" and maximize profits.[12] Although Wakefield himself responded to many of the key trends in political economy, he also lobbied for a way to realize

Adam Smith's utopian dream of settler colonies as perfect capitalist societies by giving Indigenous land "real" value via bonding it to the London credit and debt market.

Of course, Wakefield did not invent settler colonialism, but before he published his scheme, many political economists saw emigration to the settler colonies as an unacceptable drain on the economy and a burden on Britain's finances.[13] At the same time, however, Britain was widely perceived as having a problem with what liberal reformers referred to as its "surplus population" of labourers. After the Napoleonic Wars, social unrest due to unemployment and a shift toward industrialization prompted reformers such as Edwin Chadwick, a disciple of Jeremy Bentham, to see the increase in poverty as the "pauperization" of the labouring class. This social disease, according to Chadwick, transformed good able-bodied and independent labourers into paupers. One solution to the problem was relocation – moving poor people to settler colonies that had labour shortages.[14] Schemes of "assisted emigration," or "pauper shovellings," were supported by influential politicians such as Robert Wilmot-Horton, who was undersecretary of state for war and the colonies from 1821 to 1828.

In 1830, Wilmot-Horton proposed an Emigration Bill, which suggested that emigration to the settler colonies should be funded by government. The bill recommended that the government advance of approximately £1,000,000 to send 95,000 emigrants to the colonies. Denouncing the bill, John Stuart Mill wrote that he had "no faith of the efficacy of any plan of emigration," because "it implies the permanent alienation of a portion of the national capital." Yet, he called himself a "friend" to emigration and allowed for it within the competing Wakefield model.[15] Wakefield himself expressed disdain for Wilmot-Horton, referring to him as "an ignorant and meddling pretender in political economy."[16] Much to Wakefield's delight, Wilmot-Horton was appointed governor general of Ceylon during the 1830s, which effectively removed him from the emigration debates.[17] Unlike the Wilmot-Horton model and other schemes for pauper shovelling, Wakefield's proposal, in which the colony itself would fund immigration and development with its own public debt, placed the financial burden on it, not Britain. For this reason alone, it is easy to see why his plan became so popular.

The London Political Economy Club

Initially, many British political economists did not favour settler colonialism – as financing emigration could upset the equilibrium of the British economy. Nineteenth-century political economy cannot be easily generalized, but its core assumption was that an equilibrium between capital, labour, and land was desirable. Advancing ideas that revolutionized the field of political economy, David Ricardo wrote that the economy was a discrete sphere of influence on human life. According to him, it obeyed its own natural laws, existed outside of society, politics, and culture, and, importantly, could be described with principles. Ricardo implemented mathematical justifications about the natural functioning of the economy, and political economists such as William Stanley Jevons worked to sustain mathematics-centred economics. This approach echoed the way in which Newtonian physics described natural phenomena such as gravity. Centring math, Ricardo reified the "economic" as natural. In doing so, he developed ideas about relational value that had a major impact on the field of political economy. Relational value imagined a ratio between two things, or many things. The value of a thing came from its orientation to other things in a matrix of value.[18] Ratios and mathematics rely on balance, and they are expressions of relationships between things. Thus, many political economic reforms focused on what reformers saw as the "unnatural" checks to this equilibrium. If the economy were to be healthy, capital, labour, and land must be balanced. Anything that disrupted this natural equilibrium would produce an unhealthy economy.

Key political economists such as John Stuart Mill and his father, James Mill, began to consider settler colonialism and public debts during the debates and discussions held at the London Political Economy Club (LPEC), which was founded in 1821 by Thomas Tooke "to support the principles of Free Trade."[19] Later on, the LPEC credited David Ricardo's "eagerness" to be in a society of political economists as having aided in its genesis.[20] Because political economists formulated their theories with a "view to legislation,"[21] they addressed actual political and social change. LPEC members had a duty to "study the means of obtaining access to the public mind through as many as possible periodical publications of the day, and to influence as far as possible the tone of such publications in favour of just principles of Political Economy." As well as aiding the "circulation of all publications which they deem useful to the science," they were to "rectify any mistakes in regard to Political Economy in legislations."[22] Unsurprisingly, the LPEC's explicit mandate of controlling information about political economy in order to disseminate official information as widely as possible affected ideas about settler colonialism.

In a chatty letter to her aunt, novelist and social commentator Maria Edgeworth poked fun at the current popularity of political economy, writing about a certain gentleman who had joked that he would join the LPEC only if "he could find two members of it that agree in any one point."[23] Early in the nineteenth century, political economists certainly could not agree about the benefits of colonization, but this slowly changed as Wakefield and his reform ideas came to dominate the debate. Reforming the colonies became an important topic after the 1840s, seeping into both political economists' writings, public discourse, and university lectures. Unlike John Stuart Mill and others, James Mill and David Ricardo were not enthused over settler colonization. Despite his popularity, James Mill attended increasingly fewer meetings at the LPEC. Between 1826 and 1835, the club minute books record that he was present at just three meetings.[24]

Settler colonies became a target for reform because of their alleged imbalance between capital, labour, and land, as detailed in *A Letter from Sydney*. The colonies had a dearth of both capital and labour but an abundance of land. Colonial reform was a way to restore the natural balance of the world. The ideology that a healthy economy must reach a natural equilibrium between labour, capital, and land explains why colonial reform wanted British emigration (labourers and capitalists) and capital (debt instruments) to develop the abundance of land. The scheme would also benefit Britain, which would rid itself of its surplus population, and British excess capital (investments) could be employed to appropriate Indigenous land in the form of debt contracts.

In Britain, the reform Parliament of 1833–34 passed a series of acts to facilitate the flow of capital, labour, and land. For example, in 1834 it passed the Poor Law Amendment Act, also known as the New Poor Law. Political economists had cast Britain's poor laws as an unnatural element in the economy that caused pauperization. Inherited from the Elizabethan period, the laws permitted poverty-stricken individuals to apply for and obtain relief in their local parishes. As a result, to the chagrin of Adam Smith and Edwin Chadwick, they could remain in their communities and had no reason to seek work in the rapidly industrializing towns that needed cheap labour.[25] The New Poor Law of 1834 created a centralized board of poor law guardians, who assessed an individual's need on the basis of standardized criteria. Anyone who was granted relief was required to reside in a workhouse, where inmates were segregated by gender and age, which meant that families were separated. Conditions were deliberately kept harsh in hopes that anyone who had the slightest chance of obtaining employment would opt to look for it in a manufacturing town such as Manchester. Poor law reformers believed that charity relief from parishes impeded the movement of labour that should naturally settle wherever there was a demand for it. This striking erasure of humanity and remaking of people into the category of labour carried on in political economic writing.[26]

Mary Poovey states that political economists grounded their ideas about the economy in trends that were already unfolding around them. They then formulated principles that presented economic phenomena as ahistoric and universal.[27] This is precisely what the colonial reform movement did, with its assertion that the colonies could broaden the "field of employment" for British capital. Edward Wakefield's plan for systematic colonization, and particularly his ideas about colonial economic reform, appealed to political economists, who became some of his most ardent supporters. Although they did not universally agree with all his ideas, many picked up on his claim that colonialism would open up the field of employment for British capital. Wakefield argued that British capital would not have a large enough field of employment in Britain to achieve economic prosperity. The period following the Napoleonic Wars raised significant anxiety about Britain's supposedly stagnating economy. Wakefield asserted that Britain's economic sphere must expand if growth were to be facilitated.[28] The economy was incapable of growth, not because of overpopulation or other such Malthusian concerns, but because there were now no significant opportunities for investment for capital.[29]

Creating a broader field of employment required that states have national economies with responsible governments that considered market principles in decision making. In this way, such states could participate in the global market, giving Britain a broader field of employment of capital, with the result that it could avoid a stagnating economy. The economic model of many states participating in a global economy contrasted with the international economic model that was formulated by the older generation of political economists, such as Smith, James Mill, and even Ricardo. In this older model, Britain was the mother country with a bevy of satellite colonies. They depended on it to nourish their economic growth, which drained Britain's wealth. This belief clarifies why political economists such as James Mill opposed emigration schemes to the colonies. In the Wakefield model, the public debts that settler colonies took out gave them self-sufficient economies, which allowed for British investment outside of Britain's own economy. At the same time, Britain's cultural, political, and social ties with the settler colonies made them a good risk for investment. Unlike the Wilmot-Horton model, in which Britain paid for emigration and colonial development, losing both capital and labour in the process, Wakefield's model allowed for the value derived from Indigenous land to pay for colonialism, and the colonies became discrete economies and therefore sites of investment for British capital.

The assumption of equilibrium infiltrated ideas about migration, governance, taxation, and even the government debt, which Ricardo famously condemned as interfering with the natural balance of the economy.[30] The balance between capital, labour, and land always shaped political economic arguments about emigration to the colonies. Political economists asked whether too many emigrants could cause a drain on Britain, the so-called vacuum theory. They pondered whether an outflow of capital could result in a lack of capital in Britain. They also contemplated the best way to improve what were seen as wastelands. Out of these economic discussions, they began to champion settler colonialism.[31] Thanks to Edward Gibbon Wakefield and his systematic colonization, they came to see white settlement in the colonies as the highest form of colonization. Imagining a settler colonial society where land value increased endlessly, the Wakefieldian colonial reformers worked to embed that vision in legislation. Ideologically, the colonies became a "habitation" for "civilized man," as Oxford political economy professor Herman Merivale put it in 1839.[32] Political economists who supported settler colonialism did not hide their belief that it would benefit finance capitalism. For example, just before Wilmot-Horton's Emigration Bill was debated, Charles Tennant, a prominent industrialist and co-founder of the National Colonization Society, released a series of letters promoting Wakefield's scheme. He labelled the Wilmot-Horton plan as "irrational."[33] Although Tennant conceded that he was not a political economist, he wrote to them to garner their views on "proper colonization."[34] He focused his promotion of the Wakefield system on a land and colonization company called the Canada Company, to whom the British government granted approximately 2.5 million acres in Upper Canada.[35] He asked the company to implement the system, particularly fixing the price of land to concentrate settlers against its "rival landowner, the State."[36] Tennant hoped to apprise "the shareholders concerned in that Company, or in any of the other Land Companies, how greatly their interests will be advanced by the adoption of these principles of systematic colonization as a Government measure."[37] Such land companies fell out of favour in the wake of government debt financing, as Chapter 3 explores.

The LPEC limited its membership to thirty, which expanded to thirty-five in February 1847. With so few members, some idea of their general feelings toward colonial reform can be teased out.[38] Unfortunately, the LPEC rules strictly dictated that the questions or remarks made at meetings could not be read from a written or printed document. Nor could they be printed later.[39] This lack of written documentation makes it difficult to gain a clear understanding of prominent political economists' views on settler colonialism solely from the LPEC alone. Nonetheless, the club did keep minutes of its meetings, in which it recorded not only the various questions posed for debate (but not the answers), but who raised them. Thus, we can determine how often colonial reform was debated at the LPEC and which members introduced the subject.

LPEC meetings were held approximately once a month (later, they were suspended during the late summer and fall), and questions often carried over from meeting to meeting. The corn laws, the poor laws, and taxation dominated the discussion throughout the early nineteenth century.[40] On December 3, 1821, LPEC member G.H. Larpent raised the first question about the colonies when he asked "whether, under any circumstances the restrictions of the Colonial system can be beneficial to the Mother-country."[41] This question reappeared in the minute book for the next four months. Repeatedly tackling a question over so many months did occur at the LPEC, though rarely. The amount of time devoted to a question reveals how much debate it generated and also suggests its importance.

Significantly, the questions regarding the settler colonies did not exist in isolation, but rather as one aspect of several concerns that began to occupy political economists just before mid-century. For example, in December 1844 John Stuart Mill asked, "Was Ricardo correct in stating that 'the same rule which regulated the relative value of Commodities in one country, does not regulate the relative value of the Commodities exchanged between two or more countries'?" He posed that question in the context of his other inquiries about Britain's "field of employment," or expanding British capital investments outside the British economy.[42] The considerations of the colonies overlapped with many of the main economic inquiries of the time. LPEC members could debate the settler colonies as isolated problems, but many questions about Ireland, labourers, land, taxation, and population referred to them as well. As a result, simply counting the questions on colonies uncovers only a portion of the members' concerns with the subject.

Wakefield suggested that land prices should be fixed in the colonies, an idea that entered into the LPEC debate in July 1834, when Larpent asked, "Is it expedient that Government should concentrate Labour in a New Colony by laying a price on land?"[43] This question marked the starting point of LPEC interest in colonial reform. In March 1839, John Ramsay McCulloch asked, "Are there any good grounds for thinking that either the Wealth or Power of Great Britain would be at all impaired by Canada becoming independent, or being incorporated with the United States?" His query highlighted the growing acceptance of Canada as an autonomous country. Importantly, McCulloch concentrated on how its independence could potentially damage Britain.[44] The LPEC debates show that the main principles of colonial reform, which proposed to fix land prices to concentrate labour, were directly connected to the creation of a discrete settler state and that these ideas had some serious traction just before mid-century.

Even after Confederation in Canada, the questions posed at the LPEC reveal that political economists still saw Canada as a part of the empire, despite also understanding it as an autonomous nation. Club members debated whether "the existing relations between Great Britain and Canada, as parts of the same empire, [were] economically beneficial to both or either of the two Countries."[45] The settler state was not seen as a foreign country but as a particular type of statehood that remained within the sphere of the empire. This explains why the London Stock Exchange listed foreign debt markets separately from settler colonial ones. Arguably, after Confederation, Canada did not achieve full independence for more than a century. Some milestones in this process include the 1931 Statute of Westminster, which gave Canada control over its laws; the Canadian Citizenship Act of 1946–47, in which Canadians became citizens of Canada rather than British subjects; the changes in the jurisdiction of the Supreme Court of Canada; and the 1982 repatriation of the constitution.

The LPEC debated the issue of the government debt. On April 1, 1822, a few months after G.H. Larpent had raised the question of the relationship between the mother country and its colonies, club members tackled the problem of whether it were "practicable to pay the whole or a considerable part of the National Debt by a contribution on the capital of individuals; and, if practicable, would it be expedient to do so." This question generated some discussion and was still being debated in December.[46] LPEC members asked about the debt generally, when to pay it, whether it should be paid off, and how to pay it. They also contemplated whether taxes or more government loans should fund the public expenditure during times of peace. On May 5, 1828, they debated the following question: "Should any ... measures be adopted for the extinction of the National Debt?"[47] And on December 7, 1829, the club inquired, "Would a large Sinking Fund consisting of a Surplus of the Revenue of the State over its expenditure, have any tendency to raise the value of Currency and depress general prices?"[48] Members pondered whether the debt should be paid back at all through a "sinking fund," surplus revenue set aside by government to pay back the principal of a loan when its contract ended. On March 1, 1830, members questioned the benefits of implementing new taxes rather than loans to fund wars.[49] Many of the debt-related questions concentrated on how it was to be paid back, but the club eventually lost interest in this topic.

Very occasionally, the club focused on the debts of non-British governments. For example, on April 11, 1825, members considered "whether the Capital loaned from this country at the present time to the New States of South America is likely to be beneficial to the country."[50] Four decades would pass before members revisited the subject of a foreign country's debt. On December 4, 1868, a member asked whether there were "any special merits or defects in the plan adopted by the United States for proving the Interest, and reducing the principal of the National Debt."[51] LPEC member Herman Merivale dominated questions about emigration and the colonies generally, and William Newmarch asked about the debt.

For many years, Newmarch worked as the LPEC honorary treasurer and was "a most active member" of the club. He later became president of the Statistical Society and was then manager of the many-named Glyn's Bank (Glyn, Hallifax, Mills, Currie, and Company, among others). He was also director of the Grand Trunk Railway of Canada.[52] Both the bank and the railway were deeply embedded in the Canadian debt markets. The bank had the distinction, along with the Barings Bank, of funding much of the Canadian debt. Newmarch was an established presence in political economic debates about government debts. Controversially, Newmarch argued that William Pitt's substantial government loan was the best option for Britain during wartime.[53] The lack of LPEC questions about non-British government debts and the settler colonies in particular probably indicates that the national debts of foreign countries had become so normalized that they were not debated. Given that British political economists paid so much attention to their own national debt, this seems likely.

Public debts also figured into LPEC debates about colonization. By the 1850s, Merivale dominated the questions about settler colonies. An active LPEC member, he defined a colony as "a foreign possession, of which the lands are occupied wholly or partially by emigrants from the mother-country."[54] He was also permanent undersecretary (1847–60), setting the stage for Canada's post-Confederation policy regarding Indigenous peoples.[55] He developed a solution to the "Indigenous problem," which oscillated between isolation through reserves or assimilation.[56] However, assimilation was the true goal of isolation via the eventual reduction of Indian reserves. Merivale's two options were grounded in his assertion that Indigenous peoples faced four possible outcomes of settler colonization: extermination, slavery, isolation, or assimilation.[57] More generally, he believed that the Indigenous question had no solution, as it complicated the desire of settlers to achieve responsible government.[58] Merivale and his contemporaries could not imagine that Indigenous nations had a future and made it clear that resolving the Indigenous question would open up land for development. At the same time, freeing up the land would allow for more British emigration, and this population could achieve responsible government for the British North American colonies. For political economists, the Indigenous question was simply "the land question" of the colonies.[59]

Although the LPEC did not record the answers to its debate questions, part of its mandate was to approve of all political economy principles that did appear in published form, so it stands to reason that Merivale's published works about settler colonialism enjoyed some level of acceptance among club members. Merivale linked British colonization to that of ancient Greece and Rome, an unbroken chain that did more than just establish colonization as a natural occurrence. It legitimized a genocidal logic directed at Indigenous peoples, rendering their death and suffering as an unfortunate but normal outcome of colonization.[60] Merivale felt that the presence of Indigenous peoples was the "greatest moral difficulty of colonization." The colonizers of antiquity did not have to grapple with the moral issues of "extermination" or assimilation, because they did not deal with people of "another race or colour," such as the "American Indian, or the Hottentot" – a derogatory term for Khoekhoe people.[61] Notably, the possibility of not pursuing settler colonialism was never debated at the LPEC. All these ideas about colonial reform, from Wakefield to John Stuart Mill to the LPEC debates, eventually unified in the 1834 South Australia Act. After all, as Adam Smith pointed out, political economy was a "branch of the science of a statesman or legislator," and thus political economists lobbied to have its principles enacted through legislation.[62]

The South Australia Act

An early example of imperial legislation, the 1834 South Australia Act enshrined the principle of using the public debt to pay for settler colonialism. An examination of the act reveals how public debt financing functioned across the settler colonies.

The South Australia Act authorized the colony to borrow up to £200,000 with "Colonial Revenue Bonds." It stipulated that if the South Australia government were unable "to discharge the obligations of all or any of the said Bonds ... the Public Lands of the said Province ... shall be deemed a collateral security for payment of the Principal and Interest of the Said Colonial Debt."[63] Of course, "public lands" meant Indigenous land, which became the security for the loan. Almost ten years later, unable to pay its debt, the colony was teetering on the edge of bankruptcy, at which point it repealed the 1834 act and replaced it with the 1842 South Australia Act, thus becoming a Crown colony. As the following chapters will show, the British North American colonies followed a similar pattern, taking out massive loans and then almost defaulting on them. However, they simply merged together to extend their credit, a step that staved off bankruptcy.[64]

John Stuart Mill enthusiastically supported the 1834 South Australia Act. Writing in 1834, just before the act was passed, he remarked that "the enlightened views of Colonization ... are about to be realized in the formation of a Colony at the mouth of the newly-discovered river in South Australia." He praised the act as "a guarantee to the public of the honesty and patriotism of the undertaking, and many other names connected with it are a strong assurance of its probable success as an investment of capital." The new colony, "for the first time in the history of colonization," would "afford a sensible relief to the overcrowded labourers and capitalists of the mother country."[65] Mill supported settler colonialism because he thought it would create national economies that fit within a global economic ordering, a specifically "civilized" order. His unquestioned belief that white settlers had a right to Indigenous lands and waters, his emphasis on the opportunity for capital investment, and his assertion that certain Britons should simply decamp – as if they had no right to live in their home country – gave the settler public debt its meaning. No longer morally shameful, debt would facilitate the spread of an enlightened ordering of the world. Mill's framing of the 1834 South Australia Act as an opportunity for investment explains why many British political economists began to warm to settler colonization: it became a way to expand British capital investment or, in political economy terms, to expand the "field of employment" for capital. Settler colonialism was no longer a drain on British capital. In fact, it generated wealth for investors.

Not everyone saw the South Australia Act in a positive light. Some associated it with the New Poor Law of the same year. For example, on July 4, 1834, two days before Mill published an article titled "The New Colony," in which he praised the act, *The Times* printed a critical letter from an unnamed country magistrate, who bluntly stated that the act was "intimately connected with the anticipated success and the general working of the new Poor Law Bill. The Poor Law Bill will render the labouring population indifferent to their homes; and the colonization-men will be then ready to catch them, and toss them on a far distant coast."[66] The writer touched on many of the popular anti-poor-law sentiments of the time. As he suggested, the new law would detach people from their homes, compelling them to move on in search of work, not just to the industry-heavy north of England but across the oceans. A main point of the New Poor Law was the creation of a supply of cheap, mobile labour. An individual's ties to community were immaterial.

The connection between the New Poor Law and the South Australia Act was not lost on contemporaries, such as the magistrate who wrote to *The Times*. They clearly understood that both the colonization schemes and the statute achieved the same thing, rendering people as labourers who would circulate to places that were in need of workers. Increasing the numbers of labourers who competed over jobs would also keep wages low. Like the South Australia Act and the New Poor Law, the 1833 abolition of slavery "freed" labour to relocate to places that offered wage employment. If the New Poor Law pushed labour to circulate within Britain and to the settler colonies, the abolition of slavery propelled it to circulate throughout the empire.[67]

Mill struck back against the naysayers, contending that anyone who opposed the South Australia Act by distastefully associating it with the New Poor Law had "declared war against the New Colony." To defend his position, he argued that two secretaries of state for war and the colonies, George Murray (who also served as provisional lieutenant governor of Upper Canada) and Frederick John Robinson, Lord Goderich (former prime minister), "for some time had in view the adoption of … the project."[68] Mill claimed that "emigration would be paid for out of the increase to the general wealth of the world," a lofty sentiment that captured his aspirations for settler colonialism. Emigration would augment the world's general wealth by raising land value and increasing capital investment. Initially, however, the money earmarked to finance the settlers would be paid for by a "loan on the security of that future fund." This again highlights that settler colonial credit was grounded in the appropriation of Indigenous lands and waters.[69] The South Australia Act allowed for heavy government borrowing because Mill and others entertained fantasies of a desirable and achievable future. These images of the future, in which white settlers could become wealthy, affected investment. In 1837, the "South Australian Loan" market capitalization on the London Stock Exchange reached £10,000 and grew to approximately £5.5 million in 1880.[70]

Land Value, Slave Labour, and Primitive Accumulation

Unlike financing from the British government, the settler public debt more directly raised land value in the colonies. The interplay between land value, labour, development, and a settler population gestures toward the palimpsest of capitalism: layered structures that worked together to produce a final outcome, a final image. One way to understand how these layers connected with and informed each other is to look at the historical fact of slavery in British North America and particularly the liberal reforms that targeted it. Racialized chattel slavery had a long and complicated history in what became Canada.[71] From Olivier Le Jeune, the first documented enslaved African person in early seventeenth-century New France, to Lieutenant Governor John Graves Simcoe of Upper Canada and the 1793 act that limited slavery (with many caveats), and to Prince Edward Island's legalization of slavery until 1825, slavery manifested in a variety of ways and differed from region to region.

Although Simcoe's act caused chagrin among the slave-holding class, who believed that slavery was necessary for agriculture, Upper Canada became the first place in the British Empire that had an anti-slavery law. However, Afua Cooper reminds us of the important role that Black people played in the legislation. For example, she cites the violent treatment of Chloe Cooley, an enslaved Black woman, and her consequent resistance to such treatment as one of its many catalysts.[72] In his study on slavery in the Maritimes, Harvey Amani Whitfield notes that regional differences in colonial governments, Loyalist migration, and geographic access points to the Atlantic world (including the Caribbean) factored into the ways in which slavers practised slavery. Loyalists who migrated from East Florida to northern Massachusetts brought their own ideas of slavery to a British "grey zone" of slavery practice. Slavery did not have legal protection with outright pro-slavery laws, which some attempted to change. For example, Prince Edward Island passed an act to legalize it.[73] Although slavery in Atlantic Canada was not the large-scale plantation type of warmer southern environments, Whitfield asserts that "slaveholding reached into most socio-economic classes of white society" in the Maritimes.[74] Charmaine Nelson shows how slavery manifested in eighteenth- and nineteenth-century Montreal, especially in connection with slaveholders such as James McGill.[75]

Initially, slavery laid bare the brutal process of raising the market value of land in the settler colonies. Slavery and settler colonialism thrived together because they both distilled profits through a ruthless remaking of Indigenous lands into market value. Their relationship was symbiotic, not evolutionary. One did not spring from the other. Historically, European colonialism has always gone hand-in-hand with racialized chattel slavery.[76] In seventeenth-century Canada, for example, the French followed the Portuguese tradition of enslaving Indigenous people and gradually turned to enslaving Black people from Africa.[77] Historically, racialized chattel slavery has always accompanied capitalism. In the "racial twist" of the economic system of slavery, Eric Williams suggests that "racism was the consequence of slavery," not the other way around, and that capitalism emerged from this massive and unthinkably violent system of labour exploitation.[78] Racism was created to justify the exploitation of specific peoples. Europeans who engaged in the necessary cultural production to legitimize slavery concentrated on physical appearance, normalizing the idea that the melanin-rich skin, hair texture, and facial features of peoples in certain parts of Africa made them natural labour and particularly natural slaves.[79] European cultural production to justify the incomprehensible brutality of the transatlantic slave trade serviced the ideology in which some human beings were rendered as natural labour, deserving of low pay or, in the case of slavery, no pay at all. This system of white supremacy may have allowed space for the abolition of the slave trade, but it did not allow room for the continuation of languages, religions, cultural practices, government systems, and family structures that it deemed inferior to their European counterparts. New histories on racial capital and insights from Black and Indigenous studies have done much to challenge deeply ingrained assumptions in scholarship that paint capitalism as somehow divorced from or evolved past both slavery and settler colonialism. The Atlantic slave trade provided the climate that allowed capitalism to flourish. To this day, capitalist economic systems rely on slave labour, which throws doubt on arguments for an alleged shift away from slavery and toward capitalism or even a broad move from slavery toward settler colonialism.[80] Around the world, enslaved people, and many enslaved children, labour to produce the consumer products that Canadians buy. Only in July 2020 did Canadian law impose a tariff on "goods manufactured or produced by prison or forced labour," and only in late 2021 was this tariff used for the first time in intercepting personal protective equipment from China.[81]

In his analysis of slavery as the foundation of the British industrial revolution, Eric Williams connected it to capitalism because it funnelled raw materials and capital into Britain, which transformed them into manufactured goods for sale as commodities.[82] Imperial laws that made it illegal to process raw goods in the colonies reveal the intention to centre production and capital in Britain.[83] The institution of slavery also instilled a capitalist social and economic order in the settler colonies. People stolen from Africa were forced to labour for the production of capital gains, but complex legal systems also made them into capital. Slavery rendered human beings with specific physical features as both capital and labour. As Julia Ott notes, they were the "capital that made capitalism."[84] Account books recorded enslaved people as assets, and "modern" business management practices such as calculating depreciation and appreciating value of assets have a long history in slavery accounting, where, for example, the recorded market value of enslaved children increased as they aged.[85] Racialized slave labour developed a commercial economy, a complex credit and debt system including the act of mortgaging enslaved people, and importantly, it also oriented legislation toward the settler colonial quest to raise land value.[86]

For Wakefield, the "superabundance" of land in settler colonies made labour expensive, and thus he introduced his concept of a "sufficient price" of land. This may be the most analyzed aspect of his systematic colonization scheme, beginning with Karl Marx, who criticized Wakefield in his discussion of what he disdainfully christened the "modern theory of colonization."[87] Marx noted that capitalists must legislate "primitive accumulation" because the sufficient price aimed to produce wage labourers.[88] Primitive accumulation was (and is) a series of coercive efforts, such as legislation, to force people to sell their time as wages. This end could also be achieved in a roundabout way. For instance, if a city legislated against the use of front yards for growing food plants, people would be obliged to buy food if they wished to avoid starvation. To purchase food, they had to work for wages. Essentially, primitive accumulation referred to anything that sought to excise the means of production from the producers. Accumulation also worked through dispossession, as in the settler colonies.[89] According to Wakefield, the sufficient price could be calculated as "the term during which it is desirable that labourers should work for hire before they can be allowed to work as a settler" – before they could buy and "improve" land.[90] The sufficient price fixed the price of land at an amount that ensured wage earner settlers could not sustenance farm and would have to support themselves through wage labour. However, land costs that were prohibitively high would worsen what Wakefield called the "colonial curse" – the dearth of British labourers. Labourers in British North America could simply move to the United States, where wages were higher and land was cheaper.[91] Marx's focus on labour captures only one aspect of Wakefield's colonization plan that centred on increasing land value via exploited labour because this colonization needed the public debt.

Debt instruments allowed land value to circulate on money markets, an activity that could increase it, as could the labourers who would build the development projects in the colony. Despite his acerbic criticism of Wakefield's "modern colonization," Marx conceptualized settler colonies as "virgin soil." Unlike Wakefield, however, he saw them as places in which capitalism could be subverted rather than entrenched, enabling British labourers to escape wage labour and become farmers.[92] Here, ironically, Wakefield and Marx were united in foreseeing a bright future for settlers and in their dismissal of Indigenous lifeworlds.

The inhumane system of slavery buttressed the inhumane process of settler colonialism, and it conveniently solved the problem of labour shortages in the colonies. In examining the necessity of slave labour, Wakefield understood that land value could not increase without labour. In this simple fact, slavery laid bare the brutal process of what Marx referred to as "so-called primitive accumulation."[93] Dispossession included privatization of elements that were essential to life, such as water, and through processes of land enclosure, as Allan Greer details.[94] Glen Coulthard argues for the usefulness of revisiting Marx's reservations about the "primitive" in "primitive accumulation" in the Canadian settler colonial and imperial context. Coulthard easily relates the interconnectedness of slavery, wage labour, dispossession, and the theft of land when he writes, "In *Capital* these formative acts of violent *dispossession* set the stage for the emergence of capitalist accumulation and the reproduction of capitalist relations of production by tearing Indigenous societies, peasants, and other small-scale, self-sufficient agricultural producers from the source of their livelihood – *the land*."[95]

To be clear, Wakefield, Mill, and many others were absolutely explicit that they wanted to reproduce capitalist relationships in the settler colonies, which was why they focused on how the capitalist class might be encouraged to emigrate – something that Wilmot-Horton did not consider in his own plan. Wakefield accepted that the political and social "evil" of slavery could aid in making a prosperous settler colony, and he did not deny that it increased land value in America, but it came with so many evils that he could not tolerate it.[96] In opposing slavery, he contended that it hindered the capitalist class from moving to the settler colonies, it had the potential to depress the value of commodities (including land), and it obstructed the free circulation of labour. At the same time, he developed an ideology of settler colonialism that centred on moral righteousness – that it could produce and sustain a civilized society that had rooted out the evil of slavery. Wakefield and other reformers saw settler colonialism as synonymous with a civilized society and maintained that the only real way to get rid of slavery was through "proper colonization."[97] At the heart of Wakefield's theory was an ever present question: How can we institute wage labour and still increase land value? Slave labour reform extended to the prison version in penal colonies, such as New South Wales, which was also perceived as a financial burden on Britain.[98] Importantly, both types of slave labour, whether racialized or penal, did not raise land value in the colonies in a satisfactory way. Caitlin Rosenthal astutely notes that the abolition of slavery was a "triumph of market regulation," as a way to reform labour mobility for the service of capital.[99] Michael Perelman shows that market regulation was essential to the expansion of capitalism to force primitive accumulation onto societies.[100]

Land was a profitable business in settler colonies, and colonial reform sought to capitalize on the profits. In writing about the United States, Wakefield suggested that though it had a superabundance of land and not enough labourers, it had prospered nonetheless because enslaved Black people worked the land and thus increased its value. In places with so much land and not enough or no slavery, such as the British North American colonies, Wakefield stated that "not a single one of these societies has greatly prospered: Many have perished entirely."[101] Slavery did increase land value in the settler colonies, but Wakefield could not accept it in his vision of a settler colonial future. Closer inspection reveals that this seemingly paradoxical position in which slavery is seen as both a necessity and an evil materialized from the political economic assumptions about labour and land. One must be careful not to read the orthodox political economic opposition to slavery simply as humanitarianism, because this misses key historical context.[102] In settler colonies that had labour shortages, Wakefield saw slavery as essential for capital but not as the best way of increasing land value, because it discouraged capitalist emigration. If liberal political economists had the end goal of primitive accumulation to ensure an increase in land value, slavery provided the means until Wakefield suggested another way.

Wakefield wanted to transform the settler colonial relationship that increased land value from one between slavery and land into one between wage labour and land. Enslaved people increased the value of land by cultivating it and extracting resources from it, but slavery also decreased the value of commodities. For many political economists, unpaid slave labour competed unfairly with paid labour, a fact that artificially diminished prices. For example, slave-grown cotton could be cheaper than cotton produced by wage labourers. Wakefield argued that colonial reform could fix the depreciation of the market value of commodities that were produced by slave labour.[103]

He also stated that slave labour dampened capitalist emigration. He stressed that capitalists constituted "a distinct class, because it is as a distinct class that they suffer more than anybody else from the scarcity of labour for hire."[104] In a vicious cycle, slavery hindered the emigration of capitalists whose input was desperately needed to develop the land and increase its value, and the lack of capitalists allowed for slave labour to persist.[105] Due to the labour shortage in settler colonies, capitalists were often obliged to work with their own hands, an "evil" that Wakefield described at length:

> Capitalists brought up in this country [Britain] do not like to work with their own hands: they like to direct with their heads the labour of others. The necessity of working with their own hands is apt to disgust the emigrant capitalist, and to send him back to this country a discontented and complaining man. If, in order to avoid the annoyance, and, as he feels it, the degradation, of working with his own hands, and making his children work with theirs, he resorts to some sort of slavery, he is still apt to be very much annoyed. N***o slavery is detestable for the master who was not bred, born, and educated within hearing of the driving-whip. If I could find a stronger word than detestable, I would apply it to the life of a decent Englishman who has become a driver of convicts in Tasmania. "Free n****r" labour, even in domestic service, is not

> agreeable for the master, because he continually feels that the servant ought to hate him as one of the class which despises and loathes the whole n***o race.[106]

In this scenario, the "decent Englishman" is forced to choose between two unsatisfactory alternatives: the degrading exercise of working with his own hands or reluctantly availing himself of slave labour. Here, slavery springs naturally from the mismanagement of labour emigration to his colony. The sketch also expresses a deep-seated anxiety regarding the underlying violent intentions of the "free" Black person. Hence, Wakefield stressed the necessity of British, or white labourer, emigration to the colonies. Though he presented labour as both degrading and necessary, only the members of certain classes should be expected to perform it. He did recognize the social and moral evils of racialized and convict slavery, but he chose to emphasize that it embarrassed the capitalist class. It proved detrimental to the goals of systematic colonization, which needed both capitalists and labourers to increase land value.

Who should be a labourer and who would be degraded by labour was a fundamental but unspoken fact of political economy. In the nineteenth century, this division was drawn down a line of race. Race laid the foundations for class divisions because it made it acceptable to understand some people as natural labourers and others as not, and thus justifying lower wages for racialized people.[107] The idea of the "natural" extended to those who ruled as well; Sylvia Wynter points out that liberalism challenged the "natural" right of certain monarchical bloodlines to rule. However, in displacing the blood right of the aristocracy, Enlightenment liberal ideology emphasized the ability to reason. It differentiated between those who possessed reason and those who lacked it, which sustained the fantasy that some people deserved their debasement, as anyone who was capable of rational thought could easily ascend the ladder to enlightenment.[108] This ideology could also justify paying low wages to youth, people with disabilities, women – anyone whose alleged feeble grasp on reason exempted them from the jobs that only a white, male, able-bodied adult (who embodied reason) could perform. These sentiments echo in our present-day understanding of skilled and unskilled labour. For Wakefield and other political economists, the idea that some people could be degraded whereas others could not was acceptable, and socialization determined the level of acceptability.

Wakefield noted the "benefits" of the racialization process of slavery, particularly in the American states that did not practise it but that did possess Black "free" workers, whose "natural" status as an "inferior order of beings" justified their low wages. He claimed that a "black man never was, nor is he now, treated as a man by the white men of New-England." He remarked, "thus such blacks as either escaped, or were allowed to go free, from the slave states, to settle in other states, provided servants for the capitalists of those other states." The non-slave states also benefited as markets for slave-produced goods.[109] According to Mill, if British capitalist emigration were to be induced, a "*certain* supply of labour" was necessary.[110] Here, the word "certain" refers to a specific quantity of free labour from Britain that would create a capitalist society in the colonies. It also expresses an uneasiness regarding Black labour. On the one hand, Black labour was cheap, an obvious boon to capital. On the other hand, having a racialized body politic did not align with the utopian vision of settler colonies as white – and creditworthy.

Ostensibly, cheap slave labour might have seemed attractive to capitalists, but slavery also meant a loss of labour mobility. Wage earners were theorized as free to move about in search of work and would naturally congregate in places that were experiencing labour shortages, where they would compete with each other for jobs, leading to a drop in wages. By contrast, enslaved labourers could not relocate and thus could not offset a labour shortage, with the result that wages would go up and the demands of capital would not be met. Wakefield's settler colonialism, therefore, was not "a response to the loss of the 'human trade in flesh,'" but an answer to a question about how to achieve primitive accumulation without slave labour.[111] In the settler colonies, the regulatory controls placed on racialized slavery and penal labour were intended to lower wages and increase land value via labour mobility. It is no coincidence that the reform-era British Parliament that abolished slavery also passed the New Poor Law of 1834, as reformers who favoured both acts wanted to ensure the free circulation of labour. Wakefield's systematic colonization, then, solved the problem of how to achieve primitive accumulation with the most dynamic labour force possible (to keep wages low and land value high) and how to make the process palatable to capitalist emigrants, which meant an end to slavery and an opportunity to hire white labourers.

Conclusion

Despite the passing of the South Australia Act, colonial reform was far from the systematic colonization that Wakefield had hoped for; however, a transition from Wilmot-Horton's methods of emigration to Wakefield's principles clearly occurred. Interestingly, though taking out a public loan was central to Wakefield's approach, the opponents of colonial reform, such as James Mill, Thomas Malthus, and Wilmot-Horton, did not attack it. In fact, they targeted Wakefield's suggestion that the price of land be fixed, objecting that it would concentrate settlement in an unnatural way. The settler colonies, then, could pay for colonization when Britain no longer wanted to or no longer could.

Ultimately, however, as the following chapters will outline, the public debt could never be repaid, and at the same time, it relied on a system of power inequality. I want to end this first chapter with Denise Ferreira da Silva's concept of the unpayable debt, which clarifies how the power imbalance functioned. Her analysis of an unpayable debt is centred on Octavia Butler's classic novel *Kindred,* which tells the story of Dana, a twentieth-century Black woman who involuntarily travels back in time to a slave plantation in antebellum Maryland.[112] There, she saves a young white boy named Rufus from drowning. He turns out to be the plantation owner's son, and as the plot develops and time passes, he grows into a cruel and violent man. Eventually, he tries to sexually assault Dana, who fends him off and returns permanently to her own time but loses an arm due to their struggle. Like many time travel stories, the novel plays with paradox: Rufus is one of Dana's ancestors, and had she failed to save him, she herself would never have been born.

In referencing this story, Ferreira da Silva asks who, in this settler colonial context of slavery, becomes indebted to the unpayable debt? An unpayable debt is debt you pay that is not yours to pay, which you do not actually own, and "economically, Dana's is an unpayable debt because the juridical form of title governing the owner slave economic relation (property) authorizes the deployment of total violence in order to extract the total value created by slave labor, which results in descendants of slaves existing in scarcity. So, yes, Dana owns (ethically) a debt, which it is not (economically) hers to pay."[113] I want to suggest that this is a fundamental power dynamic of the credit/debt relationship in settler racial capitalism – that the owner of the debt is separate from the one who owes the debt and that this separation is produced through a constructed merging of economics and ethics and the racialization of property rights. In a capitalist economic system, all is allowable, all is ethical, if it promotes the reproduction of capital. And it is an unpayable debt in the sense that, historically, it has never been paid off. Ferreira da Silva goes on to write that this colonial/slavery relationship occurred in the "total violence," found in "each and every daily act that held the captive and the captor in relation."[114] This relationship centred on the credit/debt power differential that twisted community and kinship around racial power dynamics to put the debt owed on the one who does not owe it.

Joshua Whitehead distinguishes this type of debt from community-centred concepts of debt, such as an intellectual or other types of debt to kin in community. Such a debt is a relation of honour, not one that is "owed" in the extractivist colonial manner.[115] In settler racial capitalism, this debt is owed in a violent, exploitative way. Frantz Fanon observes that colonial governance needs total violence of land dispossession, labour exploitation, dehumanization/humiliation, and policing. As this book progresses, the context of the unpayable debt and the injustice of owing a debt that is not yours to pay will emerge from the background of a seemingly simple economic relationship. As Ferreira da Silva writes, "the marks of violence on the flesh of the captive expose that what defines the Owner is not liberty but the juridically protected right to deploy total violence in order to extract from his or her property."[116]

The relationship between debt and total colonial violence in Canada crystallizes in such property rights that sustain its ongoing colonization. Property could apply to the legally protected right to own an individual, as in slavery, or it could refer to the territories of Indigenous nations. Either way, the possessor of the property has the "juridically protected right to deploy total violence in order to extract" value. The formalization of the London Stock Exchange in 1801 facilitated the transfer of the value from Indigenous land to money markets, and as the following chapter will show, in the Canadian context this transfer of wealth tracked alongside Confederation, built on debt and exploitative systems of power.

Wastelands: Indigenous Lands as "Waste" on the London Stock Exchange

2

> Wastelands are named wastelands by the ones responsible for their devastation. Once they have devastated the earth – logged the forest bare, poisoned the water, turned our neighbourhoods into brownfields so that we must grow our vegetables in pots above the ground – once they have consumed all that they believe to be valuable, the rest is discarded. But the heart of wastelands theory is simple. Here, we understand that there is nothing and no one beyond healing. So we return again and again to the discards, gathering scraps for our bundles, and we tend to the devastation with destabilizing gentleness, carefulness, softness ... In the wastelands, our freedom comes from falling in love with the beauty in lands, places, and people where others have been taught to see only weeds and devastation.
>
> – Erica Violet Lee, "In Defence of the Wastelands"

The London Stock Exchange and Government Debt Markets

In the passage above, Nēhiyaw philosopher Erica Violet Lee asks us to consider the meaning of "wastelands," both as valueless and as apocalyptic in the wake of capitalist extractivist practices. She emphasizes a third meaning, of wastelands as imbued with the potential to heal that which is rendered useless in our market society.[1] In the mid-nineteenth century, however, the metonymy "wastelands" stood in for Indigenous territories that were outside of the market economy. When colonial reformers referred to "wastelands," they were not thinking of something that was uninhabitable and toxic but of something that was lying waste and had no market value. Rooted in John Locke's theory of property, the "wastelands" moniker could apply to all unproductive lands (and waters) where the capital potential in this liberal imagining of space went to waste. These liberal ideas of making private property – that is, land and waters that existed within a cultural, social, political, and legal regime oriented around the production of these spaces as capital – extended throughout the British Empire. Brenna Bhandar notes that land outside of systems of property value, such as Indigenous reserve land, was "dead capital,"[2] as economist Hernando de Soto puts it. Interestingly, de Soto's method to give liquidity to dead capital in land via opening up access for poor people to the credit and debt system of mortgages deeply informed a Canadian neoliberal push to privatize reserve lands in the twentieth century.[3] Long before de Soto evolved the idea of dead capital, however, there was the liberal construction of wastelands. Edward Gibbon Wakefield imagined their future as capable of market-value production once they were occupied by perfectly harmonious and socially stratified British settlers. That happy future for white settlers quickly became a nightmare for many Indigenous nations, who "disproportionally contend with the toxic legacies of late industrialism in the air."[4] Aileen Moreton-Robinson states that "white possessiveness" had several interlocking strategies, all grounded in a subjectivity that denied the humanity of Indigenous peoples and simply appropriated land without their consent.[5] Wakefield's actions and writings underscored his disinterest in consent, and just as he had disregarded consent in marrying Ellen Turner, his apathy toward Indigenous peoples coloured his settler colonial scheme. Part of this denial of Indigenous land tenure derived from the wastelands ideology.

This chapter will not rehash the well-researched land appropriation model of eighteenth- and nineteenth-century settler colonialism. Allan Greer shows how the enclosure of the "colonial commons" through such practices as fencing and importing livestock occupied space and dispossessed Indigenous peoples of their lands.[6] Other processes of claiming

Indigenous land as private property came about through changing mortgaging laws during the 1830s, which varied with each British North American government.[7] In line with this, the creation of an apartheid system in which Indigenous people were confined on reserves enabled surveillance and limited their mobility, including their access to their territories.[8] As the nineteenth century progressed, the residential school system extended this containment and surveillance to mass incarcerate Indigenous children, attempting to break their bonds to their communities and lands, and to eradicate the nation-to-nation treaty agreements.[9] Indigenous dispossession took numerous forms, and many scholars offer detailed and nuanced descriptions of it.

The British North American governments, and later the Dominion of Canada, did not use a single model to spread British sovereignty and market order throughout Indigenous territories. It was not until the nineteenth century, however, that an aggressive form of settler colonialism as land theft, brewing since the end of the Seven Years' War in 1763, took root. Brenna Bhandar states, "The imperative to quantify and measure value created an ideological juggernaut that defined people and land as unproductive," casting them as "waste and in need of improvement."[10] Bhandar points out that the ideology of improving wastelands had a long history in the British Empire, beginning with political economist William Perry and the question of Ireland.[11] As this and subsequent chapters will show, wastelands in the settler colonies could not be easily sold, or sold en masse, until they could be bought and sold via debt instruments on the LSE. The creation of land value in the colonies was not just ideological. Nor was it only the product of individual settlers putting up fences; it reflected the ability of settler societies to create land value because of new and globalizing financial structures that provided the means to alienate Indigenous lands and waters.

The importance of the London Stock Exchange (LSE) to the process of a distinct mid-nineteenth-century settler colonialism cannot be understated. The LSE facilitated a growing global securities trade in government debts. The transferable nature of the debt provided an opportunity for governments to be indebted, theoretically in perpetuity, at a low interest rate that was set in a contract, and the debtholder could choose to sell debt instruments to others, which lowered the risk associated with securities trading and investment. The LSE reduced the risk of investing in government debts, as it allowed multiple financiers to invest in one debt. This made the large long-term and low-interest public debts possible.[12]

Trading securities predated the formalization of the London Stock Exchange in 1801. In 1694, the Bank of England was founded and gave the British government a £1.2 million loan. The initial British debt in the 1690s had the long-term interest rate of 8 percent, which had dropped significantly to approximately 4 percent by the 1750s.[13] Scholars debate how much of a role the British debt played in the institutionalization of the securities market, as throughout the eighteenth century the illiquid nature of government bonds generally made trading them almost non-existent.[14] Even if inactive buyers dominated the market for the public debt, they still held the debt, which allowed the government to fund large and expensive wars.[15] In the 1690s, approximately seven hundred shareholders invested in a handful of companies, such as the British East India Company, the Hudson's Bay Company, and the Royal African Company, as well as the Bank of England. The early stock market did not have the liquidity of its nineteenth-century counterpart, as shareholders made relatively few trades each year. With respect to the three companies mentioned above, only about three hundred to four hundred trades occurred per year. This began to change during the eighteenth century, and by the nineteenth century, increased transactions from buying and selling government debt and transactions from private securities created a flurry of market activity that eventually needed a regulating body.[16] The decline of the Amsterdam Bourse in the third quarter of the eighteenth century made a space for the ascendancy of London as the global stock exchange capital.[17]

Although government borrowing existed before the founding of stock exchanges, it was generally short term, with high interest, sometimes as high as 50 percent annually.[18] Monarchs could force the population to lend money to the government or could default on these debts by manipulating the law. In 1290, Edward I infamously expelled the Jewish population from England and subsequently defaulted on debts owed to Jewish creditors, which reflects how political insecurity could lead to high interest.[19] In 1672, Charles II suspended all capital payments to his debtors in a move known as the "Stop of the Exchequer," which made betting on government debts a risky proposition. After the Glorious Revolution of 1688, acts of Parliament guaranteed an annual payment of 8 percent interest so that "shareholders who subscribed capital to the loan were therefore relieved of the precarious uncertainty that the monarch could default on payments at will," as Charles II had done.[20] In addition, a portion of future tax revenue was earmarked for debt payments.[21] This support of parliamentary statutes made investing in government debts less risky and gave bondholders a degree of confidence. For example, a late seventeenth-century bondholder named Samuel Jeake believed that investing in the British public debt would yield an 8 percent yearly interest from his investments. Before the acts of Parliament set the terms for loans, monarchs could default, sometimes with impunity.[22] As John Brewer shows, post-1688 Britain did not have the same licence to default on a debt. The British government turned to both taxes and raising voluntary loans to pay for its expenditures.[23] Brewer stresses the interconnectedness of tax and a public debt, as the security of investment in the debt relied on the investor's belief in a "strong" state and its ability to tax. In this way, tax and debt funded the growth of the "fiscal military state."[24] As this suggests, it was no coincidence that the public debts of settler governments reified settler sovereignty and concretized state structures.

Two major studies examine the demographic of British investors. P.J. Cain and A.G. Hopkins maintain that it consisted of a "gentlemanly capitalist" class.[25] H.V. Bowen shows that the people who chose to invest their surplus money in stocks rather than depositing it in savings accounts were surprisingly diverse. These stocks promoted imperial projects, such as the British East India Company. Women, particularly unmarried women, invested as well, though modestly compared to the gentlemanly capitalists who made a living from their investments.[26] The ability of financiers to invest in the budding Canadian economy ensured the development of public works, civil services, and more generally a centralized government. British investors owned a significant amount of Canadian government securities. They also owned a variety of securities from railways, telegraphs, banks, land, industry companies, and more.[27]

On a practical level, settler colonies had to find an immediate way of funding public works, civil servants, bureaucracies, and mechanisms of territorial control, which they could not do through taxes alone.[28] The LSE, more than the government-regulated French exchange or provincial British exchanges, made it possible to trade a large volume of foreign government securities from loans that financed foreign and colonial governments. Aside from the particular instance of Britain's own public debt in the late seventeenth century, the expansive global public debt market did not exist until after the rise of the LSE. British investment in non-British government bonds began after the Napoleonic Wars, when the Barings bank, along with other bankers such as the Amsterdam banking house named Hope and Company, floated a loan to France in 1817, enabling that country to pay a massive war indemnity imposed on it by the 1815 Treaty of Paris.[29] This began the first of a series of French loans to pay for war damages, a step that effectively opened up a British market for foreign government bonds. Frank Griffith Dawson argues the post–Napoleonic Wars era also created a situation in which Spain's power in Latin America declined, prompting several countries to move toward independence and, importantly, to search for the funding to attain it.[30] Between 1822 and 1825, British investors saw the opportunity to make money from commerce, emigration, and inter-oceanic communication, and they invested heavily in Latin American government securities.[31] Merging three Spanish-controlled colonies to create the Republic of Colombia, Simón Bolívar took out a loan in 1819, the first of the Latin American government loans. However, investing in emerging nation-states proved volatile, as many of the Latin American countries had to default on their loans, which sent the early Latin American debt market crashing to the ground.[32] In many ways, the public debt supported the creation of a nation-state, and in the case of the colonial public debt, it supported the creation of the settler state. It forced the state to act as a centralized government to manage economic activity through a defined loan contract and also to administer the debt in development projects or wars. James Belich refers to debt as the "alter ego" of the centralized state, and the LSE played a role in producing centralized governments.[33]

The importance of the government debt to an autonomous state government was not lost on contemporaries. In 1824, during the Greek

War of Independence, the provisional government of Greece borrowed £800,000 through the agency of Loughnan and Sons (formerly Loughnan and Son and O'Brien). According to LSE members, "that this Loan was of the greatest service to Greece, in her arduous struggle for independence, cannot be denied."[34] The interest payments for the loan soon went into arrears, which prompted the Foreign Stock Market Committee of the LSE to begin a process of debt collection by 1829. The LSE dealt with matters of importance through its General Purpose Committee and later the Foreign Stock Market Committee. These committees handled payment conflicts between individuals, as well as large debts such as that of Greece.[35] How much the LSE could enforce its own rules of payment varied greatly. In the case of the Greek debt, it had to seek the authority of the British government to try to force the payment of the debt so that the bondholders could receive their interest. The defaulted securities sometimes fell into a grey area of authority, as the government, the banks, and the LSE seemed unclear about which jurisdiction was involved.

On October 15, 1829, the Foreign Stock Market Committee recorded their appeal to the Earl of Aberdeen, secretary of state for foreign affairs. A payment that amounted to £85,000 was overdue, and the LSE members wanted to "bring this subject under consideration of [the British] government." They asked for a payment of £28,000 annually to cover the future interest needed "to solicit on behalf of the numerous body of persons who are holders of the bonds." The earl replied that he had no wish to "interfere in speculations of this kind which are of a purely financial nature" and added that the British government "cannot claim to exercise any authority with Foreign states." However, he was not unsympathetic regarding their financial loss, which the government was "far from viewing with indifference."[36] Ranald Michie points out that there was a "constant tension" between securities markets and governments. The LSE committee members wanted the British government to enforce debt repayment, which could potentially undermine British foreign relations.[37] Sometimes, the LSE supported the public debts of nations that Britain viewed with animosity, including France immediately after the Napoleonic Wars.[38] The LSE funnelled borrowed capital to many burgeoning states, and the British settler colonies flourished as capital via debt was siphoned into the hands of their governments.

The Abstraction of Indigenous Land as Waste

What underlying colonial logic legitimized the use of the territories of Indigenous nations to funnel that capital into the coffers of settler colonial governments? Colonial reformers, political economists, and colonial governments had a history of abstracting Indigenous territories as "wastelands." The framework for appropriating Indigenous land had a long genealogy in British ideology, which normalized the perception of land as value that expedited colonial governments' claims of the wastelands as assets. As the following chapters address, financiers used these claimed assets in calculating how much money they would lend and how much interest they would charge. The details about this move to abstract and to claim come to light in two significant inquiries, one in 1825 and one in 1836, which informed imperial policy regarding wastelands. The first centred on a colonization plan formulated by Robert Wilmot-Horton and the second on the Wakefieldian alternative. Two important trends emerged from these debates: the Wakefield model was accepted, and Indigenous territories were classed as security for loans.

In 1825, Wilmot-Horton introduced a Waste-Lands Bill to the House of Commons, which was to pronounce on "the sale and improvement of Waste Lands in Upper Canada." The bill suggested that a loan from the government could establish British settlers in the Canadian wastelands, which they would then develop. Some consideration was given to the Indigenous peoples who lived "in the vicinity of these waste lands," but not so far as to assert that they had an inherent right to them.[39] During the debate on the bill, the MPs favoured an American method that relied on private companies and a centralized land office to deal with land distribution.[40] When challenged that the bill was "brought in for no other purpose than to support a Joint Stock company, established to speculate on emigration," Wilmot-Horton asserted "that the principle of the bill did not relate entirely to emigration. That was an incidental part of it."[41] Such nimble use of language underscores the importance of legitimizing the version of settler colonialism that one wanted to promote, even to others who wanted to colonize. Much was at stake in how colonizers stole Indigenous lands; if joint-stock land companies made money from land grants, then, for example, perhaps the colonial government would lose an opportunity to speculate on the land via access to loans and, in this case, London bankers might lose as well. Even though Wilmot-Horton argued that Canada could "absorb the exertions of any amount of population" due to the "indefinite extent of fertile land," his bill failed to pass.[42]

In 1836, the Select Committee on the Disposal of Lands in the British Colonies investigated how properly to "dispose" of wastelands. The committee consisted of important political figures including George Grey, Francis Baring, William Gladstone, and George Julius Poulett Scrope. The correspondence included in its report showed that Indigenous peoples did factor into the planning of the disposal of lands, but only insofar as the Wakefieldian "new system" would directly benefit them. For example, the commissioners of South Australia claimed in a letter to George Grey that the principles enshrined in the South Australia Act would not have been entertained unless "they would operate beneficially, not only to the aborigines, but to the parties interested in the colony."[43] This had more to do with the "civilizing" potential of the colony than with how much money Indigenous peoples would receive from the loss of their lands. Probably, they received very little compensation, and in the British North American colonies, the money made from the sale of their land often went into a trust held by the government, which could help fund the appropriation of more land.[44]

The select committee report began with an assessment of the system used in the United States, where shifting politics regarding land resulted in the introduction of a centralized policy, with the 1812 founding of the General Land Office, whose purpose was to manage public land. Built from slavery, the American system inspired Wakefield in his own settler colonial theories.[45] In 1830, President Andrew Jackson signed the Indian Removal Act into law, which freed up desirable real estate by forcibly removing entire Indigenous nations to lands west of the Mississippi. Wholeheartedly defending the measure, John Stuart Mill criticized the "mischievous remarks" made about Jackson and took issue with those who framed the violent removal, known today as the Trail of Tears, as a "hardship" and "injustice" inflicted on Indigenous peoples. He suggested that the American government's expenditure on "civilizing" them included "sums so large, as to form a very important item in the moderate expenditure."[46] The turn toward forced removal arose from a thaw in hostilities between Britain and the United States, which occurred after the War of 1812. Before that time, the two countries had made military allies out of various Indigenous nations. In 1818, however, Britain and the United States settled their differences by signing the Anglo-American Convention, which set the international boundary at the forty-ninth parallel and ushered in a commercial relationship between the two nations. No longer necessary as military allies, Indigenous people were now seen as an impediment to white settlement. In British North America, reformers also called for relocation as part of a "civilizing mission." For example, James Givins of the Indian Department nurtured the creation of early reserves as places where Indigenous people could progress toward civilization. In the 1830s, Francis Bond Head, lieutenant governor of Upper Canada, took the removal idea to a greater extreme, advocating for the relocation of Anishinaabe peoples to the isolation of Manitoulin Island in Lake Huron.[47]

Although the emigration and loan ideas expressed in the 1836 select committee report were not directly about North America, they could be applied to and did refer to the North American colonies.[48] The report favoured a new American-style system in which land was managed by a centralized public office, not by companies. Struck by the amount of wealth that the American state could generate from the disposal of wastelands, the committee held the American process in high esteem and recommended that the colonies in the British Empire should adopt much the same system. It wanted a regular and "uniform system of sale," as well as a well-organized system with a General Land Office that had no "political duties whatsoever."[49] It argued that Australia instituted a standardized system in 1831 but that it needed a "superintendence similar to that of the United States, and with the guarantee of an Act of Parliament."[50] Throughout the report, the comparison of British colonial land management to the United States created a narrative that land in British settler colonies could generate enough revenue in the near future to pay off the principal plus interest of any loan, just as in the United States. However, as subsequent chapters will address, this could not occur in British North America for a variety of reasons. In fact, such universal standardization did not occur in the United States either.[51]

The select committee report recommended that colonies where "the climate ... is not unfavourable to the European frame" should put the revenue from land sales into an emigration fund, which would pay for people to populate them.[52] The committee assembled evidence from individuals who favoured Wakefield's colonization system, including Wakefield himself, who testified before it. Although its recommendations touted Wakefieldian ideas, they did not mention how the initial emigrants would be funded to produce the revenue from land. Nonetheless, the evidence collected by the committee did answer this question. Testifying before it, LPEC member William W. Whitmore was asked whether emigrants should be initially funded by "a Parliamentary grant" (as in the Wilmot-Horton model) or by "a loan chargeable on the future proceeds of land sales in the colony." Whitmore replied that the colonial government should raise "money in the money market."[53] When Wakefield testified before the committee, he was asked, "Do you conceive that the revenue to be derived from land sales might be anticipated with the benefit of the colonies, by the borrowing of money for the purpose of emigration, on the security of future sales?"[54] Replying that this was a "most useful means," Wakefield cited the example of the United States and its method of disposing wastelands and paying for emigration. According to him, the land fund generated by the United States had an annual revenue of $4 million. He added that the United States could "wish to borrow so much money as will enable us to bring into the United States, a number of young labourers exceeding the number of our slaves." Wakefield went so far as suggest that financing the government on the money market would play a role in the possible abolition of slavery in the United States.[55] The land would become a "pre-eminent security" if it could be leveraged to raise more funds to pay for emigrants to develop it to give it a higher market value. When asked, "How would you propose to carry your views into effect; by the anticipation of the land revenue?" In reference to the colony of South Australia's commissioners and their work on converting land into capital, Wakefield answered,

> By empowering the commissioners, who were charged with the other parts of the operation, to raise money for the purpose of immigration,

> upon the security, for each colony, of the land to be afterwards sold in that colony; and binding them, of course, to apply the sum which they raised by anticipation for each colony, in conveying emigrants to that colony, and to no other.[56]

The settler colony's public debt would provide the initial spark that would ignite what reformers hoped would become the massive wildfire of British emigration. The committee raised one objection to this plan, but not regarding the faulty logic of incurring an enormous debt based on an idea of the future profitability of unceded Indigenous territory. Suspecting that the plan would disrupt the colonial economy, the committee asked Wakefield, "Do you not think that this anticipation of the future land sales for the purpose of emigration might lead to mischievous gluts of labour in the colonies?" To which Wakefield replied, "I think not, provided that proper precautions were taken for preventing gluts of labour."[57]

Robert Torrens, chairman of the South Australia Commission, also testified before the select committee. He referred to one of the many disagreements between the colonial reformers and the Colonial Office.[58] In this case, Lord Glenelg, secretary of state for war and the colonies, had tried to change the conditions of land sales in South Australia. Torrens argued that this "excited in the minds of the colonists a very angry feeling."[59] He elaborated on a key element of the South Australia Act – that "the commissioners shall in the first place raise a loan of £20,000 for the purpose of indemnifying the government against any possible contingency of expense falling upon the mother country." When asked whether the commissioners had done so, Torrens replied that they had "raised a loan of £30,000 upon the security of future revenue, to be raised in the colony at the rate of 10 per cent."[60] However, in order to sell land, both emigrants and the colony needed immediate funds, and that money would be paid for by a "loan on the security of that future fund."[61] Torrens added that the "principle ... is already embodied in the South Australian Act, of raising loans upon the security of future sales of land." He testified that this principle could be used to ameliorate the situation in Ireland, which had a "surplus population" – or too many unemployed and low-employed people who might cause social unrest.

In his discussion of Irish emigration, he laid out exactly how the "money market" was tied to land appropriation and large-scale emigration. He explained,

> Though the system of selling land in Australia has hitherto been very imperfect, yet in the course of the last year the revenue realised from this source has been 300,000£. This is a constantly-increasing revenue, and an increasing revenue of 100,000£ per annum would pay the interest at five per cent, of a loan of two millions, therefore if the Government were to introduce an Act rendering this system permanent and universal throughout Australia, there could be no difficulty in immediately negotiating a loan of two millions applicable to Irish emigration. An emigration loan of two millions, properly applied, would take out, I think, about 200,000 individuals of all ages, to Australia. Now the introduction of so large a population would greatly increase the demand for land; the increased demand for land would occasion increased sales, and those increased sales would produce a very greatly increased emigration fund, an increased emigration fund would be again applicable to an increased emigration, and an increased emigration increasing the population of the colony, would again increase the demand for land and the emigration fund; thus there is a geometrical principle of progression in the system.[62]

In other words, the public debt gave market value to Indigenous territories that were outside of created real estate, and this value came from speculating on their future value. The money from the public debt could fund emigrants, who would then drive up the value of land through development and competition to purchase it. This increased value would allow the colony to raise a larger debt, and so the cycle of inflating the market value of land through the public debt would continue. The commissioners who formulated the South Australia Act mentioned that the money could not be raised on the money market unless the "lenders felt assured" that the fundamental principles of the statute were sound and would be faithfully adhered to. Government debt financing needed a strong central state (or at least the belief that one existed) to assure creditors that they would get their money back.[63]

For example, in the late nineteenth century, the LSE refused to recognize the debt issues of New Zealand's provincial governments, because it did not have confidence that the provincial governments were strong enough to reimburse it, a stance that forced New Zealand to issue one stock. This centralized the New Zealand government around the issue of a single government debt. Now there was only a single government debt, as opposed to multiple provincial debts.[64] The Canadian debt also consolidated with the 1867 British North America Act, which created the dominion loan. Creditors used various measures to determine the creditworthiness of a government.[65] Importantly, the perceived ability to appropriate lands added to this creditworthiness, as did the confidence that an act of the legislature would uphold debt contracts, both of which required a strong settler government.

Torrens told the select committee that he had originally objected to the Wakefield plan, along with Robert Wilmot-Horton, James Mill, and Thomas Malthus, because he believed that wastelands were inferior land. Now, however, he had realized that they were "good" and "useful," and that the market could transform them into productive land to generate future revenue. This comment emphasizes that wastelands equated to the territories of Indigenous nations, not to swamps or other areas that were not suitable for human use. Torrens noted that the objections of Wilmot-Horton, James Mill, and Malthus to the Wakefield scheme "were grounded on the received principles of political economy." The three men were opposed to the National Colonization Society (Wakefield's colonial reform group) and had published a pamphlet regarding the disadvantages of "concentrating" emigration in the colonies. Although the idea of taking out a loan based on the future revenue of wastelands that had been made profitable was central to Torrens's testimony, it did not arouse criticism from the select committee or from those who opposed colonial reform.

Torrens noted that he embraced Wakefield's methods once he saw that government debt would "permit population and capital freely to spread over the most fertile and best suited lands."[66] His testimony also reveals why the British government would accept the scheme, as it could potentially free Britain of its colonial financial burden. From these colonial reforms, and specifically from the recommendations of the select committee, the British government set up the Colonial Land and Emigration Commission, an intermediary between emigrants, colonial land management, and the Colonial Office that operated from 1840 until 1878.[67] This body regulated land sales and emigration into the settler colonies. In this extension of colonial jurisdiction to regulate land and emigration, Indigenous territories provided the security for loans and counted as government assets abstracted as wastelands. In this context, settler colonial public debts had become a discrete sector of investment on the LSE by the 1850s.

Indigenous Territories on the London Stock Exchange

Were it not for the London Stock Exchange, this public borrowing might not have scaled so rapidly. It was one thing to claim Indigenous territories as wastelands up for grabs to borrow against, and quite another to actually receive capital calculated from their perceived future value. The development of settler colonies brought an emergent global market in settler colonial public debts, and it was in this context that Canada's public debt flourished. P.J. Cain and A.G. Hopkins make a clear case for the importance of finance capital in the expansion of empire. They argue that Canada was "unlikely" to have achieved independence as a nation had it not made use of the London financial markets.[68] Even before Donald Creighton published *The Road to Confederation* in 1964, Canadian historiography debated the importance of the London securities market to Confederation.[69] However, the study of financial markets and Confederation has become somewhat synonymous with R.T. Naylor's now infamous reference to the Barings Bank – that the "Baring Brothers were the true Fathers of Confederation."[70] Although the Baring Brothers did play a key role in financing the debts, this was certainly not the whole story. Scholars have taken note of the "sudden appearance" of the colonial debt market. However, the significance of these colonial securities as an impetus for settler colonization has received little scholarly attention, and the fact that the colonies became settler states has received virtually none.[71]

The consolidated public debt in what became the Canadian settler state did not begin in isolation. Three distinct government debt markets emerged as the nineteenth century progressed: the British government debt; the foreign government debts including those of Europe, Latin America, and the United States; and the settler colonial government debts. Canada's public debt, which manifested around the same time as most other national debt, was not an anomaly; it was part of a broader pattern of government financing via debts issued as securities on the LSE. Although technically, all public debts constituted one market, contemporaries involved in the securities market distinguished between the public debts as British, foreign, and colonial. "Colonial" referred only to the settler colonies. The settler colonial government debt market technically began in the 1830s, with the first issue of the Upper Canadian, South Australian, and Van Diemen's Land loans, but it did not encompass all settler colonies until the late nineteenth century. As the next chapter will outline, the Upper Canadian debt predated its issue on the LSE, but in the 1830s it became the first of the British North American colonial debts issued as securities on the LSE, closely followed by the New Brunswick debt.[72] The Canadian debt should include the provincial debts, as section 111 of the British North America Act of 1867 stipulated that "Canada shall be liable for the Debts and Liabilities of each Province existing at the Union." Under sections 112–16, the provinces owed that debt to the Canadian government, which in turn owed the entire combined amount to debtholders.[73] However, since the provinces had amortization periods after Confederation, and since they also extended their debt contracts to make principal payments, individual provincial debts could be bought and sold long after Confederation consolidated them into the dominion debt.

The British North America Act briefly outlined the transition of public debts from colonial to dominion and provincial governments. Decades earlier, the 1841 union of Upper and Lower Canada attached Upper Canada's massive debt to Lower Canada's lesser debt and relatively high revenues from the St. Lawrence waterway.[74] With the creation of the Province of Canada, the debt centralized power in many ways. Following Confederation, in the first half of 1868, the unequal power balance between the provinces of the former Province of Canada, now Quebec and Ontario, and the dominion created tensions around which government had responsibility of paying for the debt. To sort out which government body should pay for the former Province of Canada's $62,500,000 debt at 5 percent interest, Ottawa chose arbitrators to represent each government.[75] The division of responsibility to pay the principal and interest resulted in forty-two tedious meetings between the three arbitrators; David Lewis Macpherson, who represented Ontario; Charles Dewey Day, who represented Quebec; and John Hamilton Gray, who represented the Government of Canada. The arbitration resulted in a decision to saddle Ontario with just over $9.8 million and Quebec with nearly $8.8 million.[76]

Day disagreed with the amounts assigned to Ontario and Quebec, and subsequently resigned his position as arbitrator because the loan and division of property between the two provinces, as the Speaker of the Legislative Council phrased it, "favours the Province of Ontario at the expense of the Province of Quebec."[77] Nonetheless, under the terms of an 1873 act, "Ontario and Quebec became and remained conjointly liable to Canada for any excess of debt over the former instead of the latter sum" of $73,006,088.84, instead of the original $62,500,000.00.[78] The matter ended up in the Supreme Court of Canada in 1895, highlighting the link between colonial government jurisdiction over Indigenous territories and the public debt, with this particular court case centring on the colonial land claim derived from the Robinson Treaty of 1850.[79] Originating in the early nineteenth century, Canada's public debt developed in a complex manner over colonial claims of Indigenous lands and waters.

What was the historical context of these unprecedented government debts? In 1822, the General Purpose Committee of the London Stock Exchange recorded a flurry of petitions to open a "fair Market for Foreign Securities."[80] The desire for a foreign sector on the stock exchange reflected the "immense transactions that have taken place in the Securities of Foreign Governments within the last 6 months."[81] By 1823, the LSE had established the Foreign Stock Exchange and drew strict lines of trading where "Foreign Securities should be confined to the Foreign Stock Market and dealings in the British Funds restricted to the Stock Exchange."[82] The "Foreign Stocks" printed on the front page of *The Course of the Exchange*, a popular securities list, grew significantly in number, and the worth of foreign loans swelled to £40 million between 1822 and 1825.[83] Along with both American and French government securities, foreign stocks included Austrian,

Belgian, Greek, Mexican, Peruvian, Portuguese, and Spanish bonds, and many, many more. The problems with the early loans, as in the 1820s default of Greece, made government securities an implausible, and not inevitable, outcome of a debt securities market. Notably, the expansion of the settler colonial government securities market occurred after the Latin American loan bubble burst. Financed by a public debt, Greece fought its expensive war of independence, as did the Latin American countries. Engaging in war is a risky business, with no guarantee that a nation-state will triumph and pay back the principal and the interest of its loan. This made investing in foreign government debts a form of gambling on the outcome of war and created inherent instability in the debt market. Paula Vedoveli states that this instability persisted into the late nineteenth century with the Baring Crisis, which she described as "the most dramatic financial collapse of the nineteenth century."[84] Not only did the Barings Bank issue the first Latin American loan; in 1824, it also backed many of the Canadian debts.[85] In theory at least, investing in a settler colonial government debt would be a surer bet because of the colony's perceived stability and direct connection to Britain.

As the securities market grew, so did the publications that dealt with it. Mary Poovey traces the proliferation of financial writing as a genre of the blossoming credit economy. This genre included guides that described the securities market for investors.[86] Broadsheets, newspapers, and especially *The Course of the Exchange,* a bi-weekly listing of securities and their prices, supplied investors with the latest trading information. First published in 1697, *The Course of the Exchange* had been founded by John Castaing, who was in the habit of listing stock prices on the walls of Jonathan's Coffee House, which acted as an unofficial stock exchange before the 1801 formalization of the LSE.[87] The early stockbrokers initially met at the coffee house but later moved to the larger premises at Garraway's Coffee House.[88] *The Course of the Exchange* sheds light on the public debt market for settler colonial securities and shows just how large this market became. By the 1870s, the trade in such securities had expanded to the point where *The Course of the Exchange* began to list them on its front page, which suggests that they had increased in both number and importance after 1850.[89]

Throughout the nineteenth century, *The Course of the Exchange* was always printed on both sides of a single sheet of paper. Confining itself to just one page would have been convenient and would have kept costs down, as it was printed every Tuesday and Friday. When the number of securities available for investment began to increase exponentially, especially after the Napoleonic Wars, *The Course of the Exchange* still came out on a single sheet. However, reflecting the rapid growth of the LSE, the size of the sheet expanded, moving from that typically used for a small book to a large broadsheet by the 1880s. The publication provides a snapshot of the data needed to make any serious calculations of total market capitalization, varying interests rates, market integration, or how many investors existed and what they invested in. However, scholars have found that its information corresponds with their own statistical measurements regarding market growth.[90] It clearly shows the government debts for the settler colonies market, or what it labelled "Colonial Government Securities."

In the late 1850s, *The Course of the Exchange* began to include a discrete category for the public debts of the settler colonies after the Crown agent for colonies expressed a wish to make the colonial securities "more generally sought" and requested that the LSE list the securities of Canada, New South Wales, Victoria, and South Australia as "a distinct heading, say of 'Colonial Government Securities.'" The LSE General Purpose Committee complied with the agent's request.[91] The fact that *The Course of the Exchange* chose not to label colonial government debts as "foreign" has significance, suggesting that they were categorized within Britain's economic sphere as a part of empire but also that they were distinct from the British economy. Securities were listed under certain subheadings and were grouped on either the front of the page or the back depending on their importance. The subheadings sometimes reflected major historical changes. For example, after the Napoleonic Wars, a "French Funds" subheading began to appear, and British investors had the opportunity to invest in French securities.[92] Famously, David Ricardo invested in the French rentes, making an extraordinary amount of money as a result.[93] "American Funds" had its own categorization, a subheading that had changed to "Public Securities of the United States of America" by mid-century. American and French securities were listed under the category

"Foreign Stocks," but as the number of American securities on the London market grew, they were eventually awarded their own category. The LSE always had involvement in foreign government securities in the form of government debts. For example, despite the uncertain relationship between the British and American governments in the early nineteenth century, British investors made up the majority of non-American holders of many US debt securities.[94]

Tracking the development of what *The Course of the Exchange* labelled "Colonial Securities" sheds light on Canada's early public debt. Prior to early 1857, the publication listed a few securities from what became Canada, such as the Hudson's Bay Company issues, the Canada Company (for a short period), and the Upper Canada Bonds after January 1837 in the "Miscellaneous" section, which appeared near the bottom of the back page.[95] This placement and the fact that they were not given their own category suggests that they were not seen as significant investments. By contrast, the public debts of Britain, France, and the United States were listed at the top of the front page, which also included the securities for major development and public works projects such as canals and gas light companies.[96]

On March 6, 1857, *The Course of the Exchange* introduced a category titled "Colonial Gov. Securities," which appeared on the back of the page and dealt exclusively with settler government debts.[97] The Hudson's Bay Company, for example, remained in the "Miscellaneous" category.[98] This change drew a clear line between government securities spawned from debts and the securities of private companies. The overwhelming majority of the debts listed in the new category were those of settler colonies, many of which became autonomous nation-states with centralized governments, governed by British colonizers. The new category also encompassed colonies that did not become settler states, such as Mauritius and Ceylon (Sri Lanka), which were included because they were seen as potential settler states. Various government inquiries linked both Mauritius and Ceylon to other settler colonies, such as the Cape of Good Hope.[99] The British discourse about tropical settler colonies discussed the feasibility of places such as Mauritius and Ceylon to potentially become settler zones in the same manner as South Africa.[100] This "tropical colonial development" for British settlement occurred experimentally throughout the empire, in places such as Udagamandalam in the Nilgiri Hills of Tamil Nadu.[101]

Most British attempts to settle in the tropics, however, failed to produce a settler state, though not for lack of trying. For example, the British government allowed for the clearing of massive areas in the Nilgiri Hills in present-day Tamil Nadu to establish large-scale plantations of cinchona trees, which were native to the Andes. To obtain samples of the trees, the British government (in a race against Dutch efforts to make cinchona plantations) placed smugglers in South America, who illegally collected them from Peru and elsewhere, sending them on to Kew Gardens, just outside of London, via a complicated transfer system. Eventually, an entire global industry sprang from the cinchona plantations. The British government went to so much trouble because an alkaloid extracted from cinchona bark could treat malaria. Caused by the *Plasmodium falciparum* parasite that was carried by the anopheles mosquito, malaria thwarted mass British settlement in the tropics.[102] Known as quinine, the alkaloid attacked the parasite and was so well regarded for its anti-malarial properties that the British made it into a tonic to drink as a prophylactic. Thus, the gin and tonic was born from the British desire for settlement and imperial expansion. Quinine still gives many brands of tonic water their distinct taste.[103] The immense expense and effort to transplant plants to India highlights the importance that the British government placed on white settlement in the tropics.

On January 4, 1870, *The Course of the Exchange* began to list colonial government securities on its front page. They had become so numerous and so socially important that eventually they were second only to the "British Government Funds."[104] Figure 1 charts their increase, a boom that began around the time of Confederation. The figure includes the pre-1857 Canadian securities, but technically colonial securities numbered zero since there was no listing for colonial government securities or a separated colonial government securities market until after 1857.[105] This would change as the nineteenth century wore on. The buying and selling of colonial government debt helped to finance the building of the settler nation-states. From the first official financed debt, with the South Australia loan, to the various Canadian loans, the LSE made it possible

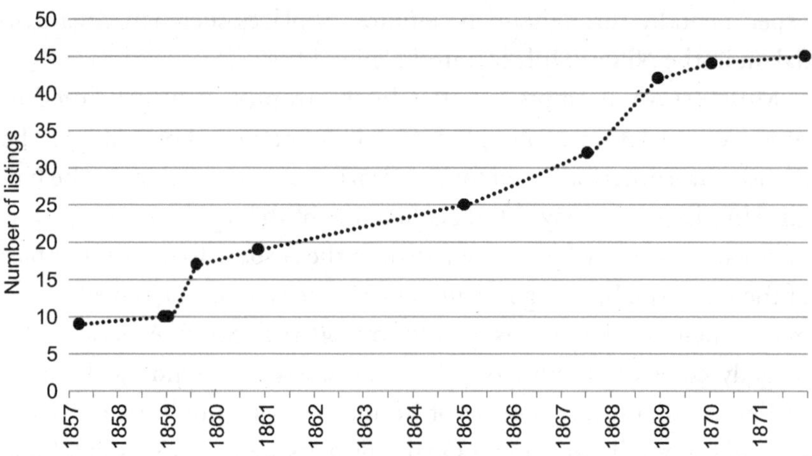

1 Growth of the colonial government securities market

for the settler colonies to fund their governments and eventually their independence as nation-states.

Different ways in which to buy the Canadian debt, such as through scrips issues, bonds, and debentures, and at differing rates of interest, also increased in number. To highlight the significance of these debts to the establishment of Canada, when Finance Minister Leonard Tilley was challenged about the growing annual expenditure in 1883, he explained that this would not pose a tax burden on the tax-paying population. Instead, land – Indigenous nations' territories in the northwest – and government access to loans could more than make up for any spending. He noted that peoples were taxed at about "13 cts. a head less than they would have been taxed for the annual expenditure between 1874 and 1878 … but, unless that increase causes an increase in taxation the people will not object, but will rather be satisfied to know that our country is prospering."[106] He continued that the Canadian government would "receive from our lands in the North-West a large a sum during this fiscal year as during last year, $1,750,000" and that if anything should happen to the inflow of money from Indigenous lands, and revenues from canals and elsewhere, then "a loan of two or three millions of dollars in Canada would be taken up readily because there are enquiries in every direction for our securities."[107] Money could be drawn from the taxpayers to cover government expenditure, but more capital in the form of securities could be drawn from debt including the appropriation of Indigenous territories as assets to raise a loan. According to an 1875 issue of *The Course of the Exchange*, the market capitalization of the Government of Canada loan totalled approximately £10 million. This did not include loans to provinces such as British Columbia, New Brunswick, Nova Scotia, Prince Edward Island, and Quebec, which had the largest provincial loan listing of £800,000.[108] In 1890, the total loan to Canada was £58.7 million.[109]

It is difficult to get a clear picture of exactly how much money flowed between the British North American colonies and Britain with the public debt. The figures of total loans and market capitalizations in the context of the annual budget can speak only to numbers that are frozen in time, as the actual monetary amounts cannot be easily assessed. For example, the total loan would include the debt over time, with interest split between differing securities. The market capitalization is merely the value given to the loan based on trading activity (the number of shares times the current market price) and can say something about the value that trade gave to the overall loan only on a specific date. The price of each share was also dependent on the number of individuals and firms trading. Given this, the particularities of the colonial loans need more in-depth research and analysis.

Each provincial debt was consolidated as the Dominion of Canada debt. The existence of the colonial provincial debts and then the Dominion of Canada debt points to the fact that Canada's public debt did not develop evenly. First, the LSE issued the Upper Canada bond in 1837. On January 1, 1839, it issued "New Brunswick Scrip" (a type of debt instrument). On March 6, 1857, New Brunswick's official public debt was listed at £166,000 at 6 percent annual interest. On March 13 of that year, the LSE listed the public debt of Nova Scotia at £250,000 at 6 percent annual interest. Nova Scotia's debt fluctuated slightly throughout the years, whereas New Brunswick's issues remained steady. Although Prince Edward Island had a large debt, as shown in Chapter 4, it was not issued on the LSE until after the island invested in the railway during the early 1870s. On January 5, 1875, it had £220,000 worth of debt listed at 6 percent yearly interest.[110]

Nearly two decades after Confederation, campaign literature issued by the Conservative Party split borrowed money into the following categories: "provincial debts assumed by the Dominion" ($107,000,000); "monies expended on railways" ($103,000,000); "money for purchase Northwest" ($1,5000,000); "Sir. Richard Cartwright's deficits" ($4,500,000); "Sir. Richard Cartwright's losses on loans obtained" ($4,800,000); "canals" ($28,543,978); "lighthouses and navigation" ($8,284,580); and "government buildings and miscellaneous public works" ($13,147,318).[111] Richard John Cartwright, in the government in many capacities including as Liberal finance minister, was responsible for two loans in 1874 and 1876 at 4 percent interest.[112] Many, including Cartwright, attempted to manage the massive debt that the dominion government had incurred through Confederation and the construction of infrastructure; however, as Chapter 3 will highlight, because such infrastructure was heavily subsidized, expenditure exceeded revenue.[113] Government debts that could be bought and sold on the LSE were initially backed by the territories of Indigenous nations, which along with British North America's close ties to Britain gave it credit. However, as Finance Minister Cartwright discovered, the loans may have built the dominion economy, but they eventually came due, and an enormous gap existed between them and the revenue that the development projects actually produced.

In his 1876 budget speech to the House of Commons, Cartwright expressed some frustration when he remarked that "we could have managed our affairs much more easily and more profitably to this country if a little more foresight had been exercised before we engaged to construct enormous public works in all parts of the Dominion in the precise years in which a large portion of our debt matured." In that year, $1,879,000 worth of debts had matured; in 1877–78, the figure would amount to $5,731,000; in 1878–79, it would rise to $7,624,000; in 1879–80, it reached $6,060,000; and a few smaller sums came due in the following years.[114] In this "embarrassed" context, Cartwright desired to "make provision far in advance" for the maturing debts.[115] Citing the "favourable condition of the English money market," he sought to borrow money in consultation with financial agents and John Rose, the former minister of finance turned investment banker in London. The result initiated a loan that included 5 percent Canadian bonds, Canadian 4 percent bonds, and £1,500,000 bonds, some of which was secured by an imperial loan guarantee. Of this money, Cartwright would use a "considerable proportion" to "pay off debts and obligations of the country, which bear a much higher rate of interest."[116] This amounted to loans to pay for more loans. Loans to pay for due principals and interest rates led to structural indebtedness. This pattern of structural indebtedness began in each colonial government's early debt history and continued to plague Canada long after Confederation.

Conclusion

Anyone who considers lending money does not make the decision solely on the basis of the borrower's current financial circumstances, but on the potential future ones as well. After all, a borrower who has access to capital has no need to take out a loan. Lenders make their decisions not on the present, but on the future. When colonial governments asked for a loan, their main future assets were the "wastelands," a word that coded the territory of Indigenous nations as available for colonial government appropriation. The amount of the loan was based on the future value of the land, a value that would prove unachievable as the debts proliferated through the decades and then through the centuries. This led to two distinct structural features of the Dominion of Canada: indebtedness and an imperative to expand to capture more Indigenous lands as security for further loans to pay off the initial ones. Soon, a discourse about structural indebtedness and its links to promoting civilization, or capitalist social and economic relationships, attempted to legitimize heavy government borrowing. In 1874, British political economist Charles Fenn praised the system of public borrowing:

> It is very clear that concomitantly with its debt, the world has grown rich; and there is this striking feature between the debt now currently contracted and that at the commencement of the present century – that, instead of being applied exclusively to war ... it is largely employed in the construction of railways, steamships, telegraphs, improvements of all kinds, at home, in our colonies, and in foreign lands, and that it now assumed, in part, although by no means wholly, that reproductive character which promises well for the borrowers as for the lenders.[117]

The "reproductive character" of debt took on new meaning. The colonial reform theory, of settler colonialism as a perpetual motion machine that could endlessly reproduce itself, needed an initial spark of debt to ignite the engine. The British colonial reformers and, even earlier, those who implemented borrowing in the British North American colonies believed that the debt could be paid off. Recall John Stuart Mill's assertion that only the first amount of money was needed to get the fire of colonization started. Fenn, on the other hand, used "reproductive" in the sense that the public debt allowed settler colonies to reproduce capitalist social and economic relationships, which justified not pursuing an economic policy to end government indebtedness. Suddenly, the rhetoric de-emphasized the necessity of paying off the debt and stressed the positive qualities of maintaining it.

By the late nineteenth century, some Canadian political economists had started to accept the federal government debt as a permanent feature of the state. In 1898, James Mavor, professor of political economy and constitutional history at the University of Toronto, wrote in praise of what he called the "Canadian policy of development" funded via public borrowing. Mavor did not fear bankruptcy, and like the provincial and dominion leaders who instituted public borrowing, he believed that it was not a concern, as long as Canada had "good credit." This belief opened up a space for borrowing unprecedented amounts of money. Mavor predicted that, as "long as the capital borrowed by Canada from Europe is wisely expended upon productive enterprises ... and as long as the interest of the debt can be easily met, there does not seem much likelihood of the adoption of any drastic system of redemption of debt."[118] Paying the interest would ensure that Canada did not default. As for the principal, when it came due, the government simply needed to borrow more, as Finance Minister Cartwright had done. This relied on a policy to "unite the forces of the state with those of private corporations."[119]

At its core, the "Canadian policy of development" equated with expansion over Indigenous land – an inherently imperialist directive. It had dire consequences for Indigenous peoples, whose territories formed the heart of the settler state structure.[120] Financed by their public debts, the British North American governments cut deep tracks of devastation across Indigenous territories. Tragically, in their efforts to domesticate the wastelands of the liberal imagination, they produced real wastelands with their policies that pursued unyielding environmental destruction.

PART II
Structural Indebtedness of the Settler State

Expansion Unbounded: Upper Canada and Public Debt Financing 3

The Government was also bound, as a compensation to the Upper provinces, to enlarge the canals, as soon as the finances of the Dominion would permit, and as this enlargement, so far as the Welland and Cornwall canals were concerned, was undertaken by the Mackenzie Government, the Liberals cannot complain it was undertaken too soon. When the Northwest was purchased, the necessity for large expenditure with a view to its development was admitted, and when British Columbia was brought into the Confederation, it was on the condition of the construction of a railway uniting the Pacific ocean with the railway system of Canada, the work to be at once commenced and continued until completion within ten years. All these obligations have been SANCTIONED BY THE PEOPLE at several general elections. In light of these obligations the increase in the public debt is not only easily explained, but is completely justified.

– Conservative Party of Canada, *Facts for the People: Character and Composition of the Dominion Debt,* 1885

Debt and Expansion, in Perpetuity

Charles Fenn's argument that public debts had transformed from a method of financing wars to a mechanism for development and James

Mavor's observation about the "Canadian policy of development" certainly reflected reality in British North America by the mid-nineteenth century. Rhetorically, the public debt and responsible government interlocked; *Facts for the People,* the piece of Tory campaign literature quoted above, claimed that "the people" had sanctioned all the debts contracted by the dominion government because "the people" had voted for politicians who used public debts, even though the franchise was quite narrow at the time. As it noted, however, both Liberal and Conservative Parties used public debts to pay for Canada, primarily because this was the only method of large-scale capital acquisition. Like John Stuart Mill and many other British political economists, Fenn saw the debt as a boon to civilization for the world precisely because it produced market value. Nowhere was this more apparent than in land reforms in settler colonies.

In the 1820s, the Upper Canadian government used its public debt to fund development projects of unprecedented scale, such as the Welland Canal. Despite great optimism, the projects failed to produce enough revenue to pay the principal and interest of the loans. Seeking more credit to access more loans, the government pursued land reform from the 1830s onward, as a way to leverage Indigenous territories as security. This model illustrates the first of the three principles of the settler state: the necessity of expansion over Indigenous homelands to promise future value for credit. The approach freed the colony from any lingering desire to "protect" Indigenous lands and waters, as the 1763 Royal Proclamation had mandated.

Land reform policy exemplified the moral ease with which colonial governments appropriated Indigenous territories, even the portions that they recognized as Indian reserves. These were held in trust by the Upper Canadian government, and Indigenous people were legally codified as wards of the state. An 1895 Supreme Court of Canada case that dealt with the Robinson Treaty of 1850 noted that in "transactions with the aborigines from the earliest colonial times in North America the Government has assumed the status of the Indian tribes to be that of distinct political communities ... [When] some legal possessory right by the tribes in actual occupation has always been recognized, then the form of the transactions has been that of a treaty" – a nation-to-nation agreement.

However, the logic of white supremacy qualified the court's definition of the nation-to-nation relationship: "It is to be taken into account that the Indians relatively to the whites are in a state of dependency or pupilage, and that the nearest legal analogy as to the relationship between their tribes and the Government is that of guardian and ward."[1] The money from the Indian reserves went into special accounts that held funds from their sales, rents, and leases, but through the legal mechanism of the trust, the Upper Canadian government could, and did, dip into them and could exert control over these spaces. Funds could be moved from the "Indian Investment Accounts" to the "Indian Accounts" and then to the "City of Toronto," the "Simcoe District," and the "Grand River Navigation Company," to name a few.[2] In this way, reform of Indian reserves, even when reformers argued to abolish them altogether, seemed less pressing than reform of the clergy reserves (as discussed below).

The Welland Canal

In the 1820s, Upper Canada set itself on building infrastructure, particularly canals, to extend trade and communications and to open up inland settlement. Prior to this, Britain had maintained its "ancient custom" of settling only on the coasts and along the St. Lawrence River in an effort to prioritize seaboard settlements and to avoid conflict with its Indigenous allies. The Royal Proclamation of 1763 meant to avoid situations such as Pontiac's Uprising, which was named after Odawa chief Obwandiyag, who led the Anishinaabe Three Fires Confederacy to push back against British incursion into its territories. The proclamation drew a north-south line along the Appalachian Mountains, forbidding settler encroachment in the Indigenous homelands to the west of it but, in fact, opening the door to settlement.[3]

The British Board of Trade and Plantations, which managed colonial affairs along with other arms of government until the emergence of the Colonial Office in the nineteenth century, and imperial policy also opposed the inland flow of British immigrants because of the fear that, unable to access shipping routes and thus send raw materials to Britain, they would naturally process them at home. When the United Empire Loyalists fled the United States, the vast majority established themselves in the Maritimes, which eventually resulted in the establishment of the colonial government of New Brunswick when it separated from the colony of Nova Scotia in 1784.[4] John Reid notes that this influx, which also led to the creation of Upper Canada, put immense pressure on Wabanaki territories. He adds that "worse was to come as Scottish settlement began" in the early nineteenth century.[5]

Population shifts after the Seven Years' and American Revolutionary Wars changed inland trade relationships as well. Canal and new waterway infrastructure such as the Trent-Severn Waterway, which connected Lake Ontario to Georgian Bay, was praised as a tool to "open up the interior of the province" to facilitate both resource extraction and settlement to increase land value.[6] American advancements in trade infrastructure, such as the Erie Canal of 1825, also pushed Upper Canada to develop its own infrastructure, so it began to borrow to pay for development.[7] As mentioned, the projects did not generate enough revenue for the colonial government.[8] They did turn a profit for some investors, however. Individuals would make or lose money depending on the amount of market speculation that inflated or deflated the value of the canal stocks they had purchased and when they chose to buy or sell. Madeline Whetung shows that elite settlers had a vested interest in building the canals because they stood to make a profit. The projects proved unprofitable in more than just their inability to make money from revenues. They caused immense destruction in both Haudenosaunee and Anishinaabe homelands, as well as in the habitats of other-than-human beings, including eels and *manoomin* (wild rice).[9]

Situated about ten kilometres west of Niagara Falls, the Welland Canal connects Lake Ontario to Lake Erie. Albert Schrauwers's detailed synopsis of its founding shows how the Welland Canal Company (WCC) moved to incorporation as a way to induce capital investment. He outlines Upper Canadian land policy and legal mechanisms, such as incorporation, as a part of this process.[10] The debt-financed construction of the Welland Canal underscores the directive to enfold Indigenous territories into the blossoming settler colony. Construction of the canal began in January 1824, after the Upper Canadian legislature passed an act to incorporate the WCC. The act granted the company permission not only to survey lands in the Niagara region, but also to select sites for mills, warehouses, and manufacturing, and to purchase those sites. It allowed the WCC to make reservoirs, tunnels, and aqueducts, and to "feed" the canal with "brooks, streams, springs, watercourses, hallows, or other repositories of water" within a thousand yards, or just under a kilometre, from "any part of the Canal" or newly made reservoirs.[11] The WCC also acquired special privileges over the acquisition of land on Indian reserves, as long as it offered *post facto* compensation. It could access land, appropriate and redirect waterways, and take raw material "without any previous treaty whatsoever with the respective owners or occupiers," as long as it "recompense for such damages to the owners and occupiers of, or other persons interested in, such lands, grounds, property or hereditaments, within the space of six calendar months next."[12]

The Welland Canal project inaugurated the long-standing Canadian tradition of decoupling treaty rights from land rights through a process of privatizing Indigenous territories, whether unrecognized or recognized as Indian reserves. For example, Governor General Charles Bagot's "Report on the Affairs of the Indians in Canada" was submitted to the Legislative Assembly. Submitted in two parts in 1845 and 1847, it called for the implementation of "civilizing" policies to gain access to Indigenous lands and recommended that the reserve system be terminated. This approach would be echoed in 1969, with Pierre Elliott Trudeau's infamous White Paper, and in 2012, with the reserve privatization schemes of Stephen Harper.[13] Such were the many tools employed by the colonial state to extend its tendrils of jurisdiction deeper into Indigenous spaces. The Six Nations of the Grand River still push back against this ongoing incursion.[14]

Development projects and the public debt did not evoke any substantial partisan sentiment. Both liberal reformers and the Family Compact (the cabal of colonial elites who dominated politics and business) supported development and the canal. However, the question of whether to acquire the money from local banks or London financiers did spark some heated debate.[15] Manu Karuka highlights that the close ties between the imperial government, the colonial government, and the corporation in settler colonies articulated a property-rights-based framework around whiteness, or "shareholder whiteness." Karuka notes, "Finance capital and whiteness ripened through a historical elaboration of relationships between imperial corporations and colonial states, forging and sustaining continental imperialism."[16] The development of the Welland Canal and the financing of such a massive project had a noticeable white political consensus.

The British Crown had initially agreed to grant the WCC a ninth of the estimated costs of building the canal, a sum that, along with funds the company could raise with its own private securities, would pay for the construction. The Upper Canadian government approved a second charter that raised the authorized amount of company stock to £200,000.[17] Individuals subscribed £93,000, of which £10,000 was forfeited due to economic issues in Upper Canada. At the time, WCC stock was not sold on the London Stock Exchange, because receiving any funds bought by investors would take an impractical amount of time.[18] This left £57,000 out of £200,000 without financial backing.

The inability of the WCC to fund itself marked the beginning of its financial troubles, which prompted the Upper Canadian government to interfere in its affairs. What this points to is that though a company could sell, or be valued at £200,000, it could not access these funds unless investors bought the securities. After work began on the Welland Canal in 1824, the Upper Canadian legislature passed an act that enabled it to invest £50,000 of WCC stocks "on behalf of the public."[19] On January 20, 1826, the government also passed a statute to raise a loan to give to the company – An Act to Authorize the Government to Borrow A Certain Sum of Money, Upon Debenture, to be Loaned to the Welland Canal Company. It enabled the government to borrow £25,000, with the public as risk-bearer for the loan, to give to the WCC.[20] On March 6, 1830, after this initial debt, the government passed An Act to Grant a Further Loan to the Welland Canal Company, and to Regulate Their Further Operations.[21] The money from the public debt, as enabled by this legislation, went to the privately owned WCC. The 1830 act noted that "as soon as the said sum of twenty-five thousand pounds, or any part thereof, shall be so raised, it shall be lawful for the Governor, Lieutenant Governor, or person administering the government of this province, to issue his warrant upon the said Receiver General for the same, in favor of the said Welland Canal Company."[22]

The public money was "granted in aid," with the expectation that it could be paid back. Furthermore, John Henry Dunn, who had been receiver general of Upper Canada since 1820, was to pay the raised funds "into the hands of the president of the said company." The money was "to be held and applied by him to and for the uses of the said company in the completion of the said canal."[23] Interestingly (but perhaps not surprisingly), from 1825 to 1833, Dunn was also the president of the WCC. Deeply embedded in colonial politics, he was appointed to the Legislative Council of Upper Canada in 1822. In 1841, he won an election to represent the city of Toronto in the first Parliament of the Province of Canada until 1844.[24] Undisturbed by Dunn's political involvement, the lieutenant governor of Upper Canada, Peregrine Maitland, remarked that his dual role as receiver general and WCC president was "sufficient assurance that everything is intended and carried on in perfect good faith."[25] Dunn's ties to prosperous merchants such as Samuel Street, one of the wealthiest men in Upper Canada at the time, made him a good choice for both positions.

The necessity of such public and private crossovers in Upper Canada reveals the difficulty that colonizers faced as they attempted to build their society. Smaller amounts of capital borrowed from rich elites such as Street could partially finance a development project, but they were never enough to pay for all of it, so the government turned to legislation to institute public debt financing for private companies such as the WCC.[26] Unsurprisingly, the WCC had many ties to government. For example, one of its directors, Colonel Joseph Wells, was a member of the Legislative Council. One director was also attorney and solicitor general, and another was a member of the Legislative Assembly. In fact, four of the seven WCC directors held prominent positions in government, which often justified its involvement in private companies by citing the public "good."[27] Public risk supported private profits, but far from being perceived as a transgression, this blurring of public and private allowed the colony to function.

In so many ways, Upper Canada tied its fiscal well-being to the success of the WCC. If the company failed, the government would lose a significant amount of money and, importantly, could not generate future revenue for debt repayment, which could damage its credit. As time passed, the private WCC slowly became owned by the colonial government. In 1837, the government passed an act to raise the capital stock to £597,300, of which it held £454,500 (£209,500 was a consolidation of previous loans and subscriptions). In 1841, on the heels of a financial panic during the late 1830s, the government purchased the WCC through an act of the legislature. Despite the disappointing shortcomings of the Welland Canal, the government built the Cornwall Canal and the Beauharnois Canal (which involved, not coincidentally, Edward Gibbon Wakefield), as well as enlarging the Lachine Canal. An enlargement of the Beauharnois Canal was completed by 1845, and the Welland Canal opened. All of this caused a temporary upsurge in revenue, as traffic on the St. Lawrence increased.[28]

The Welland Canal project cut through and greatly changed Indigenous lands, though the Indigenous peoples had never surrendered their sovereignty over the area.[29] From the British perspective, the Anishinaabe had ceded their lands via the Upper Canada treaty process, which began in the 1780s. The British then granted part of the land to the Haudenosaunee, with the Haldimand Tract. However, what the treaties actually meant and whether they encompassed waterways, the growth of settlements, and large environmentally damaging projects such as the Welland Canal have been the subject of debate. Evidence shows that they did not apply to aquatic territory.[30] Nonetheless, operating under the assumption that the Crown was entitled to both lands and waters, the Government of Upper Canada authorized the WCC to reshape both. In the case of the Six Nations of the Grand River, some parcels of land were surrendered to the town of Brantford in 1829; however, the "true value" of land for the Six Nations exceeded its market price.[31] Dunn was appointed as a manager for the Six Nations Trust throughout the 1830s.[32] In 1847, the WCC received money from the Six Nations Trust, and there is no record that it was ever paid back.[33] The Six Nations have been protesting the Welland Canal's damage that extensive flooding from the Dunnville Dam (named after John Henry Dunn) caused since the 1820s.[34] In asserting sovereignty over Indigenous lands and peoples, settler societies created wastelands that were unfit for many forms of habitation.[35]

Title to land scaffolded the aggressive colonization of Indigenous territories in what would eventually become southern Ontario, an area with a dense settler population. The Six Nations of the Grand River had the misfortune of living in what would become one of the most expensive real estate markets in Canada, a market that developed from colonial policies of expansion, resource extraction, and "improvement" projects such as the Welland Canal. The Six Nations, who continuously fought against settler incursion, were required to prove that they possessed title to their land, despite the fact that the Haldimand Proclamation had outlined clear boundaries. In 1835, the Indian Office informed the Six Nations that they must demonstrate that their chief, Joseph Brant (who had passed away in 1807), had proof "of the validity of the original claims" and the titles "by the Crown to the parties" that were under investigation in this land claims case.[36]

Canal projects failed on many levels, especially in the case of the Trent-Severn Waterway, which proved an abject failure. The canal cut through Anishinaabe territories in what is now known as the Kawartha Lakes region. Since time immemorial, the Anishinaabe had traversed its interconnected lakes and waterways, and had harvested its abundant manoomin. Madeline Whetung shows how the canal affected what she calls the "Shoreline Law" of the Michi Saagiig Anishinaabe, whose homelands are in southern Ontario. This law is a particular type of place-based relationship between water, land, other-than-human beings (including manoomin), and the Michi Saagiig. It was greatly disturbed by the construction of the Trent-Severn waterway. The Michi Saagiig homelands came under Treaty 20, which Michi Saagiig leaders and colonial officials signed in 1818. Whetung argues that the colonial interpretation of the treaty did not distinguish between land and water jurisdiction, even though the Anishinaabe made requests respecting water tenure and the protection of wildlife, which the colonial government ultimately left out of the treaty document.[37] Leanne Betasamosake Simpson states that Anishinaabe international relations included humans, plants, and animals, which the Trent-Severn Waterway and consequent dam at Bobcaygeon negatively affected.[38]

The environmental destruction wrought by the canal cannot be overemphasized, as salmon and eel populations have significantly declined in the area. The manoomin now grows in a strained habitat, exacerbated by the influx of cottagers.[39] Doug Williams, an Elder from Curve Lake

First Nation, along with Dave Mowat, Leanne Betasamosake Simpson, James Whetung, and others who work toward food sovereignty plant manoomin in an effort to restore and revitalize their lands. Simpson emphasizes the deep significance of manoomin, eels, and salmon for the Michi Saagiig, and notes that "colonialism and capitalism are based on extracting and assimilating." She laments,

> My land is seen as a resource. My relatives in the plant and animal worlds are seen as resources. My culture and knowledge is a resource. My body is a resource and my children are a resource because they are the potential to grow, maintain, and uphold the extraction-assimilation system. The act of extraction removes all of the relationships that give whatever is being extracted meaning.[40]

The Trent-Severn, which cost $24,000,000, was also one of the lengthiest public enterprises in Canadian history. The first meeting for the proposed project was held in 1833, but the waterway itself did not open until 1920, by which time transportation requirements and patterns had changed, making it superfluous to requirements. It became a playground for a few, mostly wealthy, yacht owners.[41] It is now a national historic site, a fact that merely underlines its failure to generate adequate revenue. Designating it a historic site also showcases settler nationalist pride in such development projects that facilitated colonialism and environmental destruction.

Public debt financing hid the failures of these development projects. It came to the rescue of projects that would otherwise never have progressed beyond the planning stage because they would not make enough money and would be too expensive. The use value of the project did not matter as much as raising the funds to pay for it, and this speculation generated market value. In a ghoulish way, even dying ecosystems had market value. Public debts created market value for beings and things that had the right to exist for their own sake, not as resources. As long as financiers saw the future profitability of wastelands, they continued to deem settler colonial governments creditworthy and to give out loans premised on the future value of Indigenous lands and waters. The integration between private interests and public money in a settler colonial system made the failure of such development projects the public's burden. This points to a broader issue of debt financing large development projects. For example, the WCC never accurately calculated the costs of building the canal, and the final price tag far exceeded the original estimates. At the same time, it received large sums from the Upper Canadian government because of the promise of future revenue. The cost of the canal outstripped the principal and the interest of the loan, and it could not make a profit because of the indebtedness that plagued it from the start. Roger L. Ransom argues that not all canals ultimately fail to produce a revenue that exceeds their investment, but the Welland Canal certainly did. In its case, this risk of the capital investment was placed on the settler public.[42]

The bond between private companies and colonial governments preceded colonial reform, and highlights many of the issues that colonial reform meant to fix. For example, the problems with funding the Welland Canal exemplified the lack of accessible capital for land development. The canal laid the foundation for public borrowing, and in the 1830s the Upper Canadian government had its public debt issued as securities on the LSE. Agents generally negotiated the loans, and in 1833 the British government officially created the Crown Agent Department, with two Crown agents, which remained separate from the Colonial Office until 1880.[43] Among their various activities, Crown agents were tasked with negotiating the loans for colonies and having them issued on the LSE to raise the funds.[44] The receiver general in the colonies, particularly in Upper Canada, negotiated the loans for the colonies. As receiver general from 1820 to 1843, Dunn was instrumental in moving Canada's debt to the London money markets. Dunn travelled to London, hoping to contract a government loan. He successfully contracted two loans, one in 1834 and the other in 1836. A loan of £200,000 was with Thomas Wilson and Company, and Wilson and Barings shared the second loan of £400,000. However, Upper Canada's initial financial backer, Thomas Wilson and Company, failed in 1837 with over £90,000 of Upper Canada's funds. Here, Glyn, Hallifax, Mills, and Company stepped to extend its financial services to help the Upper Canadian government avoid ruin.[45] Barings and Glyn divided the Upper Canadian account between them until 1891, when it was transferred to the Bank of Montreal.[46] In short, Dunn had managed to contract a loan in 1834 and another one in 1836 in London for £200,000 from the soon to fail Thomas Wilson and Company, and the second, a £400,000 loan, shared between Wilson and Barings.[47] Dunn took a fee for brokering the debt, to the displeasure of Attorney General John Beverly Robinson.[48] By 1838, *The Course of the Exchange* was listing the Upper Canada bond at a market value of £200,000, a considerable amount for the time and one that reflects the colonial government's indebtedness.[49] Paradoxically, Upper Canada had its debt issued as securities on the LSE during a time of sociopolitical and economic instability. The financial Panic of 1837, the Rebellions of 1837–38, and a sustained exodus of British emigrants drawn to the higher wages and cheaper land in the United States made the colony a risky bet, yet two major London banks (Barings and Glyn, Hallifax, Mills, and Company) decided to make it.[50] The loss of the settlers caused concern because they were key to colonial reform ideology, as they would ideally work on the development projects, which would raise land value in their colony. They also formed the body politic that was necessary for the creation of a white public as risk-bearer for the loans. Anxiously mentioning their loss, popular Methodist minister William Ryerson wrote to his brother Egerton Ryerson that it was the "fear of the hour."[51] For his part, Wakefield referred to low numbers of white labourers as the "colonial curse."[52]

To have a loan issued as securities on the LSE, the Upper Canadian government assured lenders that land could act as security. The imperative to appear creditworthy resulted in a pattern of development that was central to settler government land management after the 1830s: the appropriation of Indigenous territories as security for loans. Although, in theory, the Royal Proclamation of 1763 reserved this appropriation solely to the Crown, the Upper Canadian government claimed the territories nonetheless. Colonial jurisdiction expanded every time account books recorded them as assets to be offered up as security for loans and sold them away to the future. The Upper Canadian land reforms that began in the 1830s attest to this desire to claim Indigenous homelands. Development projects in Indigenous spaces required securing of the land for capital investment, and, in turn, the projects themselves ballooned colonial jurisdiction, even without a significant settler population in those spaces. Large-scale development projects such as the Welland Canal unlocked the London money market because they made real the promise of raising land value and assured investors that the colonial government could generate enough revenue to pay both interest and principal. Thus, the promise of future revenue, not revenue itself, paid for settler colonialism.[53]

Land Reform and the Expansion of Credit

In 1791, the Constitutional Act divided the Province of Quebec, previously a French territory, into Upper and Lower Canada. Attempting to manage a distinct and large French society, it addressed questions about the nature of British governance over both the French population and the influx of United Empire Loyalists, who had headed north because of the American Revolutionary War. It also created the clergy reserve system, setting aside land for the use of the Protestant clergy, and transferred land that colonizers held under French property title, both issues that would dog reformers who sought to increase land value. The clergy reserves – "for the encouragement of the Protestant religion and the maintenance and support of a Protestant clergy" – were intended as a counterweight to the land held in Quebec by the Catholic Church.[54] In Upper Canada, most clergy reserve land was allocated to the Anglican Church, with a lesser amount going to the Presbyterian Church. Prime Minister William Pitt's government passed the act and gave the colonial executive administrative authority over the reserves. Lieutenant Governor John Graves Simcoe and Surveyor General D.W. Smith began work to create them.[55] Many debates ensued, and in 1794, the imperial government accepted the plan to set aside one-seventh of Crown land as clergy reserves.[56]

The 1791 act reflected broader European practices to protect church jurisdiction over spaces. Church endowments had the legal safeguard of mortmain, which literally means "dead hand," and this property holding right extended to the clergy reserves that could not be taxed nor appropriated by secular authorities.[57] The practice of holding land in mortmain derived from medieval canon law, which even derived from Roman law, and which made such land inalienable in certain contexts.[58] It directly influenced colonization patterns, and the issue of holding Indigenous territories under mortmain conflicted with reformers' desires after the

1830s to colonize Upper Canada. Mortmain was a way to hold lands, technically, in perpetuity, and reformers targeted its use throughout the British Empire. For example, in British India, the "Hindu Undivided Family" – practices so called by the British in which families would hold lands in common rather than as private property – posed a problem for the free circulation of capital via private property, as lands stayed within family economic structures. Mortmain existed alongside the "Hindu Undivided Family," and both were subjected to complex reforms in the late nineteenth and early twentieth centuries.[59]

Alan Wilson records that the management of the clergy reserves was plagued by scandal, accusations of corruption, the incompetence of Anglican ministers who doubled as land agents, and many other issues that stemmed from their control by the church. Although Upper Canadian land reformers did feel that corruption as a concern, they saw the reserves as an impediment because they hindered the so-called free circulation on the private property market. They concentrated on releasing the capital from mortmain.

From the late 1820s onward, the Legislative Assembly attempted several times to pass a bill for the reform of the reserves, and each time the Legislative Council rejected the bill.[60] The secretary of state for war and the colonies, Frederick John Robinson, Viscount Goderich, praised the assembly's efforts, writing that he had "no hesitation whatever in stating that I entirely concur with the Assembly in thinking that they [clergy reserves] form a great obstacle to the improvement and settlement of the province."[61] Governor General Charles Poulett Thomson wrote in 1840 that the problem was "the one all-absorbing and engrossing topic of interest, and has been for years past the principal cause of the discontent and disturbance which have arisen, and under which the province laboured."[62] The debate raged throughout the 1830s and 1840s, and centred on how to support the Anglican and Presbyterian clergy without the reserves, how to appropriate the land, and how to pay for instructing the public in Protestantism. In 1840, with so much discord, the imperial government took it upon itself to introduce a bill in Parliament to resolve the question, where the MPs debated how properly to promote Protestant religious instruction in the colonies of British North America.[63]

The first Anglican bishop of Toronto, John Strachan, protested London's attempts to reform the clergy reserves. Appealing to the government to desist, he pointed out that Britain had both "the right of conquest" and the "right of cession" to the former French colony.[64] Importantly, Strachan referred not to the conquest of Indigenous nations, many of which had fought alongside the British, but to the conquest of New France. The British government unilaterally claimed that it held highest title in the conquered lands. However, it asserted jurisdiction over Crown lands, and part of the land reform process involved transferring that jurisdiction from the imperial to the colonial government. Not until 1837, when the Upper Canadian government passed the Public Lands Act, did it have more direct jurisdiction over Crown land.[65] The clergy reserves, on the other hand, proved much more difficult to secure for loans, for the simple reason that the colonial government had to respect the authority and right of the church. At least nominally, it had to follow a procedure to place the reserves under colonial jurisdiction as a way to extend credit for loans and to infuse the colony with British capital.

Bishop Strachan baulked at the idea of the colonial government alienating the clergy reserves. He framed his objection around what he saw as an imbalance of power between the Catholic Church and his own Church of England. In 1853, he raised his concerns with Henry Pelham-Clinton, the Duke of Newcastle, who was also secretary of state for war and the colonies. Why remove land from the Anglican Church, Strachan pleaded, when the Catholic Church held so many profitable acres? He calculated that it possessed over 2 million acres, which "represent a capital of 700,000." Its lands around Montreal, Trois-Rivières, and Quebec City were "worth more than half a million, and believed by many to be worth double that sum."[66] Strachan's calculations about potential capital show that opposition to land reforms did not equate with an opposition to leveraging lands to access capital. He simply wanted the Anglican clergy reserves to remain untouched. His invocation of an imbalance of power between the two churches clearly connected to the power that governing bodies derived from the control of Indigenous territories. Selling Catholic lands could tip the scales in favour of Anglican power.

Debate regarding the clergy reserves intensified when John Colborne, governor general of Upper Canada in late 1835 and early 1836, established fifty-seven rectories solely for the use of the Anglican Church, though only forty-seven became legally viable. This move fuelled the Rebellions of 1837–38 and brought victories for the reformers. Strachan defended Colborne's rectories and noted the intent to set aside part of them for settlement. Rhetorically, he claimed that the motive behind discontinuing the Anglican reserves was to "pull down the true Church of God," but his argument reflected a concern with the problem of how to raise land value, which both reformers and conservatives saw as the most pressing issue in British North America.[67] Favouring settlement, capital investment, development, and land reform, Strachan wrote at length to Robert Wilmot-Horton, lauding his emigration scheme as a "noble measure of State-policy" and "an untrodden field for the political economist."[68] Therefore, he was not opposed to the colonial government's desire to raise land value, but he wanted to ensure that the Protestant churches would have their own piece of the pie via the clergy reserves. This points to a pervasive understanding in settler ideology that land held power and that power derived from potential capital. Even non-reformers such as Strachan explicitly referred to the potential capital in land. To access this "dead capital," he favoured the Clergy Reserve Corporation of Upper Canada, which had taken over management of the clergy reserves from the Executive Council in 1819.[69]

In 1820, as the clergy reserves question burned through parliamentary debates, capitalists John Galt, Edward Ellice, and Alexander Gillespie became agents for Upper Canadians whose property had been affected by the War of 1812 and were applying to the imperial government for compensation. Galt suggested that this could be covered by a loan of £100,000, but London offered just £25,000. In 1822, Galt recommended that the government should sell the Crown and clergy reserves and use the money to pay the damage settlements.[70] In this context, the imperial government chartered the Canada Company in 1825. Helmed by Galt, it was a land and colonization company, and it concentrated on purchasing the Crown and clergy reserves of Upper Canada. A private enterprise, it modelled itself on the Australian Agricultural Company and the Dutch Holland Land Company, whose purpose was to improve wastelands.[71] The government facilitated such land and colonization companies throughout the settler colonies when it moved away from the system of land grants.

As Albert Schrauwers points out, 1825 marked a distinct change in Upper Canadian colonial governance, but it was not until Wakefield's method took hold in the 1830s that capital could really flow into the colony and make the fortunes of many elite settlers.[72] For example, by 1825, the Canada Company acted as the conduit for London capital because its securities were issued on the LSE (listed in the "Miscellaneous" category in *The Course of the Exchange*).[73] The company used money raised on the LSE to colonize, thus releasing Indigenous territories into the market. It had £1 million worth of securities for the explicit purpose of purchasing Crown and clergy reserves in Upper Canada.[74] What followed was a well-documented series of land purchases and negotiations between Strachan, the Clergy Reserve Corporation of Upper Canada, various prominent men in the colony, and Galt, as well as an immigration policy derived from the Wilmot-Horton model.[75] In fact, Wilmot-Horton's colonization schemes buttressed the philosophy behind ventures such as the Canada Company. Clarence Karr even refers to Wilmot-Horton as the "spiritual father" of the Canada Company.[76] As a method of accessing British capital for the purpose of colonization, the land company model struggled to maintain the interest of investors and did not consistently secure capital.[77] However, the Canada Company still directly tied Indigenous lands and waters to London markets through the use of securities to fund land purchases. Although the model had varying success, it points to the groundwork that such companies had put in place before colonial governments stepped in and used debt instruments to secure British capital.

Achieving land reforms in Lower Canada was an even more complex matter than in Upper Canada because elements of English property law, such as mortmain, did not map particularly well onto French property law. The seigneurial system also made the shift to British property law challenging in a variety of ways. Brought to North America during the seventeenth century, it gave Quebec its unique long rectangular lots.[78] In 1774, after having defeated France in the Seven Years' War, Britain passed the Quebec Act, whose purpose was to assist in the governance of

Lower Canada. It incorporated an English property law called "free and common socage," a system of landownership in which a person held the land in exchange for providing non-military services. In many cases, this took the form of a nominal payment to government.[79] The Constitutional Act of 1791, which created Upper and Lower Canada, took another step in installing English property law in Lower Canada. In 1825, the Canada Tenures Act made explicit the Constitution Act's implicit assumption of the legal superiority of English property law. The statute placed the free and common socage tenures under "the Law of England" and gave local legislatures the authority to modify land tenure.[80] This prompted an act from Lower Canada in 1829 (which received Royal Assent in 1831) to add flexibility to the French and English land tenure systems, so that both could exist together but that allowed for French law to preside over free and common socage.[81]

The Canada Tenures Act of 1825 allowed a seigneury to convert to free and common socage. In 1832, Edward Ellice, who held a seigneury in Beauharnois, availed himself of this provision in converting approximately half of its land to socage and allowed the landholders of the other half to opt for individual lots.[82] Allan Greer notes that merchants such as Ellis desired "the simpler, absolute, and individual form of property" in Lower Canada, as the liberal land reforms to create private property were "designed to facilitate commercial transactions in real estate."[83] The land reforms concentrated on how to make land easily alienable for quick changes in ownership, but more importantly, fee simple title allowed one to raise money through debt. For instance, an individual could take out a mortgage, or a government could count the land as a secure asset in order to request a large loan from a bank. Socage, however, attached an additional layer of responsibility to the land because it involved providing a service, which could hinder the transfer of the property.

One particularly fascinating conversion involved the massive seigneury of Lauzon, which was on the St. Lawrence River just across from Quebec City.[84] On January 15, 1636, it was granted to Simon Le Maître, a nobleman involved with the Company of New France (Compagnie des Cent-Associés). The historian of Lauzon, Edmond J. Roy, states that the grant contained a "clause que l'on voit rarement dans les documents de cette nature" and that "si M. Le Maître veut faire porter à cette étendue de terre quelque nom et titre plus honorable, y est-il dit, il pourra s'adresser au roi et au cardinal de Richelieu."[85] This "rare clause" allowed Le Maître – just two weeks after he received the seigneury – to direct notaries in Paris to pass the title to Jean de Lauzon, an original member of the Company of New France. Roy argues that Le Maître had no intention of ever travelling to New France and participating in colonization. However, de Lauzon did take possession of the seigneury and had many interactions with the Kanien'kehá:ka and other Indigenous nations such as the Wendat.[86]

In 1774, Henry Caldwell, the receiver general of Lower Canada, leased the seigneury. Between that date and 1801, the population of New France tripled, and Caldwell raised his rents to take advantage of the influx of settlers. J.I. Little reports that he enthusiastically embraced colonization, benefiting from the rents he charged.[87] Blessed with rich soil, the Lauzon seigneury was also endowed with extensive forests of pine and other profitable tree species, which both Henry and his son, John, logged and sold. After John became receiver general in 1808, he began to pay for his own development projects, such as mills, by helping himself to provincial revenues that were held in trust. Unfortunately for him, the price of timber fell sharply, and he was unable to pay back the approximately £219,000 that he had appropriated. His defalcation prompted his removal from office in 1823, and the sheriff seized the Lauzon seigneury in 1826. Caldwell appealed the decisions, but the court dismissed his claims in 1834.[88] Prompted by the notoriety of the Caldwell Affair, the colonial government established a select committee to look into the management of Lauzon. The evidence it amassed highlights contemporary discussions about land disposal, free and common socage, and resource development at seeming odds with French and medieval English land tenure systems.

The colonial government was determined to get its money back, and the issue of who should pay it ended with Caldwell losing the seigneury.[89] The select committee stifled discussion about its possible public sale, and evidence presented in its report accused a Mr. Primrose, the seigneury superintendent, of letting the mills fall into disrepair and looking the other way as people took precious timber from the land.[90] Focusing on the disrepair of the property, the committee opted to convert it to socage and recommended that it be granted to Peter McGill, railway enthusiast and president of the Bank of Montreal among other prominent business positions, and to William Price, a plank manufacturer and lumber merchant.[91] Price, in particular, was greatly interested in the timber extraction possibilities and had the experience and connections to satisfy the requirements of the free and common socage grant to continue the flow of resource extraction. For his timber business, he had set up a system of inspection, and employed and lodged men to assist him with ensuring the quality of timber shipped to England.[92] This particular instance of a seigneury converted to a socage confirms the desire for resource extraction and expansion but also shows how land tenure systems interacted with development projects. By 1854, seigneury land tenure had virtually been abolished.[93]

Upper Canada's Debt and the Durham Report

The period between 1791 and 1854 marked a series of starts and stops in land reform and attempted settler emigration. In the wake of the Rebellions of 1837–38, however, land reform swept across Upper and Lower Canada when four governors general implemented the Wakefield model. Curiously, each man was in office for only a short time before succumbing to a painful death: John George Lambton, Lord Durham, 1838–39; Charles Poulett Thomson, Baron Sydenham, 1839–41; Charles Bagot, 1841–43; and Charles Metcalfe, Baron Metcalfe, 1843–45.[94] This quick turnaround time meant that each new man had to step in and implement land reform as best he could. Each one bonded his approach to Wakefield's principles and helped to usher in the "manifesto for effective settler colonialism" – the 1839 report that urged both the unification of Upper and Lower Canada and the installation of responsible government, *Report on the Affairs of British North America*, or the Durham Report. Responsible government in the Province of Canada (the merged Upper and Lower Canada) occurred in 1848, another piece of the settler credit puzzle.[95] Chester Martin described the report as "the resplendent vision of imperial administration for the public lands" and noted that it "was probably regarded as the most constructive contribution of the Durham mission. The ablest men on the staff were assigned to it – Charles Buller himself as chief commissioner and Gibbon Wakefield as architect and draftsman."[96] Wakefield's influence on the report was palpable, and his apostle, Buller, was politically well placed to implement Wakefield's schemes.[97]

It was no coincidence that the Rebellions of 1837–38, land reform, and the event of the first Canadian debt issued as security on the LSE occurred concomitantly. Having the debt issued on the LSE in the 1830s and then grow into the 1840s and beyond was neither inevitable nor easy: it required land reform that was facilitated by the rebellions. In 1838, Prime Minister Lord Melbourne sent (or exiled) Lord Durham to Canada to investigate the causes of the rebellions, with Wakefield in tow as one of his aides. Durham resented his appointment, saying, "I did not want it. I abominated it," and accepting it only after turning it down twice.[98] His reluctance and chronic ill health made no headway with Melbourne, and he arrived in Canada on May 29, 1838.

Durham's involvement in the eventual union of Upper and Lower Canada, a bill that received Royal Assent just five days before he died, has been the subject of much scholarly attention.[99] However, a great deal of it focuses on his political ideas about responsible government, his radical ideas about democracy, and the impact of the 1839 Durham Report.[100] Until recently, little has been said about his involvement in the implementation of settler colonial policy.[101] Before visiting Canada in 1838, he had a confirmed interest in colonization, having been involved in the New Zealand Company, founded in 1837 by Edward Gibbon Wakefield, with the express purpose of appropriating Maori lands.[102] The complicated history of the company involved both Durham and Wakefield, though Wakefield eventually distanced himself from the company.[103] One of Wakefield's brothers, Felix, was also involved in "the best mode of converting into private property the waste lands" of New Zealand.[104] The New Zealand Company engaged in very questionable land purchases and prompted staunch opposition from the Colonial Office. Edward Gibbon Wakefield described Aotearoa as "the finest [country] for British settlement" and went so far as to remark that its climate had an effect on "some ladies who appeared ten years younger than when I parted from them in London."[105] Durham's association with the New Zealand Company highlights the interconnectedness of land companies and colonial reformers. One did not preclude the other, and certainly both had the same objective to capture British capital as a way to raise land value in the settler colonies.

While inquiring into the roots of the rebellions, Durham examined not only how to appropriate and develop Indigenous land, but also how to "promote emigration on the greatest possible scale." His emigration scheme included methods to "encourage the investment of surplus British capital in these colonies," echoing colonial reform's assertion of the need for British capital to pay for emigration and development. In fact, Durham claimed that mass emigration would be "a cure for political disorders" in British North America.[106] But there was a catch. Durham had learned that, of the approximately 17.0 million acres in Upper Canada, fewer than 1.6 million were as "yet unappropriated." Most of the "good" land had already been settled. In proposing a solution, Durham singled out the 3.0 million acres of clergy reserves in Upper and Lower Canada, asserting that they "retard more than any other circumstance the improvement of the colony." Freeing them up and improving them – releasing them to the market and making them produce a revenue – would go a long way toward solving the problem.[107] Furthermore, the Durham Report explained, most of the reserves were lying idle: "The great objection to reserves for the clergy is, that those for whom the land is set apart never have attempted … to cultivate or settle the property, and that, by that special appropriation, so much land is withheld from settlers, and kept in a state of waste." In fact, most reserves remained "entirely wild to this day."[108]

Durham stayed in Canada for only five months, resigning his position and sailing for home on November 1, 1838.[109] When Durham passed away in 1840, his quest to reform the reserves lived on. His successor, Charles Poulett Thomson, the first governor general of the Province of Canada, continued the mission of instituting land reform, which meant capital investment and British settlers. By 1847, hoping to alienate the church-held land, the Province of Canada converted clergy funds to Canadian debentures and secularized the reserves in 1854. Alan Wilson aptly links responsible government to the takeover of the reserves and the government's ability to access capital, but this revelation needs to be taken one step farther: the government could access capital only through debt. Wilson notes that "transferring the Reserves fund to Canadian debentures released a large amount of new capital just at the beginning of the speculative fifties. The struggle to achieve this transfer of resources and responsibilities bore a direct relation to the struggle for Responsible Government."[110] The slow legislative acquisition of the reserves occurred so that the "dead capital" in that land could be used as credit.

The Durham Report also commented on Upper Canada's massive debt, proposing that the union between the two Canadas could ameliorate the situation. It depicted the debt in a positive light, as a necessity to build infrastructure, and argued that the French Canadians lacked financial modernization, as exemplified by their minimal debt and "underdeveloped" institutions. It noted that as early as the 1820s, union between the Canadas would have improved Upper Canada's financial problems by giving it access to Lower Canada's revenue from customs duties.[111] Lower Canada's yearly revenue was £150,140, and it owed approximately £6,769 in interest payments, which it could pay if it reduced its expenditure (Sydenham proposed a drastic reduction of money to the rural and urban police force). By contrast, Upper Canada's yearly revenue was £122,520. In 1841, the balance owed from the interest on its debt was £56,837, with £8,931 owed in the future, resulting in a total of £65,768 in interest alone. This sum would affect the cost of maintaining its public works, colonial administration, and other expenditures.[112] Michael Piva argues that the financial crisis with Upper Canada's massive debt was a "primary motive" for union in Upper Canada.[113] To access more credit, the Upper Canadian government expanded to include Lower Canada, and the newly formed Province of Canada had an increased borrowing capacity.

The British government took Upper Canada's financial problems seriously. During a private meeting on August 21, 1839, Prime Minister Melbourne's cabinet recommended that a proposal be submitted to Parliament to guarantee a new loan to the colony. The loan, for "a sum not exceeding £1,500,000," would be "for the purpose of diminishing the Interest on the Debt, and of continuing the Public Works."[114] The meeting noted that "this sum will be secured on the Revenues of the Upper Province," which assumed that the colonial government could appropriate Indigenous land to generate revenue for debt repayment.[115] However, this did not alleviate the credit problems, and in the early 1840s

Sydenham became fearful that interest rates would have to rise from 5–6 percent to 8–9 percent if any semblance of creditworthiness were to be maintained on the London money markets.[116] As the Speaker of the Assembly at the first session of the Legislative Council of the Province of Canada in 1841, he emphasized the interconnection between paying back the debt, large-scale British immigration, and the disposal of public lands as "subjects of deep importance" that demanded "early attention."[117] During the session, Sydenham pledged the services of the British government to ensure that Canada would not only avoid imminent bankruptcy, but prosper. To emphasize the aid from London, he stressed to the Legislative Council and House that "the eyes of England are anxiously fixed upon the result of this great experiment" of accessing capital and importing British settlers, eerily echoing Puritan John Winthrop's 1630 lecture "A Model of Christian Charity," which stated that "the eyes of all people are upon us" in the great scheme of "civilization."[118]

Sydenham pleaded with Lord John Russell, secretary of state for war and the colonies, to convince the government to offer an imperial loan guarantee of £1.5 million to the colony. With a loan guarantee, London pledged to pay the loan itself if the colony defaulted, which assured creditors that they would receive their payments. It would not grant the colonial government immediate money, but it would restore its credit so that it could again raise funds on the London money markets but with a lower interest rate. The statute authorizing the loan guarantee of £1.5 million received Royal Assent on September 18, 1841, and included a potential loan amount of £1,659,689.[119] The British Parliament discussed passing an act to "employ the credit of this country for the benefit of the finances of Canada," to guarantee a loan that did not exceed "the sum of One Million Five Hundred Thousand Pounds in the whole" as a way to stave off another financial crisis in the Province of Canada. This effectively ensured that the Canadian government could not default on its debt. It also protected government bonds so they would not lose value, because shareholders received a guarantee of interest payments from the British government.[120] The Canada guaranteed loan passed in 1842, pledged Britain to guarantee interest payments of 4 percent per year, and this loan guarantee set a precedent for colonial loan guarantees, as Chapter 5 explores in greater detail.[121]

On both sides of the Atlantic Ocean, the imperial and colonial governments assumed that the development of lands would pay back the loans, but this idea still had a few outspoken critics. For example, C.E. Trevelyan, assistant secretary of the British Treasury, condemned the excessive spending on public works that had no guarantee of even paying for themselves. The stimulus of public loans to private companies between 1841 and 1867 contributed to an artificial prosperity followed by economic stagnation and depression when the loans could not be repaid.[122] Land reform became necessary to pay for the loans, and Sydenham was told that the Upper Canadian legislature should resolve "the question of Clergy Reserves" as "a sine qua non to the promise of a Loan."[123] Alienating the reserve lands would strengthen colonial credit. This logic allowed for the consolidation of Crown and clergy land sales and rents as assets for the Province of Canada. In May of 1853, an act passed that allowed the colonial legislature – with few limitations on interfering with existing interests derived by some clergymen – access to lands for the "Appropriation and Application of such Clergy Reserves, Proceeds, Investments, Interest, Dividends, Rents, and Profits."[124] This authorized the colonial legislature to discontinue the clergy reserves. The land could be appropriated and sold as the legislature saw fit.

Guarantees through legislation also formed a part of the debt process with the Colonial Stock Act of 1877, which made the colonial market technically more secure, as securities could be inscribed. Despite these guarantees, much of the success of the colonial securities had to do with the practice of underwriting them. This indicates that colonial governments had difficulty in obtaining investors.[125] Syndicates or groups of brokers would often underwrite new issues. They would raise the capital for the debt and then resell the issues. This placed the responsibility for any losses on the syndicates, rather than on the individual investor, which made the debt a safer investment. Large syndicate firms bought massive volumes of securities. This practice had a clear influence on the success of stocks. For example, in 1891 no syndicates bid for South Australia, Victoria, or Queensland stock, all of which failed.[126] Lance Davis and Robert Huttenback find that the Crown agents who acted through these few firms between 1860 and 1914, primarily Scrimgeour and Company, marketed almost £85 million in long-term government loans.[127] By the turn of the twentieth century, a few of these firms had monopolized the colonial securities market, with R. Nivison and Company underwriting Australian, Canadian, and South African government securities.[128] Without the practice of underwriting and deliberate government intervention in emigration, a settler colony had neither the capital nor the labour to establish itself.

Conclusion

Although the governments of the various British North American colonies all had their debts issued as securities on the LSE throughout the mid- to late nineteenth century, each one had to surmount its own unique barriers before this could occur. For the Upper Canadian government, inland British settlement and support of private development projects allowed it to appropriate an unprecedented amount of Indigenous territories. "The only resource of a new country is its lands," a report from the select committee on the disposing of Crown, clergy, and other lands noted. It went on to stress that "the first duty of a Government is to appropriate [its lands], so as the confer the earliest benefit and most equitable distribution to the entire population."[129] This report and others on the appropriation of the territories of Indigenous nations framed such colonization as a public good. The "public" here explicitly meant those within British subjecthood. Much of the quagmire of Upper Canada's land policy can be linked to the inequities and injustices wrought through the Family Compact, which resulted in the Rebellions of 1837–38. Reformers argued that land reform could ameliorate such inequalities within colonial societies.[130] Money, however, did not appear out of nowhere to pay for the establishment of a settler society predicated on capital accumulation. Colonial reformers, elites such as Strachan, and many others made it abundantly clear that capital acquisition was necessary, and that land appropriation was the key to accessing that capital. The Upper Canadian government eventually chose to rely on London capital and could do so because it claimed Indigenous lands and waters as security for the loans. Land reform did not occur strictly because of ideology, but out of necessity in order to borrow. Optimistic predictions regarding the amount of revenue that debt-financed development projects could produce did not align with the disappointing reality, and Upper Canada found itself unable to keep up with interest payments or to pay back the principal when debentures came due. To strengthen its credit, so as to borrow more, it consolidated with Lower Canada, and the resulting Province of Canada appeared more creditworthy.

In Harold Innis's words, Confederation was a "credit instrument" that extended the credit line of the British North American colonies.[131] The public debt exerted a centripetal force on the colonies. First, Upper and Lower Canada came together in 1841 with a "united debt,"[132] the Province of Canada, New Brunswick and Nova Scotia came together at Confederation in 1867, Rupert's Land was purchased in 1869, and British Columbia and Prince Edward Island joined Confederation in 1871 and 1873, respectively. In each of these steps of union, the public debt played a key role. Larger governments would appear more stable and thus more creditworthy to investors. Because consolidated colonial governments had more credit than smaller ones, the London Stock Exchange sometimes asked for colonies to join together to make the investment less risky for investors. In the case of New Zealand, the LSE would not issue its debt unless the provinces came together and agreed to have one "New Zealand" debt issue.[133]

The late 1840s were a precarious time for the Province of Canada. In 1846, Britain repealed its corn (cereal crop) laws, whose purpose had been to protect British agriculture from foreign competition. The corn laws had also favoured the privileged duties for the British North American colonies, but that ended when they were repealed. This, coupled with the lack of inland transportation for the grain and a railway system that was rudimentary at best, left the future of Canadian wheat sales up in the air. To make matters worse, the government debt increased by approximately 67 percent from 1850 to 1859.[134] Hoping to develop its dismal canal system and make it profitable, the Province of Canada wanted the imperial government to enter into a free trade agreement with its old enemy, the United States. In 1854, it did so with the Reciprocity Treaty with Washington.[135]

Britain agreed to the free trade deal for both politically strategic and commercial reasons. Governor General James Bruce, the Earl of Elgin, made a convincing argument that if it failed to do so, the colonies would be susceptible to absorption into the United States.[136] The treaty brought the British North American colonies together and also allowed them to remain distinct from their southern neighbour. It legislated two primary goals: to develop the coastal fisheries and to make the British North American canals profitable. The 1818 Anglo-American Convention had limited free trade between British North America and the United States, but now the Reciprocity Treaty allowed American fishers access to the entire east coast, and British fishers access to the coast north of the thirty-sixth parallel.[137] Under its terms, Americans could fish and make landfall on the lands Britain claimed, where fishers could dry their nets and process their catch in a virtually unrestricted manner, as long as they did not interfere with private property.[138] Both they and the British colonists could take any fish except shellfish, and the previous restrictions that prohibited fishing within three nautical miles from shore were voided.[139]

As for the canals, they could make a profit only if a certain number of cargo-laden ships passed through them. Supporters of free trade posited that opening up the Welland Canal to the United States would generate revenue from American usage and would stream American capital into British North America. Accordingly, the treaty gave American citizens the same rights as British subjects to use the canals.[140] Rather ironically, after all the claims that the Reciprocity Treaty would force the canals to generate revenue, free trade had the opposite effect. In the first year of the treaty, the St. Lawrence trade fell by approximately 47 percent, and it averaged about a 33 percent loss until the treaty was abrogated in 1866.[141] The picture was not entirely bleak, however: free trade facilitated the sale of Prince Edward Island oats to the United States, with the result that it benefited the Atlantic province more than the rest of British North America.[142]

Expansion of colonial governments to consume Indigenous territories for credit also consolidated the British North American colonies through a shared economy. As Brittany Luby suggests, reciprocity "revealed that international cooperation" between British settler nations "could facilitate joint economic growth" to the detriment of Indigenous nations.[143] Land gave colonies credit on the London money market, and so did bodies of water and waterways. In 1867, the British North America Act allowed the new dominion to engage in heavier borrowing. Finally, perhaps most infamously, Prince Edward Island's unique land reform and substantial debt played a key role in its decision to join Confederation. Far from being an outlier, the island followed the same trajectory as the other British North American colonies that were funded with a public debt, saving themselves from default by merging with a larger government system. As the following chapter will outline, the island's struggle to have its debt issued as securities on the London Stock Exchange exemplified a core principle of debt financing settler colonialism: the necessity of generating market value for land to access capital.

The Island's Gambit: Mi'kmaw Territory and the Land Question

4

> I don't think you should ever, ever give [lands] up, never give them up, but lease them, get some kind of payment for it, but don't ever give it up, because your power lies in land.
>
> – Lennox Island resident, 2019

Desperately Seeking Capital

In 1851, a tragic natural disaster occurred off the north shore of Epekwitk, or Prince Edward Island, as the British had called it since 1799.[1] Intense winds blew from October 3 to 5, killing approximately 160 people and destroying 74 vessels.[2] Among the dead were a substantial number of Americans who were fishing off the coast, with the result that the storm became known as the Yankee Gale. In terms of lives lost and ships wrecked, it was – and remains – one of the worst storm tragedies in the island's recorded history. Alexander Bannerman, a Scottish-born merchant, banker, manufacturer, and eleventh lieutenant governor of Prince Edward Island, used the event in an attempt to persuade the imperial government to make a free trade agreement with the United States. According to Bannerman, the island offered a unique opportunity for financiers to invest in the creation of a commercial fishing industry.[3] His plan involved allowing American fishers unfettered access to its ocean waters as a way to induce capital investment for fisheries development. The island's Legislative Council and House of Assembly "unanimously agreed" to allow Americans open access to fish and to come ashore to process their catch.[4] To make his case, Bannerman remarked on an undercurrent of violence in the fisheries question, warning that islanders threatened to "take the law into their own hands" if the Americans insisted on fishing in their waters.[5] Partially in response to Bannerman's plea, London negotiated the 1854 Reciprocity Treaty with Washington. Both the island government and the Province of Canada sought access to American capital and trade, and reciprocity pulled the heterogeneous British North American colonies together into one economic sphere.[6]

The fisheries question in the Maritimes is still fraught with violence. In November 2021, arson at a Mi'kmaw lobster warehouse in New Edinburgh, Nova Scotia, reduced the building to rubble. An angry mob of settler fishers had vandalized the warehouse a year earlier.[7] Elsewhere in the Maritimes, such crowds have attacked similar structures that facilitate Indigenous fishing. Because the Mi'kmaq are members of the Wabanaki Confederacy (along with the Abenaki, Passamaquoddy, Penobscot, and Wəlastəkwey Nations), their commercial fishing and hunting rights are protected under the Peace and Friendship Treaties of the eighteenth century. However, the rights were not fully recognized by Canada until 1999, when, in a Supreme Court of Canada ruling known as the Marshall Decision, the court stated that "moderate livelihood" could be had through fishing and hunting. Unfortunately, since the 1999 advent of the moderate livelihood fisheries, Indigenous fishers have often been the targets of violence.

In 1767, the British government divided Prince Edward Island into sixty-seven lots of approximately twenty thousand acres each, which it granted by lottery to a small number of private owners, many of whom did not live on the island. In exchange for the land, the recipients promised to pay a sizeable quitrent (a tax) to the Crown and to improve and populate their lots by sending out colonists who would pay them rent, but many failed to do so. Thus was born the "land question" that would dominate Prince Edward Island politics until the colony joined Confederation in 1873.[8] Under the lot system, a few small spaces were designated as reserves for fisheries, and others came under the ownership of the island government.[9] The vast majority were privately owned, their claims grounded in a British legal system whose general purpose was to uphold the property rights of white middle- and upper-class men.[10] As the government could not resolve the land question simply by appropriating the lots, it had to acquire them "by purchase" or by a method known as escheat.[11]

Escheat was a legal process that transferred title to the Crown if the owners were convicted in court of failing to uphold the terms of their land grants. Although many lot owners had defaulted on their promises, they could avail themselves of legal and even political recourse should the island government threaten to escheat their land or even to tax it. In 1853, a few years after the implementation of responsible government, the colonial government attempted to pass two bills that essentially taxed landlords and proprietors, but the imperial government that "seldom interposed in the internal affairs of a colony to which representative institutions had been granted" had "found [the bills] to be so bad in principle and defective in machinery that the then Colonial Secretary (Sir. G. Grey) felt himself bound in November, 1855, to disallow them both."[12] As a result, the government did not succeed in escheating much land. William Stewart MacNutt points out that even when responsible government came to Prince Edward Island in 1851, legislating land changes was still subject to restrictions.[13] This contrasted starkly with the way in which the British and island governments dealt with Mi'kmaw land and water tenure. Both behaved as if the Mi'kmaq had no legal claim to the island after the lot system was imposed in 1767.[14] The white supremacist ordering in British governance systems saw "civilized" governments as justified and legitimate and Mi'kmaw governance systems as illegitimate and available for colonization. Ultimately, land reform on the island centred on securing title so that the colonial government could borrow from London financiers, a method of capital investment that depended heavily on the second principle of public debt financing: the necessity of generating market value for land to access capital. For the island government, accessing capital meant securing land title and generating value though speculative ventures.

However, many people were critical of speculation and saw the activities of the London Stock Exchange as a form of gambling. Popular opinion linked the LSE with "stock jobbing" – participating in the market solely for the sake of profit, rather than for the more noble purpose of investing in worthy ventures. The strict rules about who was allowed to trade and the limited number of LSE members certainly did little to offset the suspicion that the LSE was little more than a gambling den that catered to an elite few.[15] This negative view also applied to land speculation in British North America, where speculators drew much ire for hindering the "improvement" of the colonies. In Upper Canada, they invested in land with the intent of maximizing their profits, selling only when the price went up, a practice that hindered the settlement of British immigrants.[16]

The island government's struggle to have its public debt issued as securities on the LSE shows that speculation on secured lands created value – if done through the appropriate channels.[17] It could both make an extraordinary amount of profit and make "real" value in land, or "the making present and materializing of uncertain futures."[18] Reformers lobbied to have gambling acts changed, particularly limitations on futures contracts, as the LSE ushered in a new era of finance capitalism that relied on bets on the future, not just in Britain but throughout the British Empire.[19] When a colonial government made a bet that it could pay the principal and interest on a public loan at some point in the future, that bet recorded actual amounts of capital that transferred hands for a particular price of land without that land actually being sold to individual settlers. This was the island's gambit, a move that sacrificed treaty rights, displaced Mi'kmaw communities, and failed to protect a place to live as a legal right, even for white settler tenants.

The island needed money to purchase land from its owners, but its credit was poor. Without secure title, the government could not convince London financiers to invest in the colony, as Attorney General Joseph Hensley discovered in June 1867, when he sailed to England, with the intent of securing a public loan. Upon arriving, he learned that the government's inability to settle the land question made investment in the island distasteful. Islander William Henry Pope, a staunch Tory who favoured Confederation, made it very clear that the failure of the Liberal government to secure a loan in Britain or elsewhere would mean joining the union. He even went to some effort to make the imperial government see that the island was unfit for investment.[20]

On the island, both Confederation and the land question were complicated issues that excited much division among elite political parties and grassroots opposition to landlords, such as the Tenant League.[21] However, both liberals and conservatives were concerned about public credit. Broadly speaking, the former felt that retaining strong ties to the British Empire would extend island government credit, whereas the latter wanted to join Confederation, so that Canada could back the credit.[22] Colonies that amalgamated had certainly expanded their credit, as was the case for Upper and Lower Canada in 1841 and those who joined Confederation in 1867. Peter J. Smith shows that both Tories, such as John Strachan, and Whigs, such as Lord Durham, agreed that a union of the British North American colonies would increase public credit.[23] Echoing Harold Innis, Smith shows that union was "a credit instrument to alleviate public debt and promote political stability." This contention evoked similar arguments from Adam Smith, who suggested that a union of England, Ireland, and America would swell public credit.[24] Political debate on the island certainly understood that joining the government's credit to either Canada or Britain would strengthen its own poor credit. The question of whether to enter Confederation was, then, also a question of how to increase credit to let capital flow into the island via debt instruments.

The Island under Colonial Rule

In his correspondence with the Colonial Office, Lieutenant Governor Alexander Bannerman failed to mention that the Mi'kmaq had fished in the waters of Epekwitk since time immemorial. The Peace and Friendship Treaties guaranteed protection of Mi'kmaw fishing rights, and the Mi'kmaq themselves had never ceded or surrendered the island, which meant that their jurisdiction extended to the fisheries.[25] Bannerman's program of fisheries appropriation centred on searching for capital investment, and from the moment it attained responsible government, the island mobilized a policy of capital investment to grow its economy at the expense of Mi'kmaw treaty rights. For example, though the treaty agreements were legally binding, the Reciprocity Treaty of

1854 supplanted colonial treaty responsibility to the Mi'kmaq Nation. This slow "forgetting" of treaty responsibility had culminated with the criminalization of Mi'kmaw treaty rights by the twentieth century.[26]

Known to the French as L'île Saint-Jean, Prince Edward Island had borne Mi'kmaw names for thousands of years before the first Europeans arrived. According to Chief William Benoit Paul's recorded teaching of 1933, Epekwitk means "the-side-of-a-boat-when-you-see-it-along-way-off-and-it-seems-to-be-low-in-the-water." He also mentioned an older name, Ookchiktoolnoo (Kjiktu'lnu), which means "Our Great Boat."[27] Keptin John Joe Sark suggests that the name of the island links the Mi'kmaq to that place from the end of the last Ice Age, about twelve thousand years ago – a time when it was covered in ice.[28] Paul's teaching emphasizes just how long the Mi'kmaq had lived on Epekwitk, as the complex and lengthy process of deglaciation or ice retreat of the last Ice Age could expose new land masses, such as the island.[29] Archaeological evidence from the Greenwich area of Prince Edward Island National Park includes objects that date back ten thousand years to the present, which suggests continual occupation.[30] Epekwitk is also translated as "lying in the water," and some translations of the name come from the Mi'kmaw story of Glooscap, who lay down the island "like a cradle in the waves."[31]

Michelle Lelièvre shows that Mi'kmaw land and water tenure systems, which she links with mobility rather than with the culturally loaded term "seasonal migration," provoked an intense anxiety in British colonizers, who wanted to surveil Indigenous peoples. Lelièvre argues that a sedentarist ideology began to permeate the British imagination in the nineteenth century, which rendered mobile peoples as uncivilized. Its binary of settled versus wandering saturated British reports that often characterized Indigenous peoples as nomadic. This logic propagated the myth that Indigenous nations did not attach themselves to any particular place, which delegitimized their rights to land and water.[32] In fact, Mi'kmaw Elders from Epekwitk describe a mobile tenure system that saw both land and waterways as homelands.[33] Patrick J. Augustine states that though "islands are cut-off from the land, they remain inclusive of the homeland."[34] Accounts from Elders are clear that the tenure system was passed down from generations through families and communities. Certain families used particular areas. The common Mi'kmaw surnames on the island, Bernard, Francis, Knockwood, Labobe, Sark, Thomas, Toney, and Tuplin, also act as a legend for a map of land and water tenure. Certain Mi'kmaw names, such as Augustine, which is also common on the mainland, highlight the relationships between people from Epekwitk Aqq Piktuk and other districts of Mi'kma'ki.

In an 1838 letter to Lord Glenelg at the Colonial Office, Lieutenant Governor Charles A. Fitzroy wrote that the Mi'kmaq were "scattered" throughout the island, suggesting that their "wandering" rendered their rights to it as irrelevant.[35] Historians have asserted that the Mi'kmaq used Epekwitk largely or only as a "summer home," which supports settler claims that they have no real right to their territories.[36] To be clear, the Mi'kmaq do not have land "claims": they have inherent rights to their territories, which are upheld by their own legal system, nation-to-nation treaties, and even the Supreme Court of Canada. Furthermore, their land rights are valid regardless of whether they are recognized by the island government.[37] The summer home myth shows the impacts of settler history making on Indigenous communities. For example, when I interviewed Saul Jacobs, a member of Lennox Island First Nation who attended school off-reserve, he said that he was told that "really all of PEI was more of summer camping, more like a vacation spot for the Mi'kmaq." Jacobs said he learned this from an islander school. The idea of the summer home did not originate with a single historian or settler. It is a belief system that informs how Mi'kmaw land and water tenure is generally perceived on the island, and it is embedded in racist narratives about Indigenous peoples and white possession more generally.[38]

The histories of Mi'kmaw Elders highlight the mobile land and water tenure system that concentrated on Malpeque Bay and the Hillsborough River.[39] At the same time, extensive archaeological evidence shows that the Mi'kmaq lived throughout the island.[40] At Malpeque Bay, certain Mi'kmaw families lived at Gategagoneg, which British settlers named Indian River (see Figure 2). Prince Edward Island has four First Nations reserves. The three Abegweit Nation reserves, Rocky Point, Scotchfort, and Morell, are near or along the Hillsborough River. To the west, the fourth, Lennox Island, is across the water from Gategagoneg.

Two burial sites underscore that generations of Mi'kmaq have lived at or near the Hillsborough and Indian Rivers. Elder Maria Labobe recalled

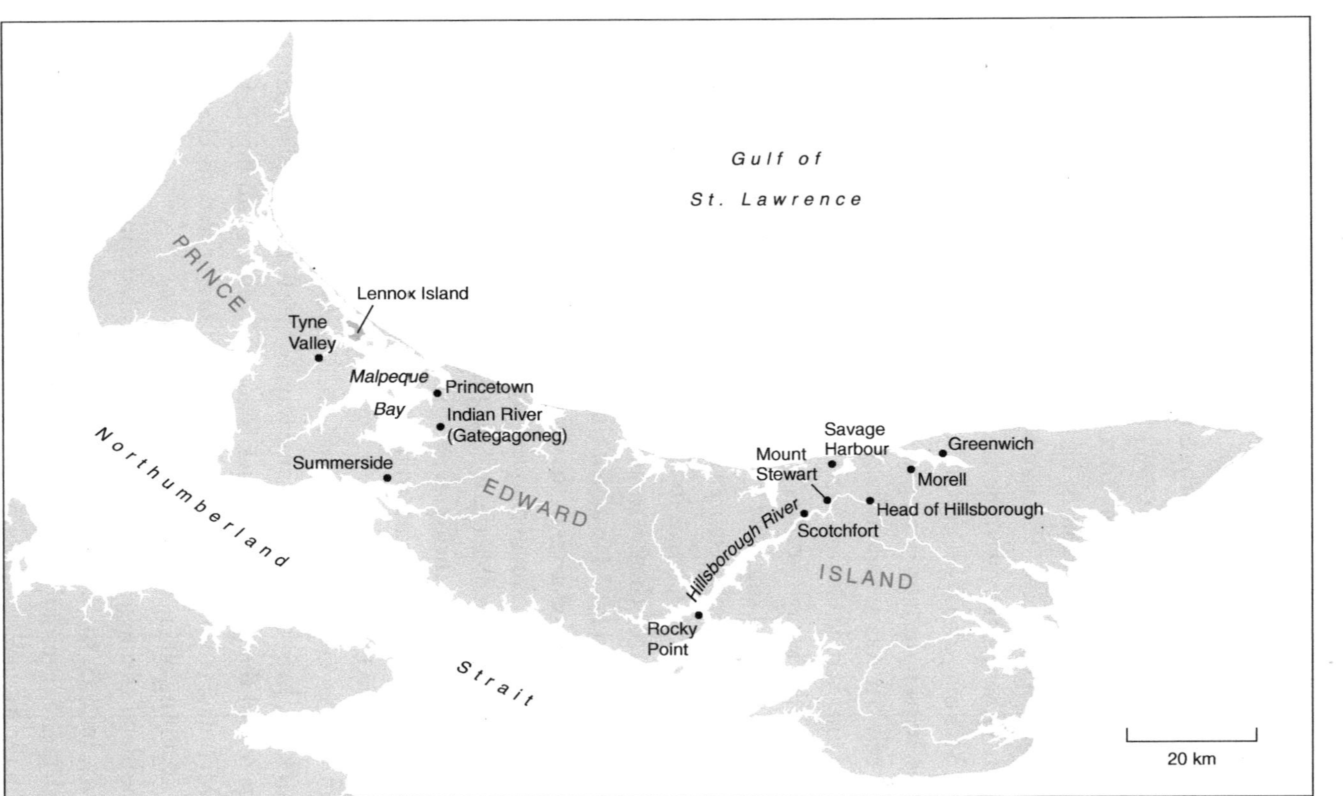

2 Map of Epekwitk. Cartography by Eric Leinberger.

the finding of Mi'kmaw ancestors who were buried at Savage Harbour, north of the Hillsborough. They were discovered "down along Savage Harbour banks and they were wrapped up in leather and then birch bark on the top of that and laid into the ground and that's how they found them."[41] According to Elder Cathy Sark, the "Hillsborough river being so busy that was like the main way of travel a long time ago before the roads, it was up and down the river on the canoes, on their boats and everything, and they [ancestors] had built a fort when the first settlers came which were French." She noted that seals and walruses would swim up the river, where they were hunted by the Mi'kmaq.[42]

The Mi'kmaq also used eels, which were best caught in the winter months. In fact, the word Gategagoneg roughly translates to "the place of the eels." It was a winter living space, contradicting the summer home claim. Settler George MacDonald recalled his friendships with a few of the Mi'kmaw families at Gategagoneg in the early twentieth century. He said that since 1842, "a lot of the Indian people were buried there," and he remembered another burial site made a "few thousand feet" from St. Mary's Church in the area. He did not know how many people were interred there but said that "there are many – you can tell by the way the land is." He added that, in an early twentieth-century gravesite, Mi'kmaw relatives of the deceased had "placed a fence around it [the graveyard] and a small plaque." The anecdotal evidence makes the proximity of the two cemeteries to Gategagoneg unclear, but one site had "iron Crosses put near their graves."[43] The burial sites clearly establish a continued tenure and return to living spaces over generations, which both Mi'kmaw Elders and settlers affirmed. In addition, settler place names, such as Savage Harbour and Indian River, were chosen because the Mi'kmaq lived there. In the same way, N***er Point and Black Sam's bridge record the presence of Black islanders.[44] Elders also highlighted that Mi'kmaw families could sometimes circumvent state mechanisms such as closing off lands as private property.[45]

The island's demographics changed significantly during the eighteenth century. In 1755, the British expelled the Acadians, removing a strong French presence from the island, though it did persist in enclaves, particularly in the west. When Britain lost the American Revolutionary War in 1783, United Empire Loyalists streamed north to the Maritimes, wanting land. In Nova Scotia and New Brunswick, they had considerable success in obtaining it, as both colonies had courts of escheat, whose work freed up land to grant to Loyalists. For example, Nova Scotia escheated nearly 2.5 million acres between 1783 and 1788. As mentioned above, escheat was largely a dead letter on Prince Edward Island, where property owners could block its application.[46]

After the 1767 division of the island into the lot system, Mi'kmaw families tended to live as they had always done but both around and with the growing settler population. In some cases, landowners did not enforce British-based legal property codes where the Mi'kmaq were concerned and even took steps to protect Mi'kmaw land use. This changed when the government used its public debt to gain possession of land, as was the case with an enormous 100,000-acre estate on the northeast of the island.[47] It belonged to Charles Worrell, whose family wealth was partially generated by the use of slave labour for sugar production in Barbados.[48] The link between the West Indies sugar plantations, slavery, and the island unfortunately remains an understudied subject.[49]

The Worrells had not attempted to evict the Mi'kmaq.[50] In fact, Charles Worrell had granted eight Mi'kmaw families and their descendants a tract of land on the estate. But when the island government used its public debt to buy part of the estate, it did not protect the Mi'kmaw families who lived there. White squatters had moved in, and the government chose to sell the land to them. In an attempt to ameliorate the situation, in 1859, the colonial government selected 204 acres on Lot 39 (part of the Worrell Estate) and moved the Mi'kmaw families who lived outside of this specific acreage there. This small part of Lot 39 became the Morell reserve. In typical colonial fashion, surveyors had "discovered that one half of it was totally unfit for any practical purpose"; the most fertile lands went to British colonists and the least fertile went to Indigenous peoples and, even in the case of land grants, Black settlers.[51] The Mi'kmaw families brought a "complaint" to the colonial government "on the part of the Indians." The complaint noted "that the land thus assigned them is less in quality, and ninety-nine acres thereof inferior in quality to that left them by Mr. Worrell," and they argued that "as good and sufficient land should be granted to them as was taken from them."[52] Several layers of appropriation and dispossession mark this particular case, in which white settlers "owned" the land and the island government used aggressive measures to increase its value.

The colonial system made it virtually impossible for the Mi'kmaq to own land title in the British sense. The purchase of Lennox Island as the first official Indian reserve accentuates the difficulties the Mi'kmaq encountered in defending their territories. In 1772, Lennox Island had been attached to Lot 12 and granted to James Montgomery, but by about 1860 it belonged to David Stewart. After the island government created the position of Indian commissioner in 1861, Commissioner Theophilus Stewart lobbied it to buy Lennox Island for the Mi'kmaq.[53] The Aborigines Protection Society (APS) in London offered to do so. However, desire for the underlying title framed this humanitarian venture. In 1867, the APS applied to the treasurer of the New England Company (NEC), asking for a £400 loan to purchase the island. The NEC had been incorporated by the British government in 1649, with the mandate of propagating "the Gospel of Jesus Christ amongst these poor heathen."[54] It used various tools such as schools to indoctrinate Indigenous children.[55] The NEC colonization model of acquiring land rights to Indigenous territory extended far beyond the island.[56] The NEC agreed to lend the money for the purchase of Lennox Island on the condition that it, not the APS, held the land in trust. It also wanted the purchase to be in its own name, not that of the APS. The deal collapsed once the NEC discovered that due to the land question, uncertainties regarding title might eventually lead to litigation.[57] Finally, in 1870, the APS bought the island for the use of the Mi'kmaq.[58]

The settler historical literature stresses the benevolence in the acquisition of the reserve, usually concentrating on Theophilus Stewart, the Native Benevolent Society, whose members included Robert Hutchinson, future mayor of Charlottetown, and future premier George Coles, who managed to raise some money for the Mi'kmaq. The island government also made a few attempts to persuade London to buy the island for the Mi'kmaq. Such histories, however, ignore that this "help" centred on obtaining land rights to Mi'kmaw homelands and the isolation of the Mi'kmaq on a remote island or non-arable lands for reserves. They do not ask why such solutions to the "Indigenous problem" did not involve, for example, the legal codification of Mi'kmaw treaty rights.[59]

The Lennox Island purchase and the benevolence of humanitarians resonated differently on Lennox Island itself. When I interviewed community members, I wanted to focus on two main points: the establishment of the reserve and Mi'kmaw treaty rights. Generally speaking, their history of the making of the reserve lined up with the settler narratives. However, their explanation as to why it was created did not. When I asked about it, I received various responses:

> *Teresa Williamson:* When Lennox Island was bought, it was bought for, like, four hundred pounds or something like that back in the day. That part I think from other people is true … So normally, [Mi'kmaw] people would be all throughout Prince Edward Island, and these people [settlers] just come and say of this little piece of land that's, like, the last left over basically, out of all of these lots that we split up PEI one is for you guys [the Mi'kmaw], which is, like, the least –
>
> *Saul Jacobs:* Swampiest lands. *(agreement around the room)*
>
> *Teresa Williamson:* Swampiest, grossest land left to the people who were originally here to begin with.
>
> *Mary Garner:* Well, we have artifacts over at the cultural centre that date back ten thousand years, that's a long, long time, ten thousand years. Here on Lennox Island, there are two neighbouring islands, Hog Island and Bird Island [two islands that are a part of Pituamkek, a sacred sandhill ecoystem[60]] …
>
> *Saul Jacobs:* If the bridge [bridge and causeway that connects Lennox Island to Epekwitk] would have been here before they were setting up lots, we wouldn't be here – It was terribly inconvenient for anyone to get over here, so this is a –
>
> *Mary Garner:* We're on an island, on an island.
>
> *Saul Jacobs:* I kind of think they thought it might be a good way to wipe everybody out. They got TB.[61]

Saul Jacobs's suspicion regarding tuberculosis is reflected in the literature about the eradication of Indigenous peoples through the intentional spread of diseases.[62] The community members emphasized that Lennox

Island was chosen to get them out of the way. It had little prospect as farmland and was also subject to harsh weather, such as the intense nor'easters (as in the Yankee Gale tragedy), where storm surges can erode precious coastline.[63] The history of Lennox Island makes visible how the island government made Mi'kmaw treaty rights invisible. Neither eighteenth- nor nineteenth-century debates about the land question default to designating the ownership of the island to the Mi'kmaq, an approach that persists in current historical scholarship. The perception of the land question in both the literature and contemporary British settler and imperial understandings set up a dichotomy between an agitation for settler sovereignty with responsible government and the rights of elite British landowners.

The Land Purchase Act

When the fervour for land reform hit Upper Canada, Lord Durham pointed to Prince Edward Island as a regrettable example of an inefficient system that simply maintained land "in a state of wilderness."[64] Something had to be done to release its potential capital. In 1839, the island's Legislative Council split into the Executive Council and the Legislative Council, giving the government a tripartite system, namely the lieutenant governor and the Executive Council, the Legislative Council, and the House of Assembly. These changes led to a session in 1840 that discussed both the land question and the constitution of the island.[65] The issue of landownership was the key problematic for the developing colony. It was more than just ideological: it stained the government's creditworthiness. In this context, the government turned to a public debt.

The year 1851 marked the beginning of the government's venture into public debt financing. In that year, it passed the Act to Authorise a Loan for the Use of this Island, and Also to Make Provisions Respecting the Payment of Treasury Bonds and Warrants and the Interest Thereon, which made it lawful for the colonial government to open a loan account of £10,000 with the Treasury and to borrow at an annual interest rate of 5 percent.[66] Although government loans existed prior to 1851, with financial instruments such as warrants, the warrants acted differently from debentures and other methods to secure funds. Warrants could be used by governments to make payments in lieu of a cheque. This was not an uncommon way for colonial governments to raise money quickly.[67] Debentures, on the other hand, explicitly raised funds through debts. According to the 1851 act, all persons, corporations, or companies were allowed to invest in the island government. It earmarked this money for the payment of previous warrants, and this effectively used a debt to pay for a debt. The act set the payment of the warrants from the Treasury in succession of when they were issued according to their date.[68] Such acts that authorized raising capital via loans laid down the legal framework for paying back the loans.

If colonial legislatures wished to incur a public debt, they had to enact it through the legislature. Thus, an examination of their legislation reveals the amount of the debts and their purpose. However, if an act authorized the government to raise £10,000, this did not automatically mean that the full amount was ever raised. To get a complete picture of the amount owed, both the provincial Treasury records and banking house records would need to be consulted, as well as calculations about compounded interest, loan amounts, and market capitalization. The statutes do contain important information about how the loans would be paid. For example, the government could cancel interest if, after it called in a debenture and advertised it in the *Royal Gazette* for a specified period, no one came forward to claim it. At the same time, some acts authorized loans whose purpose was to pay debts that had now come due. Thus, as new debts were piled on top of old debts, the island government avoided default and bankruptcy, but determining its actual deficit at any given moment is difficult.

In 1853, the Liberal Party government under Premier George Coles passed the Land Purchase Act, which empowered the government to purchase land from willing owners and sell portions of it to the tenants as private property. A loan account would be opened in the Treasury, and the treasurer would be authorized to borrow up to £30,000, which would be used to buy the land. Selling the property did not mean that the government relinquished the highest land title, only that the tenants could purchase the limited title. The act was overseen by Dominick Daly during his time as lieutenant governor (1854–59). Ultimately, it set the government on a downward spiral into a deep deficit that it eventually resolved with the island's 1873 entry into Confederation, a decision that increased its credit. Running a deficit is not the same as nearing bankruptcy: as long as the indebted party can maintain credit for further borrowing, bankruptcy can be avoided.[69] For example, expanding territory and assimilating increasing amounts of Indigenous land into government assets would strengthen credit regardless of how much actual money the government owed. Nor should the government deficit be confused with an economic downturn. The fear of bankruptcy did enter political discussion, but colonial elites such as Strachan stressed that public debts were troublesome only if governments ran into credit trouble.[70]

The Land Purchase Act created the office of the commissioner of the public lands, who was responsible to the Executive Council to the lieutenant governor. He had the authority to determine the price of land and to purchase and sell it, and had the jurisdiction to handle money for the sales.[71] He worked with the treasurer, who opened the debt account and paid it off, as well as issuing debentures.[72] The act stipulated that the government would not pay more than seven shillings and sixpence per acre, which created a ceiling for land purchases. However, because the rate could vary, this did not quite constitute price fixing and thus did not equate with Wakefield's concept of the sufficient price. On top of this, the government wanted to sell the land "at as low a rate as possible."[73]

The Land Purchase Act made the government's objectives quite clear: it wanted to own title and then manage the land. The public lands commissioner would take the loan funds to buy land. The debt would pay for the purchases, and the security for the borrowed money came from money earmarked from land sales, rents, and profits, and the act stated that the government "pledged and rendered liable" these assets.[74] Public funds, money, and securities were also used as collateral. The hope was that tenants could purchase "the wilderness and unoccupied lands," which reinforced a "discovery" rights framework, even though the Peace and Friendship Treaties had established the island as unceded.[75] The Land Purchase Act made it explicit that the colonial government would take out a public debt to appropriate Mi'kmaw territory that it coded as "wilderness" and "unoccupied" lands.[76]

Not everyone was on board with the government's solution to the land question. Escheat leader William Cooper stated that it would "incur a debt of £300,000 to be paid by labouring people." Even at this early point, Cooper understood that the public – the "labouring people" – would act as risk-bearers for the loan and would have to pay it off. Cooper favoured escheat to solve the land question and suggested that the government should investigate the original land titles to determine which ones could be revoked, or escheated.[77] In the end, though Cooper's figure of £300,000 was only slightly overstated, his prediction that the island could incur a massive debt proved accurate: from land purchases alone, its borrowing capacity was raised to £229,000 by the 1870s.[78]

The *Islander*, a local newspaper, was also critical of the Land Purchase Act. No friend to the Liberal Party, it warned that "the Bill is not simply an electioneering humbug – it is something worse." It calculated that the government would have £30,000 issued in debentures with £10,000 afloat, which pushed the loan to £40,000, with an annual interest of £2,900. Although the paper's figures were correct, it accused government members of forming a "compact" and a "clique," loaded words that evoked Upper Canada's Family Compact and Lower Canada's Château Clique. Even worse, it alleged that the public debt scheme was simply a device to enable certain government members to off-load their useless bog land. In passing the legislation, their purpose was "to draw from the Treasury a price for their worthless land of more than ten or twenty times its value." After all, the Land Purchase Act set the price of the land, the point of which, the *Islander* insisted, was to raise the value of the "worthless" properties.[79] Although this attack was meant to discredit the Liberals, it also reveals much about how land value was made real in settler colonies via debt instruments. Land did not have inherent market value – a fact that many mid-nineteenth-century liberal colonial reformers frequently lamented. It had to be made into capital, and in this case given liquidity with debt instruments.[80]

The debt-funded purchase of a portion of the Worrell estate created more than a few headaches for the colonial government, as landlords criticized the purchase. They argued that tampering with landownership and land prices would reduce the "value of real estate."[81] Understandably, the government wanted to pay the lowest possible price for land, but doing so could drive down its market value. Buying land with a public loan raised three serious issues for the government: buying at low cost devalued the land; the sales, which proved disappointing, meant that not enough revenue was generated to repay the debt; and the interest on the debt seriously hindered the government's ability to keep up its payments.

Settler tenants did not immediately leap to purchase the newly freed-up land. Between 1855 and 1857, few people did so, and not all of them paid in full. Tenant Thomas Gleason bought forty-one acres at two different rates based on the assessment of their quality. James MacIsaac bought twenty-five acres.[82] The ledger kept by the public lands commissioner reveals that most of the purchasers were men. Many people who bought land did so modestly, at around 50 acres, though some purchased more and some less. Taking 50 acres as a generous estimate of the median of lands purchased per person between 1855 and 1857, roughly 3,450 acres were purchased by individuals. If we assume that they paid twelve shillings and sixpence per acre, the maximum permitted under the Land Purchase Act, the total for land sales would have amounted to approximately £2,156, or only about 7 percent of the £30,000 debt allowed for in the act. Even if we greatly inflate the price of the 3,450 acres, it would be difficult to arrive at a figure that would cover the debt, including its annual interest.[83] According to the 1848 census, the island had 6,099 tenants in leasehold. Nearly half of them held 999-year leases, and the rest held 30-, 50-, or 100-year leases.[84] Such long leases could point to one reason why tenants did not buy out their landlords and had to keep on paying rent: they did not have the upfront money.

With leaseholders purchasing fewer parcels of land than expected, and with the imperial government blocking land tax legislation at the behest of landowners, the island government options to generate revenue from land dwindled into mid-century.[85] After Henry Labouchere became secretary of state for war and the colonies in 1855, he wrote to Lieutenant Governor Daly, proposing two solutions to the land question. Initially, he suggested that the colonial government should find a way to have the tenants buy the land in fee simple. Then, in December 1855, he suggested that the island should raise a larger loan, which London would "take into consideration."[86] In 1856, he advised the colony to ask London for an imperial loan guarantee.[87] Just as for the Province of Canada in the previous decade, this form of guarantee ensured that Britain would cover the colonial government's loan if it defaulted. The guarantee would make investment in the small colonial government a safer bet for financiers and could enable it to borrow larger sums of money at lower interest rates. Due to the seasonal disruption in the mail services, a month elapsed before Daly replied to Labouchere, and his palpable excitement at the prospect of a loan guarantee is easy to detect in his letter.[88] He assured Labouchere that he would bring up the matter during the next session of the legislature, which he had scheduled for February 14.[89] Perhaps Labouchere looked favourably on settler colonies taking out massive public debts because he was related to the Baring family and had married Frances Baring in 1840. The Barings Bank had lent to many governments, including those of British North America.[90] For whatever reason, Labouchere assured Daly that if he wanted to purchase the land, which Daly desperately did, London would "give a favourable consideration" to granting the loan guarantee.[91]

The Council Chamber and the House of Assembly sent correspondence addressed to the Queen on behalf of the Legislative Council and House of Assembly. It noted that Labouchere appeared to be unaware of the 1853 Land Purchase Act, which capped the island's borrowing limit at £30,000. They also warned Labouchere that the statute dedicated the island's revenues to the payment of that loan. Nonetheless, they stressed that this amount was too insignificant to resolve the land question. At this time, resolving the land questions meant that the island government would own the highest title to land under British property law.[92] Labouchere understood that the island government wanted the "state" to be in possession "of the fee-simple."[93] At Labouchere's suggestion, the council and the assembly jumped at the opportunity to access larger loans. Positioning themselves as a "loyal colony," they argued that they would finally have the revenue to pay back the initial land purchase loan if the government could buy all the township lands with a larger loan. If it could own the lands all at once, "the advantages would be incalculable," and they asked the Queen for a loan guarantee.[94]

Labouchere responded that "adjustments" could be made to the Land Purchase Act to increase the amount of money that the island government could borrow. However, before that could occur, the government would have to propose a loan amount and provide London with a detailed statement of its finances, as well as a comprehensive plan to pay off the principal and the interest of a larger loan.[95] Daly responded to Labouchere's loan guarantee in two ways: he claimed that the Land Purchase Act worked to produce the "effects" of both increasing the value of land and bringing a "large portion of the wild lands, by whomsoever owned, within reach of actual settlers, to the advantage of all concerned."[96] He envisioned a settler colonial future for the island, in which settlers could own lands according to British private property law, with the Crown holding highest title. "Wild lands" would become productive and, importantly, land value would continually increase. Notably, Mi'kmaw self-determination and treaty rights did not factor into his vision of the future.

The committee of the Executive Council looked into the loan guarantee. It decided that a loan of £100,000 sterling, or £150,000 island pounds, would suffice at 4 percent interest.[97] Both the assembly and the council agreed to this and proposed an amortization period of twenty years.[98] To acquire the loan guarantee, the government had to submit reports to London regarding its expenditures. According to its report of 1856, it had a positive balance of approximately £6,521. However, it arrived at this figure "after taking credit to the colony for the value of government lands estimated at a low rate, and charging it with all debentures afloat, and with £7,666 l 13 s 4 d Treasury notes afloat, not bearing interest." In other words, it calculated this positive balance by including an estimated value of "government" lands, or unceded and surrendered Mi'kmaw territories. This, it reasoned, made the colony "out of debt" and at a surplus of revenue. It claimed a positive balance of over £6,000, when its revenue in 1854 was £30,689, which barely covered the full principal amount of the potential £30,000 of debt from the Land Purchase Act alone.

The colonies included land as part of their assets. This practice rendered their debts invisible because the calculated value of the land was greater than the debts.[99] At the same time, accounting conventions such as double-entry bookkeeping balanced credits and debits, and account books do not list negative numbers, or deficits, and instead record liabilities in positive numbers. Furthermore, listing land as an asset, as if it could immediately be liquidated to pay bills, became a settler colonial economic fiction. Colonial land could not be easily, or at all, liquidated for revenue, and this fact was the primary reason that settler colonial governments needed to finance themselves through public debts in the first place. Debt instruments could quickly circulate for exchange, but not land. The island government claimed richness from land, but that wealth needed to be extracted into money markets first. At no time did Mi'kmaw territorial rights enter the equation, an exclusion that cleaved along racial lines embedded in British cultural assumptions about land title and who had the right to extend jurisdiction over such lands.[100]

Labouchere requested that the "proceeds of the lands to be purchased, as well as a first charge on the general revenue of the province, should be secured by Legislative enactments for the payment of principal and interest."[101] He also asked the colonial government to frame its proposed legislation for the loan guarantee around an 1852 statute of the Legislature of Jamaica, probably because this was a recent and exemplary colonial request for a loan guarantee.[102] Obviously encouraged by its positive correspondence with Labouchere, the government passed an act in April 1857 that outlined the terms for the guarantee. It did so before London granted its permission for an imperial loan guarantee, which was not an uncommon practice for the colonial legislature.[103] Labouchere had first mentioned the possibility of the loan guarantee in July 1856, but the prospect was growing dim by August 1857. When the island government requested confirmation, he responded vaguely, stating that "circumstances" had made the question of the guarantee impossible to discuss in the present parliamentary session but that he would try again. Daly replied that the tenantry and others expressed disappointment at the delay. He added that agents who worked for one of the absentee landowners, Lord Selkirk, would not consider selling the land or even submitting preliminary papers such as land titles to the colonial government until the guarantee had been secured.[104] In early January 1858, after months of silence from Labouchere, Daly wrote to him again and sent a copy of the act the island government had passed on April 15, 1857, to receive an imperial loan guarantee, in anticipation of a corresponding imperial act to authorize the guarantee.[105] In Britain, the House of Lords seemed to agree to a resolution to guarantee a loan of £100,000 to the island government, but some noted that "Parliament had objected entirely to the principle." It was suggested that "the most simple way" forward would be to negate the resolution and to not give the island government the guarantee.[106] Still, the secretary of state for the colonies at the time, Lord Stanley, introduced a bill to guarantee a "Loan for the service of Prince Edward Island."[107] The bill, however, was withdrawn[108] and therefore rejected the island government's proposal in 1858.[109] Two years later, the island government tried again, setting up a Land Commission in 1860, with the hope of finally solving the land question.[110]

The request for a loan guarantee had encountered a cool reception in the British House of Commons, where a speaker stated that "the general opinion" of the House was "that Imperial guarantees of loans raised for colonial purposes were objectionable in principle." The guarantees became both "dangerous" and "embarrassing to the Imperial finances." The point of the settler colonies taking out public debts was to raise capital on their own and in part to relieve Britain of financial duties to the colonies. Undaunted, the Prince Edward Island government continued to advocate for a guarantee and insisted that the island was in a unique situation, one created in 1767 by London itself, when it divided the island into sixty-seven lots and granted them to absentee landlords. In addition, it had exacerbated the problem by not systematically enforcing the payment of the quitrents, a failure that had hindered development. The pleas about fairness and hindrances to colonial improvement, however, did not change imperial minds.[111]

Loans that financed the colony easily bifurcated into additional loans when debts came due and the government could not pay them. The practice of borrowing money to pay for borrowed money became structural, and the government's debt increased exponentially due to its efforts to purchase land directly from its owners. After London refused to grant the loan guarantee in the late 1850s, the island government immediately grappled with the problem of how to pay the principal on loans that the Land Purchase Act had authorized. The statute had enabled it to raise £30,000, and of this amount it successfully sold £18,000 worth of debentures, £12,000 of which went to purchase approximately 84,000 acres of the Worrell estate.[112] However, the future crept up fast, and the due date for the debentures began to loom. Because so few tenants had purchased land, the government was not in a position to pay back the £18,000. In 1864, just six months before the debentures came due, it passed another act to borrow yet more money. An Act to Provide for the Payment of Certain Debentures made it clear that the debentures used to purchase the Worrell estate could not be paid by the December due date. It noted that the sales from lands had not "yielded sufficient" revenue and that the government could not pay the debentures. To solve this problem, the statute allowed the government to raise £19,000 at 6 percent interest to pay back the original £18,000.[113] This act was a clear example of borrowing money to pay for previous borrowing, thus snowballing the public debt.

Many of the acts to raise money had to do with the original Land Purchase Act, to pay back its debentures or to increase the amount of the debt. Not all of the statutes that increased the public debt had a direct tie to the Land Purchase Act, as was the case for An Act to Assist Leaseholders in the Purchase of the Fee-Simple of their Farms, which was passed in April 1865.[114] Under the terms of this act, any leaseholder who wished to purchase land applied to the public lands commissioner, who would then investigate the title and calculate the price of the property. Once the commissioner deemed everything acceptable, the tenant paid 50 percent of the price to the government, which then chipped in the remaining half to buy the property directly from the owner. The tenant was expected to reimburse the government for its outlay. The commissioner issued a deed of conveyance with a memorandum or defeasance specifying how much the tenant owed to the government, with an interest rate of 6 percent per year. Under this act, the public lands commissioner sold the property, and the tenant, now its owner, was to pay ten equal annual installments, with interest, and had the option to pay the amount in full to the government. The act stipulated that the surplus money from the sale of land "purchased under this act" would repay all the money borrowed, including the interest. It also specified that no tenant could pay more than sixteen shillings and eight pence per acre, and therefore it fixed the price to a certain degree.[115]

In many ways, the circular debt logic of settler colonial governments becomes clearest with this act. The government used a public debt to raise money to lend to leaseholders so that they could purchase half the land. However, the government used the public debt to raise money so that it could purchase the land in the first place. In a way, lending borrowed money to the leaseholders stimulated the purchase of land on which the government owed money.

In May 1866, the government passed An Act in Addition to and In Further Amendment of the Land Purchase Act, which authorized the lieutenant governor to borrow from any persons or bodies corporate or politic. The act wasted no time in getting to the core of the problem: the government needed more money to buy land. It authorized the government to raise £110,000 in addition to the £30,000 and £10,000 in the previous two amendments to the Land Purchase Act.[116] Thus, from the amendments of the Land Purchase Act alone, the public debt that the island could raise amounted to £150,000.[117] Altogether, the government elevated its ability to debt finance from £10,000 in 1853 to £229,000 in 1866. It needs emphasizing that the purpose of all these acts was to purchase land.

In 1871, the government added to its substantial public debt by embarking on the construction of the Prince Edward Island Railway, an ambitious – and onerously expensive – initiative that ran tip-to-tip along the entire island. To enable the venture, the General Assembly passed An Act to Authorise the Construction of a Railroad through Prince Edward Island, which included the provision that the government could raise an undisclosed sum of money to pay for the railway.[118] Poorly planned, the project overspent its budget by such an enormous amount that the colony had reached the verge of economic disaster by 1872, a fact that partially prompted its entry into Confederation on July 1, 1873.

It did so on the clear understanding that joining Canada would entail an extension of its credit and that it would receive a loan from the dominion.[119] This debt payment agreement had four major components – the Dominion of Canada debt account, the Dominion of Canada subsidy account, money for railway land damages, and a land purchase account.[120] Becoming a province of Canada effectively and immediately solved the island's debt problem. Ottawa allowed it a debt of $50 per capita, which amounted to $4,701,050.[121] It also received a subsidy that equalled 80 cents per head of the population (94,021 people), along with an annual $30,000 for legislation and 5 percent on the railway debt. However, the railway made only a portion of the combined debt, as Ottawa pledged 5 percent interest for the purchase of lands that amounted to $900,000 ($800,000 paid in cash, and interest charged on $100,000), which made the interest $22,500 per year. After these numbers and the island's public debt were calculated, Ottawa deposited $140,841.50 in the island account.[122] The debt was not as simple as a $900,000 loan: it included payment of interest methods, money to purchase land, and money for railway damages.

When Prince Edward Island joined Confederation, it had a debt of $4,701,050.[123] Confederation buttressed its credit through debt relief. Speculation on the railways built on newly secured government-owned lands had solved its bad credit. In July 1873, a private bank in London, Morton, Rose and Company, or Bartholomew House, financed the loan, with the result that the island government had its debt issued as securities on the London Stock Exchange. The LSE issued the securities because the province now had the "security of the whole Dominion." This allowed the island to raise £220,000 at 6 percent interest on the LSE, which opened up its debt to the global market.[124] Finally, after decades of failed attempts, it could directly access capital on the London money market.

Conclusion

Arjun Appadurai describes capitalism as the "dreamwork of industrial modernity" and refers to speculation as the "the motor of this dream-work."[125] In Prince Edward Island, land reformers pursued their dream of a world where capital flowed unhindered into the island. Early on, this took the form of American capital and fisheries development, with the Reciprocity Treaty, and then British capital via government loans. Edward Gibbon Wakefield, John Stuart Mill, Alexander Bannerman, Dominick Daly, and many others may have envisioned a future in which land in settler colonies increased in market value, but they did so at the expense of the Mi'kmaq, treaty law, and the stewardship of other-than-human beings and the environment. The territories of Indigenous nations were an asset to colonial expansion.[126] The fact that the island was under the protection of the Peace and Friendship Treaties and had not been ceded by the Mi'kmaq meant that the colonial government did not have to follow its own legal framework, as it did when purchasing real estate from British owners. After all, who would hold it accountable to the Mi'kmaq?

The Mi'kmaq did attempt to defend their homelands. In the 1830s, Chief Oliver LeBone petitioned the imperial government to intervene in settler incursions, as did Chief Charles Bernard of Lennox Island many decades later.[127] Some Indigenous leaders in the Maritimes wanted to join Confederation to alleviate the harsh treatment of the colonial governments.[128] Other Indigenous leaders launched international appeals of their own to fight against colonialism, many of which carry into the present day. For example, Sandra Lovelace and Freda Huson presented their cases to the United Nations, seeking to hold the Canadian government accountable for settler colonial policy and invasion.[129] The intentional framing of the Mi'kmaq as unworthy of land rights, or as too few in number, or as having merely summered on the island made the bitter truth of land theft easier to swallow for any settlers who found it objectionable. Whereas Theophilus Stewart, the Aborigines Protection Society, and various settlers attempted to help the Mi'kmaq, it is difficult to find evidence where they clearly argued for the cessation of colonization.

The history of Epekwitk, as a microcosm in which to study British-imposed property rights as land theft, reveals many truths about the formation of the Canadian state and how the dominion built itself with debt. The island government had bad credit because, under British law, it did not own the land and thus did not have secure land title to claim it as an asset when it asked for a loan. Bad credit, or the belief that principle plus interest could not be paid back and would "embarrass" the imperial government, made it impossible to secure even a loan guarantee. Not until Confederation finally made the island a safer bet and the railway opened up a space to speculate on its future value could it have its public debt issued as securities on the London Stock Exchange. Clearly, public borrowing intensified throughout the late nineteenth century and paid for the establishment of a settler society. At the same time, the island government could not pay back its loans and thus borrowed more money to cover them, digging itself ever deeper into a cycle of borrowing to pay for borrowing and falling into the familiar settler colonial pattern of structural indebtedness.

The public debt, in fact, made "real" the fictitious commodity of land in the settler colonies. It did so through the circulation of debt instruments secured with land value, which made lands appear liquid, but speculation also made land value real because it created a market for such land. The railway project enabled the island government to access London capital via loans – it gave the government credit because it became a thing that could, in theory, produce future value. Working on the history of Prince Edward Island invariably raises two questions: Why would the government chose to invest in a railroad? What was its true purpose? The point was not so much that the railway would serve a practical purpose in moving people and goods but that it provided an opportunity to speculate on money markets.

Richard White highlights the unthinking growth of the railways, an investment opportunity that trumped any rational decisions about where the lines should run, how to maximize benefits, or how to avoid environmental destruction. He notes that the bison "became the first victims" of this irrational economic growth, as railways made it easier to export their hides to market and facilitated the destruction of their habitat. For a few individuals, the sacrifice of animals, environment, Indigenous peoples, racialized labour, and even the settler public did result in fortunes that exceeded their wildest dreams. For many others, the result was little more than a nightmare. For many Indigenous peoples who found themselves in the way of Canada's aggressive westward expansion after the 1870s, the railway ushered in a heightened catastrophic settler colonial future.[130]

5 The New Canadian Empire: Imperial Credit and the Transfer of Sovereignty

When we pledge the credit of England, we are laying an additional burden on the financial resources of this country. It matters not whether in a particular instance there will or will not be a call for the actual payment of the money. The principle is clear that a guarantee is a real obligation and burden undertaken by us ... This plan for the construction of a railway, for which we are now asked to guarantee a loan to the Colonial Government, has been associated with and incorporated in the scheme of Confederation itself. Consider it with reference to this scheme of Confederation, and if you believe the objects of that Confederation are such as are vitally important and beneficial to the relations of this country with our North-American Colonies, give the benefit of that consideration to the proposal now made. It is only on grounds of that kind that I support the proposal before the House. The general system of colonial guarantees is one which has come into just discredit within the walls of Parliament; and I would hope that only motives of the highest order will induce any Government to make proposals to the House of Commons for such guarantees. I believe the present guarantee does depend upon motives of policy belonging to a very high order, and intimately and inseparably

> associated with most just and most enlightened views of the true interests of the Empire.
>
> – William Ewart Gladstone, debate on Canada Railway Loan bill, House of Commons (UK), March 28, 1867

The Transfer of Imperial Power

The early major works in Canadian history examined, and examined well, many of the threads that knotted into Confederation in 1867. Colonial union had been whispered about in the 1820s, but many developments of the 1860s, often involving fear of the United States, resulted in the loud passage of the British North America Act in 1867.[1] In 1861, the American Civil War engulfed the country in a struggle that claimed thousands of lives and could potentially spill over the northern border. Also during that year, the Trent Affair, in which an American ship intercepted an unarmed British steamer, threatened the peace between the United States and British North America. Between 1866 and 1871, a US-based Irish republican organization known as the Fenian Brotherhood repeatedly raided into Canada. The lands to the west were a subject of constant uncertainty. And the fear of American annexation made holding on to the colonies undesirable for the government in London. As Britain had learned once again during the Crimean War, fought with Russia between 1853 and 1856, armed conflict was a costly business. A clash between the colonies and the United States would be very costly. But no matter the causes of Confederation, one underlying fact never changed: executing it took an exorbitant amount of money. This chapter does not revisit the well-trodden ground regarding the ideologies and politics of the men who argued for and against colonial union. It does, however, focus on how Canada's public debt made Confederation possible.

As the opening quote highlights, only borrowed money could pay for it. Unprecedented access to British credit gave life to Confederation, illustrating the third principle of public debt financing: the necessity for settler colonies to consolidate to obtain credit. This chapter focuses on three debt-financed projects – the Intercolonial Railway, the purchase of Rupert's Land, and the Canadian Pacific Railway – and though they are discussed separately, they were so intertwined that together they constituted a single scheme of imperial expansion. Railway infrastructure and land appropriation went hand-in-hand. All three projects were made possible only because Britain granted an imperial loan guarantee. This meant that the colonies could have access to lower interest rates, which made capital cheaper.[2]

Until the 1860s, whether a colonial parliament or a British one would govern Indigenous territories remained unclear, but Confederation launched a slow transition of power, as the new "criminal empire" took over the imperial jurisdiction of Britain.[3] Loans paid for the Canadian government to take up the yoke of imperialism. Some of the early studies in Canadian history allude to this transfer as a shift from the "liberal imperialism of Britain" to the "national imperialism of Canada."[4] However, they commonly present the expansionist tendencies of the Fathers of Confederation as a natural order of things, instead of a deliberate policy choice to institute capitalist relationships and acquire Indigenous land. Canadian imperialism intended, and still intends, to assert sovereignty over Indigenous nations, as Andrea Bear Nicholas points out.[5] Confederation was not an endpoint. It was just one constellation in a galaxy of stars that revolved around the governance of Indigenous nations and access to their land.

Colonial Loans, Revenues, and Taxes

Determining how to pay for colonization was a deeply complex issue, and arguments raged over how colonial government finances were being used or, according to some, misused. Calculating the expenditures of colonial governments is not as simple as adding up their revenues, taxes, and debts, because of double-entry bookkeeping, but also because of the nature of a debt-financed government expenditure, where some believed that a financial transaction would create more debt, whereas others believed that it would reduce the debt. Michael Piva writes that the merger of Upper and Lower Canada relieved the former of its bad credit because it now had access to the lucrative revenues and custom duties collected from controlling traffic on the St. Lawrence. Even so, revenue could not cover the interest or the principal of loans, the development of resource-extractive projects, and the maintenance of the colony – but credit could. For example, the cash books of the receiver general for the Province of Canada note total revenues in excess of £200,000 in November 1844 and again in January 1845.[6] This revenue came from public works, customs revenue collected in cities such as Montreal, Kingston, and Toronto, and money going into such funds as the "lunatic asylum fund," where the Province of Canada deposited just over £188 pounds in September 1844.[7] The government used eight banks, with the Bank of Montreal holding the most money and the Bank of British North America a close second.[8] The receiver general's cash and debenture statement books give a broader picture of the ratio of debt to revenue. According to the statements "on the balance of public monies" in June 1849, the government had slightly over £10,500 spread between the eight banks, as well as £366,000 of debentures issued with £236,000 returned, which left £130,000 in circulation.[9] The balance of this money could fluctuate quite a bit, and in September 1849 it amounted to a touch over £58,500.[10] By May 1851, it had grown significantly, shooting up to over £480,000.[11] Revenue could not exist prior to development and, for this obvious reason, the colonial government could not use it to pay for development of public works. More importantly, however, and perhaps less obviously, the amount of debt in total exceeded yearly revenue. Credit, on the other hand, allowed colonial governments to borrow, even if their debts exceeded their revenues. All credit derived from access to the territories of Indigenous nations or, to be more precise, from the racialized order of landownership that gave the settler government the presumed right to claim Indigenous lands as an asset.

Under legislated debt contracts, revenues often had to be pledged and rendered liable for the loan, revenues that derived from theft of Indigenous land. In August 1848, the receiver general's journal recorded loans to thirty-eight incorporated companies, mostly canal, road, and navigation companies, which amounted to just over £1.9 million. Nearly £504,000 went to the Welland Canal Company, with just over £2,052 collected from "Welland Canal tolls." On the credit side of things, or revenues, the "Clergy Reserves Fund" for both Canada East and Canada West approximated £90,000, with "new sales" at around £10,700. Both tavern licences and marriage licences also contributed to revenues: licences for taverns in Canada East and West amounted to nearly £23,000 and marriage licences to just under £3,000. Public works revenue amounted to a little over £4,600.[12] These numbers reveal an important point: most of the revenue was derived from claiming unsurrendered Indigenous territories as colonial land, as in the case of the clergy reserve fund, development projects such as the Welland Canal, licensing and taxing the settler population, and holding Indigenous land in trust. What percentage of expenditure the colonial government paid for from revenue versus public loans loses importance as a site of inquiry when we concentrate on the entire picture offered by the colonial account books. Colonial governments could extract value from Indigenous land and render it as capital through such accounting and the use of circulating debt instruments, but violence authorized these transactions, clearing away Indigenous peoples to make room for the Welland Canal's small revenue, to make way for settlers setting up taverns and getting married – to make way for a market economy.

In 1882, Finance Minister Leonard Tilley delivered his budget speech in the Canadian House of Commons. His speech reflects the complexity of government spending, revenue, and taxation; even the MPs of his time (much like today) could not agree on exactly what constituted the correct calculations in financial assessments of the government. Debt-financed expenditure requires estimates and attempts to represent future numbers, particularly about the projected future value of land after development. Tilley noted that in 1880, Canada had collected $19,910,100.01 in taxes from a population of 4.282,300 people. Taxes between July 1879 and July 1881 had amounted to $4.88 per person, but that the figure had dropped to $4.05 per person after July 1881. He mentioned that expenditure was $50,350,806, with an average annual expenditure of $25,178,113.[13] In other words, if one trusts Tilley's calculations, the government had collected $19 million in taxes but had spent $25 million, which created a shortfall of $6 million. Keep in mind that the calculation of the debit side of the ledger included interest and any monies directed toward sinking funds but not the entire principal of loan payments owed. Taxes could pay part of the public debt lent as capital to finance companies, but if no settlers occupied Indigenous territories, they could not be raised. Money raised from Indigenous lands and waters, whether in the form of property taxes paid by settlers or revenue generated by the Welland Canal, did not go to Indigenous nations to pay for the use of their land. The receiver general's journals include no evidence that such payments were made, only that the colonial government held Indigenous lands in trust and put any money from these lands into government accounts, lending it out or using it to speculate on money markets.[14] The ability to raise loans, revenue, and taxes to pay for colonization existed because of colonization and the appropriation of Indigenous land. Analyzing the exact breakdown of these three sources of capital would be useful for further study.

The Intercolonial Railway

MP Alexander Tilloch Galt suggested the scheme of colonial union, but an 1858 session of the Parliament of Canada marked the official in-earnest attempt to achieve it. Historians have long argued that British North American governments built the road to Confederation with railway ties and iron, and Galt's involvement in both Confederation and the Grand Trunk Railway exemplifies this fact. His career, which centred on uniting the colonies and promoting British emigration, as well as his role in the Grand Trunk Railway and in the establishment of Lethbridge, Alberta, embodies the settler colonial project of capital, labour, and expansion over Indigenous territories.[15] Much like Edward Gibbon Wakefield, Galt made his mark in pursuing an aggressive colonization plan. The Grand Trunk Railway, which connected Montreal and Toronto, continued the scheme of British expansion, with the big banks Glyn, Hallifax, and Company and the Barings Bank, Lombard Street financiers, the Colonial Office, and others working with British North America to help pay for imperialism.[16]

Union between the British North American colonies entailed more than political amalgamation. The Confederation package included the construction of the Intercolonial and Canadian Pacific Railways, the acquisition of the vast expanse of Rupert's Land, and the installation of telecommunication infrastructure to connect the disparate patches of British and French settlement. Each node on the Confederation triad of railway, land, and telegraph could not exist alone, and all of them cost money – money the Province of Canada, Nova Scotia, and New Brunswick did not have. More accurately, they did not have good credit and, deeply in debt, could not access enough money at interest rates that were low enough.

Despite its indebtedness, the Legislative Assembly of the Province of Canada passed the Guarantee Act in 1849. Approved by an overwhelming vote of sixty-two to four, an "extraordinary consensus," it secured a 6 percent return for investors in any railway venture that was more than 120 kilometres long and more than half completed.[17] As the vote in the assembly reveals, there was virtually no opposition to using a public deficit to support development, as was the case for the Prince Edward Island government. Arguably, this measure was so normalized that even the authors of profoundly rich historical studies on Confederation have failed to recognize the public debt as intentional policy that underscored a white supremacist and heteropatriarchal capitalist ordering of governance. When the Province of Canada passed the Guarantee Act, it had done what colonial legislatures had always done since the 1820s: use public money to finance private businesses. After all, public money secured by government was cheaper money. The act ushered in the "golden age" of the Canadian railway.

In 1848, Secretary of State for War and the Colonies Henry George Grey acknowledged the necessity of linking the Maritime provinces to Canada via an intercolonial railway and asked how the provinces would work together "to co-operate in its execution."[18] In January 1849, the New Brunswick Legislative Council passed a series of resolutions that referred to an intercolonial railway as the "greatest moment for the permanency of British interests in this Continent." Much like other proponents of the railway, the council stressed that the project would enhance military prowess, protect the colonies from American annexation, impede the loss of British settlers to the United States, and facilitate inland settlement, which would generate wealth. The railway, however, did not necessarily lead to Confederation, and those who pushed for it concentrated on how it would benefit the British Empire.[19]

In 1858, the Legislature of the Province of Canada insisted that the intercolonial railway was "essential to the interests of the Empire at large." It would "place the whole British possessions in America within the ready access and easy protection of Great Britain, whilst by the facilities for internal communication thus afforded, the prosperity of those great dependencies would be promoted, their strength consolidated and added to the strength of the Empire, and their permanent union with the Mother-Country secured."[20] But a paradox rested at the heart of the railway project: it would both consolidate the British North American colonies and strengthen the British Empire in Canada. Refusing to finance the railway outright, London offered "to the Provincial Governments an imperial guarantee of interest towards enabling them to raise by public loan, if they should desire it, at a moderate rate, the requisite funds for constructing the Railway."[21]

On September 30, 1861, the three colonial governments held a railway conference in the Executive Council Chamber in Quebec City, where fifteen delegates discussed the loan and possible loan guarantee.[22] Four were from New Brunswick, three from Nova Scotia, and eight from Canada, including Alexander Tilloch Galt, George-Étienne Cartier, and John A. Macdonald. Galt had made colonial union a topic of consideration, but the railway, or rather the shared debt contract for its construction, brought the three governments together before political union was settled. The delegates met to "renew the offers made to the Imperial Government on the 26th day of October, 1858, to aid in the construction of an Intercolonial Railway to connect Halifax with Quebec."[23] After the conference, some travelled to England to submit their proposal to the colonial secretary when the news broke in England about the Trent Affair of November 1861. After the conference, discourse on the Trent Affair emphasized the very real possibility of a war between Britain (and its colonies) and the United States, which was only narrowly averted. However, in preparation for war, troops had to traverse a vast distance, so a desire for quick military action further legitimized the railway project.[24]

By 1867, the loan guarantee seemed so inevitable that section 145 of the British North America Act could boldly state, "it shall be the Duty of the Government and Parliament of Canada to provide for the Commencement, within Six Months after the Union, of a Railway connecting the River St. Lawrence with the City of Halifax in Nova Scotia."[25] Even though the British Parliament clearly wanted to steer away from giving the British North American governments guarantees on loans after the 1840s, the British North America Act had bound the intercolonial railway to Confederation. London's abhorrence of imperial loan guarantees came into conflict with its desire to end "a vicious system of dependence" and it sought to trigger "a spirit of independence in financial matters" in what would become Canada.[26] Although it was paradoxical that loan guarantees would grant independence, an imperial loan guarantee to ensure the success of Confederation was seen as a British imperial venture worth financing. Thus, the logic that informed the debates about the loan guarantee, that the British government needed to pay in order to extract itself from "the vicious system" of colonial dependence, was not a contradiction but a necessity.[27]

Once it became obvious that London had no intention of footing the bill for the intercolonial railway, despite pleas and veiled threats about the need to transport British troops in the event of an American invasion, an imperial loan guarantee became the chosen method to support the credit of the three provinces. London authorized the loan in its 1867 Canada Railway Loan Act, as a complement to the British North America Act.[28] Ottawa and London negotiated a £3,000,000 imperial loan guarantee; £1,500,000 of the imperial guaranteed and £500,000 in unguaranteed Canadian bonds got the intercolonial railway from Halifax to Quebec started.[29] In 1872, Finance Minister Charles Tupper requested the remaining half of the guaranteed bonds.[30] The final act put in place, "to promote the interests of the British Empire," a guarantee on £3,000,000 at 4 percent interest with a sinking fund charge of 1 percent per annum on the principal amount. Such management of public funds was written into the British North America Act. The railway loan guarantee immediately charged the Canadian consolidated revenue fund for sections 103, 104, and 105 of the act to pay for the "public service of Canada" as the first charge, to meet the annual interest on the public debts of New Brunswick, Nova Scotia, and the Province of Canada as the second charge, and to pay the governor general's salary as the third charge. Section 102 created the Canadian consolidated revenue fund.[31]

Arthur H. Gordon, lieutenant governor of New Brunswick, reported "with great satisfaction" that, on September 12, 1862, the railway loan bill passed both the House of Assembly and the Legislative Council, with only two votes against it.[32] The imperial government would eventually approve the sentiment in this bill in the form of the 1867 railway loan. In the report to the imperial government on the need for such a loan, the "specially deputed" delegates "representing the Government of Canada" wrote to the Secretary of State for the Colonies, Henry Pelham-Clinton (the Duke of Newcastle), in 1862. They outlined the merits of the railway and requested a loan guarantee from London to the tune of £3,000,000, eventually approved by the imperial government.[33] The reasoning in the report underscores the importance of the railway to Canadian imperialism. The report notes that while it was "possible that the railroad may cost half a million or more above this fixed sum" of £3,000,000, it asserted that the railway would serve "military advantages and upon consideration certainly as Imperial as Colonial."[34] The entire justification of the railway revolved around colonial expansion and imperial power, exemplified in the report's argument that

> the question of the public defences of the Colonies, as integral parts of the Empire; the question of the maintenance, of the extension of the political and social influence of England over the whole of her immense possessions in North America; the economical questions of so vast magnitude to the welfare of the nation; the question of unemployed capital, of surplus labour, underlie every link of the great and national road which Canada is anxious to build by the largest and most liberal contribution, from the Atlantic to the Pacific.[35]

The railway was intentionally used to implement capitalist social relationships that would ensure that "unemployed capital" had a place for investment (the railway) so it did not go to waste, and that "surplus labour" also had employment (the railway) so that they did not disrupt the social order. Elite anxieties about employing people centred on the fear that the unemployed or undereymployed, in their alledged idleness, would attempt to rise up against the injustice of their socially stratified positions in life as they had done in the first half of the nineteenth century in Britain.[36] The railway served a purpose beyond simple transportation or military strategy. It quite explicitly, according to contemporaries, advanced the social relationships vital to a capitalist society. In the settler-state of Canada, then, it becomes apparent that settler colonialism and capitalism were actually one and the same by the time of Confederation: two sides of the same coin or, more aptly, the machine that stamped out the coinage. The end of capitalism, then, would necessitate the end of colonialism.

It took several years of colonial lobbying to obtain London's offer of a loan guarantee for the intercolonial railway through the 1867 British act, and it came with a tinge of bitterness. It also highlights the difficulties and unequal power dynamics between the four colonial governments that would become the first provinces of the dominion. The shared debt forced each government to create a "uniformity of legislation in all the Provinces" in October 1862.[37] Originally, a sinking fund with a high annual payment of 4 percent of the principal amount was agreed on; however, the Province of Canada (that would split into Ontario and Quebec in 1867) stalled the proceedings to push for better terms for the loan guarantee, mainly to reduce the obligation to pay into a sinking fund. As it vacillated, New Brunswick and Nova Scotia asked London to "permit the imperial Guarantee to operate as regards the capital required to be expended on the first link of the railway, viz., that between Truro and 'the Bend' [Moncton]."[38] On September 18, 1863, the Province of Canada suddenly announced that it would step away from the loan agreement and begin the process anew. Outraged by this betrayal, Maritime newspapers condemned the move, calling it an unmanly breach of trust and contract.[39] In the end, however, the three governments agreed to renewed loan guarantee terms and borrowed for the Intercolonial Railway. This was not the last time the Maritime governments complained about their partner in Confederation. The three governments had hired Joseph Nelson as their agent in London to "secure petitions and memorials to parliament" in favour of obtaining the loan guarantee, but the Province of Canada did not "bear her fair share" in paying him, as Nova Scotia and New Brunswick paid £100 each for his services.[40]

Imperial loan guarantees allowed for reduced interest rates on loans, which gave the colonial government access to cheaper money. Britain, however, did not easily extend its credit, and many British MPs argued that giving loan guarantees to the settler colonies would be a burden on British taxpayers. At the same time, "lending" credit could damage imperial credit. In 1870, Scottish MP David Wedderburn decried the system of colonial guarantees as "pernicious and dangerous." He observed, "we enabled the Canadians to borrow money at 4 per cent instead of 6 per cent, but in proportion as we raised their credit we depressed our own."[41] The point of the loan guarantee was to break the financial ties between British North America and the mother country, but instead they had the potential to damage British credit. London granted several guarantees, such as the Greek loan, the Sardinian loan, and the Russian-Dutch loan. An 1869 estimate stated that it had granted about twelve more. With a loan guarantee, Britain shouldered the risk of the loans, and such loans leaned against its credit, which could negatively impact British interest rates and borrowing capacity. Given this, those who opposed loan guarantees saw the "tax-payers of this country" as the ones who paid "the interest, and of which they would have to pay the principal in the end. It was highly impolitic and injurious to the interests of the country that we should embark in these guarantees at all."[42] The Intercolonial Railway loan, however, passed through the complicated approval process of the imperial and colonial governments, with an interest payment due on January 1, 1869.[43] Because the loan stipulated a sinking fund, the Privy Council of Canada appointed Thomas Baring and George Carr Glyn to act as its trustees on behalf of the Government of Canada.[44]

Once the loan guarantee was in place, the railway venture could move on to practical considerations. Its engineer in chief, Sandford Fleming, favoured the Chaleur Bay route, which linked Halifax to Quebec by snaking along the northwestern shores of Mi'kma'ki through Wəlastəkwey territory and into the territories of other Indigenous nations. The project would naturally involve the construction of many bridges, and though the use of wood had been proposed as a cost-cutting measure, Fleming rejected it because wooden bridges would need frequent repairs. Furthermore, a local supply of the necessary timber, white pine, simply did not exist, as logging had depleted the forests in the area surrounding the proposed railway route. Fleming wrote, "on an overland journey from Halifax to Quebec by any travelled route, the eye can scarcely detect a single pine tree."[45] He predicted the "almost total destruction, at no distant day, of pine timber in these Provinces."[46] Given this dismal situation, it would be "a very grave error to build the bridges of wood," so Fleming argued for iron bridges that would cost less to repair in the longer term.[47]

The mechanics of building the railway bedevilled the colonial governments, but so did financing it. Sharing a loan was complicated. Commissioners had to be paid, services acquired, and banks had to have their commissions for sorting out the bonds. The bonds themselves had to be sent overseas and to be signed by the receiver general, or in some cases agents in London would sign them to make things easier. Issuing bonds and debentures took time, not just for the necessary negotiations, but also to physically move payment and securities across the Atlantic Ocean.[48] The debt burdens and varied credit of each colonial government complicated the loan as well. Of the £3,000,000 loan guarantee, the Province of Canada took the liability for five-twelfths, with New Brunswick and Nova Scotia each liable for three and a half twelfths.[49] The consequent payments, debentures, interest rates, and sinking fund schedule bound the three governments together, forcing them to rely on each other's good faith, good credit practice, and ability to make good on railway construction. Since one government could not contract a loan without the other two passing bills, any delay in one affected all three.

The imperial loan guarantee granted to the Province of Canada in 1842 was cited as a shining example of the benefits of such guarantees but also as proof that they menaced imperial finances.[50] In a positive report on Canadian revenues, Undersecretary of State for the Colonies Frederic Rogers claimed that the Province of Canada paid off its 1842 imperial loan guarantee debt in 1859–60, nine years before it became due. For this reason, he believed that "Canada both can and will perform her part in this matter" and "that Parliament may now properly be asked to authorise their Lordships to give the proposed guarantee."[51] Rogers argued that Canada paid off the 1842 loan "not from the proceeds of a fresh loan but from revenue."[52]

Although it was true that Canada did not contract a fresh loan to pay off its 1841 debt, Rogers's assertion that it had done so with cash was not entirely accurate. In 1859, it dealt with its repayment problem by passing an act that reduced sinking fund payments from 4 percent to 2 percent and, importantly, that allowed for the renewal of debentures.[53] Other settler colonies that suffered under their great public debts also renewed debentures, which required an act of Parliament to modify the terms of the original loan agreement. Not everyone bought into the logic that renewing a debenture for the purpose of reducing interest did not constitute an additional loan. For example, a heated 1895 parliamentary debate in New South Wales made it plain that altering a debt contract with renewals simply repackaged an old debt as paid off. Statutes passed to restructure the terms of the original debt, however, "paid" the loan off when the debentures or bonds became due. A New South Wales MP defended government borrowing as, in fact, a savings scheme that "saved the country £35,000 a year by advancing £1,000,000 to the loan account, instead of raising debentures." He claimed that the "present Government have not raised a single pound of loans for public works since we took office. We have had a loan to renew debentures in London, but not a single penny have we raised by loan since we came into office." An unnamed MP, thoroughly unconvinced by this argument, shouted out, "You borrowed money!" To which the speaker replied,

> If I have £1,000,000 lying idle, on which by law I am compelled to pay 3 per cent. interest, would it not be a mad transaction on my part to borrow another £1,000,000, and pay another 3 1/2 per cent. on it, when I am paying interest on an idle £1,000,000? That is common-sense. I do not know if it was ever done before, but that is what I have done. Having to pay 3 per cent. on £1,000,000 which I have at my disposal, I made use of it, and advanced it to the loan fund, and I could only debit it to the consolidated revenue, and that made my revenue look bad; but in point of fact it was good financing, and saved the country £35,000 a year. Going away from that, there is another imputation which has been constantly levelled against the Government, especially against myself, that we were debauching this country by the amount of loan money that we are spending in the country.[54]

Although the MP was unaware of whether such debt restructuring schemes had already been tried, they were not new. They plagued the settler colonies that could not meet their contractual obligations to pay back the loans that they had acquired because they could lean on imperial credit and because they claimed title to Indigenous lands. In defending his government's spending, the MP proposed that it "raise a loan in London shortly to the amount of £3,727,000. That loan is entirely for renewals ... to renew debentures falling due in 1896."[55] Technically, a renewal was not a fresh loan, as both the Australian MP and Frederic Rogers were at pains to point out. In actuality, however, it amounted to a restructuring of debt, not to paying it off.

The British North America Act legislated expansion over the homelands of Indigenous nations, which cemented Canadian imperialism. However, Canada had to pay for the venture, but its dearth of capital impeded its dreams of empire. Turning to Britain, it received a loan guarantee of up to £3,000,000 with the Canada Railway Loan, which helped to realize the dream.[56] The railway pulled together the Canadian settler state and did more than just physically connect the colonies: it bonded their economies as well.

A Constitution of Imperialism

Imperial loan guarantees added an extra layer of complication to the already complicated problem of how to pay for colonialism, particularly with respect to the murky waters of jurisdiction. The British North America Act was a legally binding document between the imperial, dominion, and provincial governments that outlined which one possessed what rights in the colonies – which government had the right to exploit and extract value from the land. In short, which government had the right of imperial power. Thus, it showcases the transfer of power from Britain to the new dominion.

Public debts fell under the jurisdiction of Ottawa, but a disagreement regarding its use of British guaranteed funds for the Intercolonial Railway emphasizes the muddied jurisdictional rights in this transfer of power. The incident began on August 27, 1868, when the Privy Council of Canada put out a minute that redirected the funds, some raised with the railway loan, to other avenues of investments and debt repayments. In London, Robert Sinclair Aytoun, MP for the Fife burghs, had called into question how the Canadian finance minister, John Rose, had used the money raised from the imperial loan guarantee. Rose moved money from the railway loan to pay off other debts, and though London found this alarming, the British North America Act stipulated that it could not directly intervene in the financial affairs of the dominion. Section 91 of the act explicitly stated that "exclusive Legislative Authority of the Parliament of Canada" extended to "the Public Debt and Property" and "the borrowing of Money on the Public Credit."[57] In London, MPs reflected on whether the minute had followed the "spirit of the Canadian Railway Loan Act," reaching the broad consensus that it had not. The House put forward a motion that "no further guarantee should be given by the Commissioners of Her Majesty's Treasury, except in such form and manner as should insure the direct application of the money so guaranteed to the construction of the Intercolonial Railway." Although the motion was quickly withdrawn, this punitive approach did not go over well in Canada. The criticisms lobbed at Rose from across the Atlantic had softened any implication of wrongdoing by emphasizing that he had acted in "good faith," but his reputation was nonetheless at stake. In London, the House agreed to discuss stricter terms of loan agreements to ensure that the loan money "should not stick to anyone's fingers in its progress to that charming railway that was to be constructed."[58]

Earl Granville, secretary of state for the colonies, requested that Governor General John Young explain the meaning of the August 27, 1868, minute. Apparently, Rose had "temporarily applied" the monies raised with the railway loan guarantee "to the purpose of defraying the general debts of the Dominion." Governor General Charles Monck had approved the minute, but he had left office a few months later. His successor, John Young, then had to respond to the ire of "Her Majesty's Government," which deemed the use of the funds "not to be justifiable."[59] Granville explained that he "never had any intention to call in question the financial integrity and upright dealing of the Dominion of Canada, still less the personal honour of Mr. Rose and his colleagues." Instead, he focused his attention on the decision of the law officers of the Crown that Canada had misused loan funds, but he also stressed that "no unfriendly feeling" carried with the judgment about inappropriate spending. Investigating whether Rose's decision to shift railway loan funds to dominion debts of the highest interest rates "was in contravention to the Canada Railway Loan Act," the law officers concluded that they could not advise that "the investment of the money under the Minute of the Privy Council of Canada is in conformity with the

Imperial Act." Taking this one step farther, they argued that London had not intended the loan to be used for investment and therefore concluded that "the spirit and intention of the Canada Railway Loan Act, 1867, has not been complied with."[60]

When Ottawa began to receive funds backed with the credit of the imperial government, Rose sought the advice of Baring and Glyn because "it became the obvious duty" to "place the money received, as that an undue loss of interest might be avoided."[61] With three-quarters of the £2 million the government initially raised bearing 4 percent interest and the other quarter at 5 percent interest, Rose wanted to invest the loan to reduce overall interest payment costs. Initially, he wanted to make an investment with the "best rates they could," unrealistically hoping to invest the money at a high interest rate but with "perfect security and immediate convertibility." Unsurprisingly, Baring and Glyn informed him that this was unlikely "in the present state of the money market." The best he could hope for was an annual interest rate of 1 percent. Money sitting in an account that paid 1 percent interest did not make much money, essentially becoming "dead" or "unproductive" capital. Being out of circulation made it "unemployed," and the government would have acted "wantonly" had it chosen that option. So, Rose turned to the "perfect security" of Canada's other securities that were meant to provide funds for "certain engagements of the Dominion, which it was desirable to fund or otherwise meet." He took the railway loan "moneys lying comparatively unproductive, until these moneys were required to be disbursed to the contractors on the works" and "invested" them in Canada's public debt.[62]

London raised its hackles over this use of the railway funds, but Ottawa claimed that it had the constitutional authority to do so. It asserted control over its own finances, even in connection with money borrowed on imperial credit, and thus took the reins of imperial expansion from London. It linked control over borrowing to "the consolidation of British interests in North America, by the union of new provinces, and the acquisition and government of new territories," each of which created "exceptional strain on the resources of this country." Despite the insistence of the Crown law officers that Ottawa, and specifically the finance minister, must stop investing imperial loan monies to pay off dominion debt – even temporarily – a telegram from Rose's successor Francis Hincks stated that he "intended to disregard the opinion of the Law Officers of England as to the appropriation of the Intercolonial Railway Loan."[63] This episode in financing pushed Canada to dictate what it did with borrowed funds, even if its access to imperial credit had made such funds possible.

The movement of funds, debenture renewals, and exchequer bills for debt repayment set up an increasingly complicated system to manage the public debt.[64] Tracking the government debt after the 1860s becomes difficult because of the movement of money between debt accounts but also because of the bifurcation of debts when debentures became due, where strategies such as renewal, reinvestment, and even bond buying flourished. As the conflict over the appropriate use of the railway loan guarantee reveals, not everyone bought into these schemes, and they understood the movement of funds for what it was: using debt to pay for debt. The specific railway money redeemed part of the dominion debt when Rose acquired Canadian securities because, as a Privy Council report argued, no "other investment is either so available at a like rate of interest as the securities of Canada."[65] To capture a favourable interest rate, the dominion government was "compelled to avail themselves of the only safe investment which offered – their own Bonds."[66]

Prime Minister John A. Macdonald authorized agents to use the railway loan money deposited in London to pay for the interest on the dominion public debt. Doing so did not incur the costs of exchange that would have arisen if Canada had sent the money across the Atlantic, but it also pushed down the interest rate on loans.[67] Some even went so far as to claim that not one cent of the railway loan was actually used, while avoiding charges associated with transporting funds across the Atlantic. Rose claimed that no imperial loan money was used in such a matter, but his successor Francis Hincks "could not agree with him that the loan had not been used in redeeming the Dominion Debt."[68] Such accounting disputes reveal the virtual impossibility of calculating actual numbers of the movement of loan money; the account books gave no clear answers for contemporaries who could not agree on just one transaction, let alone multiple transactions. The railway account held slightly more that £10,000,000, but this included investments, not just cash. The money went into the investment of Canada's own debt instruments, nearly a quarter of a million pounds of Canadian securities bought in London and just over £27,000 in Canadian securities bought in Canada. The railway account also invested £1.5 million in the Bank of Montreal and the highest amount of £7,627,910 in Exchequer bills – another debt instrument. The dominion government invested in itself through the purchase of debt instruments, and it also invested just over £680,000 in India bonds, or the public debt of India. The account recorded approximately £152,000 from "interest accrued on investment."[69] The previous debt had made it necessary, since it paid a rate of 7 percent interest on its public debt, 5 percent to Ontario, and "a like rate on any balance due to the Fiscal agents in London." Rose's solution to high interest rates included asking Baring and Glyn to put up £250,000 for credit and the Bank of Montreal to put up £500,000 credit. All these complicated actions had the goal of reducing the high interest public debt of 7 percent.[70] The internal circulation of debt to reduce interest rates created the illusion that the Canadian government could pay off previous loans.

Rupert's Land

The intercolonial railway, however, could not go anywhere until the Canadian government acquired the title of the land. North and west of the Province of Canada lay the vast space the British called Rupert's Land. Similar to the way the management of finances over the complicated railway loan underscores a transfer of imperial power from Britain to Canada, the purchase of Rupert's Land also reflects such a shift in imperial power. On May 2, 1670, King Charles II granted the Hudson's Bay Company (HBC) a royal charter. With one stroke of the pen, he awarded the company a trading monopoly that applied to the entire Hudson Bay drainage system. Consisting of almost 4 million square kilometres and encompassing the territory of a multiplicity of Indigenous nations, it was known as Rupert's Land, named after the king's cousin Prince Rupert, who was also the first governor of the HBC.[71]

During the next two hundred years, the HBC created a fur-trade empire of its own. Its account books could rival those of a colonial government, as it managed its affairs in several factories, or outposts, which maintained detailed records such as "Indian debt books." This account keeping documented items that Indigenous people bought from the HBC, even such minor commodities as a "1 lbs gun powder" or a "plain blanket."[72] Sometimes individuals, such as Innu traders, could arbitrage furs to receive higher payments between posts, and in the early days these trades could occur with a type of beaver pelt currency called "made beaver."[73]

In 1869–70, however, the HBC sold Rupert's Land to the fledging Dominion of Canada for the bargain price of £300,000. With its eye on westward expansion, the dominion saw the HBC charter rights, in which the company held land in free and common socage tenure, as an impediment.[74] As mentioned earlier, land tenure holdings such as mortmain and free and common socage did not fit well with liberal private property regimes that needed to liquidate land in markets to produce and increase its value. When Canada purchased Rupert's Land in 1870, that dead capital immediately became available as leverage for loans, with the risk of the loans transferred to the Canadian public. This meant that the British government, and the British public, was not responsible for the loans. At least, that was the goal, but Canada needed an imperial loan guarantee to fund the transfer, which did place some of the risk onto the British public.

Interestingly, neither the dominion purchase of Rupert's Land nor its consequent expansion over Indigenous territories were inevitable. In the early 1860s, the HBC made several overtures to the imperial government, offering its aid in securing the west for Britain. It proposed that it would pay for settler colonial expansion. It would become a quasi-colonization company, such as those favoured in the 1820s, and would transport settlers and install telecommunications infrastructure while maintaining its rights to the land. It also floated the idea of granting land to a private company, which would then develop it. However, London rejected both scenarios, knowing that the HBC would need a great deal of financial support if it were to achieve its expansionary goals. Because the HBC was a private company, not a government, it did not hold Crown title to the land, which it held in free and common socage. Thus, technically, it could not raise a loan on the potential future value of Indigenous territories. Nor did it have the rights of preemption, which the British Crown had granted to itself in the Royal Proclamation of 1763. This inability to raise loans from land hints at why colonization companies fell out of favour. Eventually, however, the HBC directors, and most of the shareholders, began to see that private companies did not have the means to put colonization in place, and they sold the unceded and unsurrendered Indigenous lands to Canada, with several qualifications.[75]

Ultimately, the HBC could not compete with other interests that were deeply invested in settler colonialism. Those old hands at financing colonization, Thomas Baring, George Carr Glyn, and other interested parties, formed a company whose purpose was to help the spread of the British Empire over Indigenous homelands by establishing a telegraph system and a method of transporting passengers and goods to the Pacific coast. In 1862, they wrote to Henry Pelham-Clinton, the Duke of New-castle and colonial secretary, asking for aid:

> Parliament is naturally averse to the increase of the national burdens, and it may be that a money grant might be out of the question: but, without adding to the expenditure of the country, there are large resources available in the shape of Territory. Would, therefore, the Government, if approving such an attempt, be ready to grant any sound and sufficient Company a considerable tract of land?[76]

A group organized by certain influential capitalists in London that styled itself as the Atlantic and Pacific Transit and Telegraph Company (APTTC) expressed its hope to establish a telegraph and mail service from Lake Superior to New Westminster in British Columbia. In the 1860s, the railway was not yet the exclusive choice for transportation, which explains why the company name referred to transit rather than to a railway as the mode for moving white settlers inland.[77] Writing on behalf of the HBC, HBC governor H.H. Berens replied that "the Directors of the Hudson's Bay Company will have no objection to make such free grant of land to any Association."[78] This serious discussion about the future of HBC rights over Rupert's Land reveals the enormous discrepancy between westward expansion and "progress" talk, and the actual funds to achieve it. The uncertainty about the future of colonization shows that the possibility of putting Rupert's Land under the management of a private company, not a colonial government, had some weight to it. Given the financial powerhouses behind the APTTC and even the HBC, who also sought British-protected rights to the development and settling of Rupert's Land, how the dominion came to purchase it for the measly sum of £300,000 raises many questions.

In 1863, the HBC went through a radical transformation, in which its major proprietors sold their shares to the International Financial Association (IFA). Many IFA members were closely associated with both the Glyn and Barings Banks. The HBC sold so many shares to the IFA that many relinquished their shareholder rights.[79] This restructuring was so drastic that it prompted the law officers of the Crown to investigate whether the HBC charter actually allowed for it. Ultimately, they found that the company had not transgressed its charter limits. The HBC shareholders sold to the IFA "with the object of enlarging the operations of the Company," and so the HBC began to focus its efforts on expansion into the west via settlement, telecommunication, and transportation.[80]

At this point, due to this mandate, the HBC had become a direct competitor of the APTTC. Under Governor Berens, it had been happy to grant land to the APTTC for the good of the empire, but that changed after the restructuring and when Edmund Head was elected governor in July 1863. The company began to negotiate itself into the westward path of colonialism. Writing to the Colonial Office in November 11, 1863, Head proposed that the HBC should build the telegraph line itself: "the Hudson's Bay Company should have the sole right to erect and should bind themselves to complete within five years an Electric Telegraph to connect British Columbia and Canada." The line would "be maintained by the Company, who would, of course, engage to convey the messages of the Imperial and Colonial Governments at a fixed and moderate rate."[81] Baulking at the idea of the HBC as the centre of westward colonization, the Colonial Office replied with a resounding "no" and stated bluntly that "any appropriation of Imperial funds by vote of Parliament to the compensation of the Company must be considered as out of the question."[82] The problem of taxation was the crux of the refusal. Responding to Head's letter in 1864, the Colonial Office explained that "in an unsettled colony there is no effectual mode of taxation for purposes of government and improvement, and the whole progress of the Colony depends on the liberal and prudent disposal of its land. These considerations afford decisive reasons against leaving that land in the possession of a corporation."[83] Westward expansion needed a colonial government that could tax settlers (a key to creditworthiness) and that, far from holding on to land for the sake of speculation, would try to sell it to settlers as quickly as possible. The Colonial Office pointed to the lamentable example of Prince Edward Island, where private landownership without the Crown right of preemption impeded colonization: on "Prince Edward Island the right of property was more recently disjoined from that of Government, but the result has not been such as to invite imitation."[84]

To make matters worse for the HBC, the Province of Canada began to petition London for possession of the Lake of the Woods region, which was in Rupert's Land. It was Anishinaabe territory and had never been ceded, but Canada based its claim on the 1763 Treaty of Paris, which had concluded the Seven Years' War.[85] Such colonial fictions of possession wrote and rewrote themselves over the territories of Indigenous nations. Neither the HBC charter, the French possession of the land, nor Canada's claim involved the surrendering of lands, sovereignty, or self-determination by Indigenous nations. Canada's claim to the Lake of the Woods area rested on the right-of-conquest logic that had been applied to Indigenous sovereignty on Epekwitk, which also involved the British defeat of France after the Seven Years' War. Layers of colonial stories to legitimize European claims to Indigenous territories created a palimpsest of land rights that do not necessarily fit into a dispossession narrative. Technically, the Anishinaabe were not dispossessed of their homelands as a result of the dispute between the HBC and Canada, but it became the foundation on which the province of Ontario would eventually claim jurisdiction over their land. The Anishinaabe would experience colonial violence well past the nineteenth century, especially after the Second World War, when an economic boom planted a hydroelectric dam on Lake of the Woods, which had a strongly negative impact on their lives and those of other-than-human beings.[86]

In 1864, Governor Edmund Head seemed to see the writing on the wall – that it would be difficult for the HBC to engage in westward colonization. Making the best of a bad situation, the company offered to sell it, initially approaching the imperial government. Posing the rhetorical question, "What are we to obtain for this cession of our rights in so large a Territory?" the HBC outlined what it expected to get. It asked for a monetary payment, which factored in a recent discovery of gold, but this was not its main objective: for every fifty thousand acres that it sold, it would be entitled to five thousand acres of "wild land" of its choice.[87] The Colonial Office rejected this scheme.

In the fall of 1864, delegates from the colonial governments attended a conference in Quebec City to hammer out the terms of Confederation, one of which was that Rupert's Land would eventually join the union. The HBC scrambled to obtain an advantage from this development. Now, it suggested that, as "the colonization of the country proceeded rapidly under the new government," it "would receive blocks of land of moderate size in the vicinity of the new settlements, which would possess an actual value in the market."[88] Only colonization could raise the market value of the land, as the HBC shareholders fully understood, so they manoeuvred to benefit from it. To be clear, the HBC was "strongly adverse to any arrangement for the cession of the Company's territorial rights which did not secure the payment as compensation of a sum of hard money," but the cession of the rights also involved payment of another kind: the future value of the land after colonization.[89]

Only a consolidated government that could take on public debt could pay for colonization in such a direct and relentless way as to raise the value of land. However paradoxically, the HBC appeared to have realized that the best way of profiting from Rupert's Land was to give it up: the dominion government would take over its administration, and it, or rather the tax-paying public, would shoulder the financial risks associated with development and settlement. For its part, the HBC would possess blocks of land near any new settlements, which would only increase in value as colonization progressed.

First, though, Rupert's Land had to be surrendered to London and then accepted into the dominion. Passed in 1868, the Rupert's Land Act set the terms for this process.[90] Once the surrender occurred, an Order-in-Council of 1870 directed Ottawa to pay the HBC £300,000 "into the Bank of England to the credit of the Company within six calendar months after acceptance of the surrender aforesaid, with interest on the said sum at the rate of 5 per cent. per annum, computed from the date of such acceptance until the time of such payment."[91] The Order-in-Council admitted both Rupert's Land and the North-Western Territory, a very large area to its northwest, into Canada. The Métis Nation, however, had not been consulted or even considered in the handover and had no desire simply to be absorbed into the new dominion. The resulting Red River Resistance of 1869–70 founded a provisional government to negotiate terms of entry into Confederation. Eventually, Ottawa crushed the resistance by sending in troops, but the uprising created "complications" for the dominion because it delayed Parliament from passing legislation to secure an imperial loan guarantee.[92] Not everyone in Parliament agreed to the acquisition of Rupert's Land, though when the House was asked to contemplate whether it were "inexpedient to acquire a Territory likely to involve this Dominion in a heavy expense without any prospect of adequate remuneration," only 15 of the 136 MPs who expressed an opinion agreed that it was.[93]

As the HBC negotiated with London to give up its charter rights, the newly formed dominion government needed to pay for the purchase of Rupert's Land, so it donned the old hat of asking for an imperial loan guarantee. In London, the House passed the Rupert's Land Loan Bill, stating that "in this Bill the provisions with regard to the appropriation were sufficient" and offering a guarantee of £300,000.[94] However, like the Intercolonial Railway loan, the Rupert's Land loan was not so easily given. Some British MPs expressed concern about the spending of loan monies and wanted to include "words which secured us against any arrangement which could impose a burden upon the tax-payers of this country." Even critics deemed the loan guarantee necessary, but some asked a perfectly reasonable question: If "the territory ceded to Canada were really valuable, as it was represented to be, why should any charge be thrown upon us, and why should not the Canadian Government undertake the liability which the arrangement involved?"[95] In other words, why could Canada not raise its own loan? In fact, Canada's credit was stretched thin. Perhaps it could have secured a loan without the guarantee from London, but whether it could have done so at such a low interest rate was questionable.

Aside from the £300,000 payout, the HBC received payment in land. This would be in the Fertile Belt, an area of choice land running from Red River to the Rocky Mountains. Under the terms of the agreement, "The

Hudson's Bay Company may, for fifty years after the surrender claim in any Township or District within the Fertile Belt in which land is set out for settlement, select grants of land not exceeding one-twentieth part of the land so set out."[96] The payment in land near potential settlement sites explains why the cash payment was so tiny. Frank Tough states that this "great property" benefited the HBC more than the £300,000.[97]

London's instructive experience with the Intercolonial Railway, in which the Canadian finance minister had redirected funds to pay high-interest debts, prompted suggestions in the House that "some stringent provisions" be attached to the Rupert's Land loan guarantee to ensure "that the money should not be spent for other purposes – that it should not stick to the fingers of those who had to handle it."[98] Despite some pushback during the readings of the Rupert's Land Loan Bill, An Act for Authorizing a Guarantee of a Loan to be Raised by Canada for a payment in respect of the Transfer of Rupert's Land was passed on August 11, 1869.[99] Also known as the Canada (Rupert's Land) Loan Act, it authorized the British Treasury to guarantee the interest not exceeding 4 percent on an amount not exceeding £300,000. The act made the loan chargeable to the consolidated revenue fund of Canada, with a sinking fund of 1 percent per year of the whole loan amount. Furthermore, if the consolidated fund of Britain had to cover any costs, these would be charged to the consolidated revenue fund of Canada at 5 percent interest per year. Investment of money from the sinking fund came with the caveat that both the Government of Canada and the British Treasury had to agree on the type of securities for investment, with "the resulting income" to be "invested and applied as part of such sinking fund."[100] The purchase of Rupert's Land relied on a public debt in two ways: a loan guarantee enabled Ottawa to raise the necessary sum, and the HBC would benefit from the development of white settlements, as the Canadian public debt paid for the increase in the market value of Indigenous land, though only in the future.

Conclusion

In August 1869, during the second reading of the Rupert's Land Loan Bill, a British MP commented that the loan guarantee "was not to be a beginning, but an end." He justified the use of the imperial loan guarantee, now firmly out of favour, because it would "put an end to the old system once and for all." The imperial Government made arrangements with Canada that bound them to assist the fledgling settler state with imperial credit in order to colonize. The MP stated that the British North American colonies had been "entangled in a vicious system of dependence" and that Britain "wished to engender in them a spirit of independence in financial matters."[101] Essentially, the end of the "old system" of British imperialism marked the advent of the new Canadian version, grounded in the use of a public debt, a practice that had become deeply entrenched by the time of Confederation.

Rupert's Land, however, was not the end of the imperial loan guarantee saga. In 1871, delegates from Canada, the United States, and Britain met to negotiate the Treaty of Washington, which dealt with several issues, including fisheries. Although Canada was now an independent country, it took a backseat during the deliberations. The treaty granted the United States access to Canadian inshore fisheries, a measure that was not popular in Canada. During the 1872 parliamentary session, Prime Minister John A. Macdonald, who had been a treaty delegate, was criticized for the fishery concessions.[102] In this context, hoping to lure Canada into accepting the treaty, London offered Ottawa an imperial loan guarantee for £2,500,000, which would pay "for certain improvements in Canada," primarily for the construction of the Canadian Pacific Railway.[103] Debating the loan bill in London's House of Commons, MPs contemplated the wisdom of granting the guarantee, given that "the credit of this country [was] involved to so great an extent." Tory MP Benjamin Disraeli wondered how the loan would be affected if the treaty did not become law. Would the British government still be on the hook to provide it?[104]

The loan bill fared well once it reached the House of Lords. On its second reading in July 1873, Liberal politician John Wodehouse argued that an "imperial guarantee would enable Canada to effect a loan at lower interest than would otherwise be necessary, and her finances were in a condition which caused no misgiving as to her ability to bear the expense. It was not unreasonable, therefore, that we should to a certain extent help her with our own credit."[105] The loan was duly approved under the Canada (Public Works) Loan Act of 1873.[106] Now that the federal government had its loan guarantee, it could proceed with the construction of the Canadian Pacific Railway, which was a condition for British Columbia's entry into Confederation. The statute also made null the 1870 Canada Defences Loan Act, under which no money had been raised. The act ultimately provided a guarantee of up to £2,500,000 on the condition that Ottawa passed an act to raise £8,000,000.[107] The three imperial loan guarantees – the Intercolonial Railway loan of £3,000,000, the Rupert's Land loan of £300,000, and the Canada (Public Works) Loan Act for £2,500,000 – paid for Canadian imperial expansion at a low interest rate. The fact that Canada needed them also reveals its seemingly never-ending entanglement with British credit to lower the interest rate on loans.

Loans for colonization fused the emerging Canadian economy to a model of structural indebtedness. The three loan guarantee acts had some method of repayment of the principal, such as a sinking fund, and the repayment was chargeable to "the consolidated revenue fund of Canada," which did not burden Britain's own funds with principal and interest payments.[108] However, all these borrowed funds to build white settler Canada on the territories of Indigenous nations had an end date. For the three main loans, the Intercolonial, Rupert's Land, and the 1873 loan from the Canada (Public Works) Loan Act, that reckoning arrived in 1903, when they matured. The sinking fund for each loan had funds – in some cases 1 percent was charged to the sinking fund – but sinking funds did not have liquidity. Shifting funds in and out of accounts was "required of the Sinking Funds held for the several loans." For example, one sinking fund held "investments in the Loans of 1875, 1876, 1878/9," showing that the government used the sinking fund itself for investments. Moving funds between accounts was a plan for the "general conversion scheme on the market" to create some liquidity in held assets in order to pay some liabilities with cash.[109]

The repayment schedule was complicated, and though the Department of Finance could claim that the dominion had available payments in sinking funds accounts, those funds were not all cash but included other Canadian securities from other loans. The other method for cash was to use Treasury bills, essentially a delayed payment and another debt instrument. The Bank of Montreal would take a Treasury bills deposit of some £1,250,000 and could "carry another million of Bills for six months or a year." When the Glyn and Barings Banks acted as the "financial agents of the Government of Canada, there was always an understanding that two million sterling could be provided for by temporary overdrafts, or by Treasury Bills." Another source of cash came from the future sales of land made by the Canadian Pacific Railway to redeem its loan of $15,000,000, though the probable "income from this source" was "uncertain."[110] Ultimately, asking a bondholder who held mature bonds to "come into a renewal scheme" with the offer of some "bonus" might allow for the restructuring of debt repayment as renewals.[111] As the years wore on, these debt repayments with debt schemes became increasingly complicated.

The transfer of imperial sovereignty to the dominion bound together railways, telegraphs, and the white settlement of the west.[112] After the Canadas united in 1841 to provide debt relief for Upper Canada, the public debt had exploded exponentially, needing more and more capital to pay interest and principal amounts that Confederation, the railway, and the assimilation of Rupert's Land and the North-Western Territory made possible. The demand for capital involved a struggle between Ottawa and London regarding financial jurisdiction that ended when London let go of Canadian finances and the dominion assumed more control over its economy. In the management of colonial economies, once the purview of Britain, Canada sought control and used the imperial loan monies as it saw fit, despite strong objections from Britain and the undercurrent of illegality. The Intercolonial Railway loan highlights the slow transfer of power from Britain to Canada, a drawn-out process of assuming imperial control over Indigenous territories that ended with the 1982 repatriation of the constitution. What Canada's public debt history tells us, then, is not how Canada became a nation-state, but how it became an imperial power, a settler state turned toward the unyielding destruction of Indigenous nations.

This policy had a long history and did not begin with Confederation. The Ontario Free Grant and Homestead Act of 1868 was intended to attract British settlers and to encourage them to appropriate Indigenous lands. In this endeavour, Canada had to compete with the United States, which had passed its own Homestead Act in 1862. Two years after it had acquired Rupert's Land and the North-Western Territory, Ottawa carved up the west by passing the Dominion Lands Act, whose purpose was to encourage the settlement of the prairies. It relegated Indigenous nations to reserves and made it easy for European settlers to homestead by lowering the age at which people could apply for land grants, cutting the cost of application, and even allowing some women to apply.[113] As for the Métis, Ottawa implemented scrip, a system of promissory notes that could be used to purchase a homestead but that, along with the creation of Manitoba in 1870, simply facilitated the land grab.[114] In 1873, Ottawa tightened the net by passing an act to establish the North-West Mounted Police, which fundamentally altered its relationship with Indigenous nations. Accompanied by notions of the "last best west" and claims about human progress, all these statutes were instruments of dispossession.[115] In particular, the Dominion Lands Act of 1872 and the creation of the North-West Mounted Police in 1873 make clear the violent tactics used to open up the west.[116]

Drawing on Achille Mbembe's concept of necropolitics, Sandrina de Finney notes that in the Canadian colonial state, "rurality is quintessentially necropolitical" – a "technology of colonial nation building that has eliminated hundreds of thousands of Indigenous bodies from their homelands to accommodate white occupation."[117] During a House debate of 1882, a decade after the passage of the Dominion Lands Act, John A. Macdonald addressed the problem of how to control the Indigenous nations of the west. Hunger was a cheap and effective weapon: he told the House that "Indians so long as they are fed will not work" and stated that "refusing food until the Indians are on the verge of starvation" would "reduce the expense." He added that though the buffalo had virtually disappeared, "some few cases came over this year, and although their arrival relieved the Indians, I was rather sorry, looking to the future ... as the Blackfoot, Bloods and Piegans who had settled on reserves at once returned to their nomadic habits." He regretted the "frequent disappointments in the way of civilizing them."[118] Macdonald's comment ties in to all the other methods by which the Canadian government engaged in genocide, such as the residential school system in which Indigenous children were incarcerated and indoctrinated in British modes of existence, to "civilize" them. Finally, with the 1876

Indian Act, the federal government assumed control over Indigenous peoples.[119] Nothing short of genocide, then, ushered in a new era of ruthless expansion and the relentless assault on Indigenous lives, communities, knowledges, languages, arts, sciences, technologies, lands, waters, *ad infinitum,* in an attempt to create a market-based universal Canadian nation *a mari usque ad mare.*

Conclusion: Debt and Decolonization

> Well, some worlds are built on a fault line of pain, held up by nightmares. Don't lament when those worlds fall. Rage that they were built doomed in the first place.
>
> – N.K. Jemisin, *The Stone Sky*

"I am a historian," Rebecca Hall writes, "and I am haunted."[1] In the colonial archives, the extreme limits of human pain and suffering flash across old and tattered documents in the most mundane ways.[2] Government account books, snippets of colonization schemes in private diaries, the force behind imperial and colonial legislation, the inhumane assumptions in House of Commons debates, and a million other examples of colonial archival evidence recorded Black, Indigenous, and "colonized" trauma in a profoundly dull and disarming way: a boring dystopia. All the bells and whistles of a fictionalized apocalypse produced for leisurely consumption in settler states do nothing but reiterate what has already been done, a million times over, to the very real lives of those who now haunt us, for those who have felt injustices that should never have been imagined in the first place.[3] Apocalypses have already happened to so many, and here I refer only to their human victims. Historians ask of their subject living through unprecedented times, "I wonder if you knew?" We should ask instead, "I wonder how we know?" Dystopias, the colonial archive tells us, could be truly boring.[4]

According to Laura Ishiguro, the "British investment in an imagined settler future" manifested in a multifaceted way and included culture, politics, and economy: a historical imagining of the future that persists in our present.[5] How can we dream of a future together as our miracle planet is slowly degraded into an environment that is unfit for so much life? Our blue skies are becoming drenched in orange and red. One might think that the job of a historian is not to indulge in fantasies about future making, but every chapter in this book is about the future – the debt-purchased future of a settler state.[6] Edward Gibbon Wakefield and the colonial reformers had an image of the desirable future – one in which Indigenous land could have significant market value that would perpetually increase – and they put structures in place to attain it. The British North America government officials who took on a public debt imagined that they could pay it back at some point in the future because by then British settlers would have taken over and developed Indigenous lands. We now live in the future that those men worked so hard to achieve. But, none of this is news, especially not to those who inhale the smoke from the massively destructive forest fires that occur every summer, those who experience heat domes, those who cannot drink the poisoned water.[7] We live in the nuclear fallout of Wakefield's dreams; we and our children, and their children, are quite literally paying for those debts, the lucky ones with their taxes and the unlucky ones with their lives.

Every hegemonic order, however, has cracks. Indigenous peoples are rebuilding their communities and revitalizing their knowledge systems, our culture is sustained with critical work from Black scholars and artistic expressions of Black joy, disability rights activists are creating an inclusive space for everyone, and the pandemic has unexpectedly birthed an anti-work movement where folks simply and steadfastly refuse to participate in the exploitation of their labour.[8]

One critical aspect of decolonization in Canada centres on a movement named Land Back, or land rematriation.[9] The gambling off the future value of Indigenous lands on the money markets complicates the issue. Land rematriation is not about "allowing" Indigenous peoples to live on the land. It prevents federal and provincial governments from interfering with Indigenous sovereignty.[10] Land rematriation movements recognize Canada's historical context to understand the structural changes needed to rematriate lands outside of federal and provincial colonial sovereignty.

Indigenous peoples need their land to sustain their communities. Mishuana Goeman shows that land means more than just property and revenue production: "Experiences of land become expressions of self, and, through the shared experience of naming, connections to others are formed."[11] Thomas King writes that "land contains the languages, the stories, and the histories of a people. It provides water, air, shelter, and food. Land participates in the ceremonies and the songs. Land is home."[12] Space assigns meaning to people, as the landscape imprints a sense of self and language blooms through descriptions of and relationships with the environment. When land is understood as more than property, its rematriation has the capacity to heal and to revitalize. Settler anxieties about a defaced Canada in which spaces of Indigenous self-governments cannot be included in a map of the country simply do not reflect historical or contemporary circumstances. As Chelsea Vowel quips about a Canada "marked" with Indigenous sovereign governments, "What is so terrifying about that exactly?"[13]

The terrifying part would be that the Canadian government would no longer possess Crown rights of preemption over all the land. Without the exclusive rights to land, development projects such as the canals that supported Canada's economy through capital investment via the public debt would have no state guarantee. But, as a Canadian, I need to ask myself, who is benefiting from this development? Why should we hold on so tightly to such a system that produces so much harm? Harm to people made marginal by such a system, yes, but harm to ourselves as well. Harm to the air that we breathe and harm to the water that we drink. Harm that we pay for. It is not reasonable to expect a system designed to produce a specific outcome (extraction/destruction for profits) to then produce another outcome (care/sustainability for living beings). Land Back is just one method of many that works to find a path out of this old colonial system. Currently, privately owned land can change its legal status in a few ways, such as being converted to a trust or being given as an ecological gift.[14] A trust has legal requirements of incorporation as a non-profit, which would, in part, place restrictions on any attempts to alienate the land to global markets and to remake it into real estate. However, it would not protect the land in perpetuity. Legally, the Crown still holds the highest title to land and can appropriate it in a number of circumstances.

On Epekwitk, the Mi'kmaq have attempted to establish a Mi'kmaw legal presence over Crown lands. In 2017, the island government sold about 130 hectares of Crown land, known as the Mill River properties, to Don McDougall, a business owner. Both the Lennox Island and Abegweit First Nations argued that the government had not adequately consulted them regarding the sale. The duty to consult is not the same as the principle of seeking free, prior, and informed consent.[15] For its part, the government claimed that it had sufficiently consulted. A month after the sale, the First Nations applied to the Supreme Court of Prince Edward Island for a judicial review of the matter. Notably, they did not attempt to obtain title to the property: they wanted the government to honour its duty to consult when selling Crown land. During the judicial review hearing of January 2018, McDougall testified that the negotiations between the government and the Mi'kmaq were "none of his business."[16] Speaking to a CBC journalist, David Rosenberg, the lawyer for the two First Nations, raised some questions regarding Aboriginal title (as it is known in Canadian law) that reflected many settler anxieties:

> What happens when a First Nation gets a declaration of Aboriginal title to land that's privately held, or what would happen, for example, to fee simple title holders who just own their own piece of property in Prince Edward Island or elsewhere in Canada? What happens to their rights when a First Nation comes along and gets that declaration of title from the courts to that land? ... That's an unresolved question.[17]

The instability of land title unsecured with Canadian private property rights challenges settler notions of ownership. At the same time, however, Land Back, like the Mill River case, targets Crown lands, not private property. Land rematriation is not about depriving private individuals of their fee simple title.

In the end, the Supreme Court of Prince Edward Island decided that the government had met its duty to consult in connection with Mill River, and the provincial Court of Appeal subsequently upheld that decision. Shortly afterward, Chief Darlene Bernard of Lennox Island and Chief Roderick Gould Jr. of the Abegweit First Nation took the case to the Supreme Court of Canada, which dismissed it in April 2020, thus quashing this particular Mi'kmaw attempt to exercise a modicum of land rights.[18]

When I spoke with members of Lennox Island First Nation in 2019, they underlined that they saw no evidence that the government took the duty to consult seriously. Many people had clear ideas about the Mill River decision:

> *Jimmy Reese:* I think in the last few years, we developed a pretty good relationship with the provincial government ... Like, there's a bunch of different properties in the last ten, fifteen years that have been turned back ... They recognize that they do owe us something.
>
> *Saul Jacobs:* Any time they do business with Crown land, they're supposed to consult ... And we saw what happened at Mill River.
>
> *Anne Warren:* I was just about to say Mill River, yeah.
>
> *Saul Jacobs:* And it was just, like, dismissed; they had no grounds. *(agreement around the room)*
>
> *Jimmy Reese:* They did consult, but it just wasn't good enough consultation ... But the judge said they did consult. No one has a definition on what the proper consultation is *(interrupted)*.
>
> *Saul Jacobs:* But they consulted, they informed them [the First Nations] that this was going to be done, and they got a letter back that said, "No, we want to do more talks about it," but they just went ahead and did it anyway. So is that called consulting? *(laughter around the room)*
>
> *Anne Warren:* That's informing.
>
> *Saul Jacobs:* That's informing, saying that we're going to do this ... That's not consultation.

> MARY GARNER: Then they can check it off in their little boxes, that First Nations were *(interrupted by laughter)*.
>
> TERESA WILLIAMSON: Yeah, check.[19]

Lennox Island members identified the Mill River "consultation" process as unacceptable, reflecting Audra Simpson's formulation of the "ruse of consent." Although almost two hundred years separate the sale of the Mill River property from Edward Gibbon Wakefield's marriage to Ellen Turner, both hinged on the pretense of consent made possible by a relationship of unequal power and are not so very different.

So, what do I think *The Debt of a Nation* can tell us about the future? This book tells us how Indigenous territories were sold and attached to the global market economy to aid Canadian capital exploitation in violation of a multiplicity of treaty laws. It stresses that the public debt was a relatively recent phenomenon. Neither natural nor neutral, it was a set of practices and policies whose purpose was to capture the territories of Indigenous nations, to generate market value for a select few, and to produce a white settler state. Technically, Crown lands could be returned to Indigenous nations, but in reality they have been sold to the future (or will be) and tied firmly to global debt markets. Instead of the current practice of Canadian credit derived from speculation on the future value of Indigenous land, another way to funnel capital back into our local economies might facilitate decolonization. For example, we could think about methods that can decouple Indigenous lands and waters from global debt markets. If public credit on the municipal, provincial, and national levels exists to aid large corporations in making profits, then we can think together, in our local communities, about questions that address the necessity of public credit. Do you and I really need a credit card to help corporations achieve their profit margins? A more direct and immediate method to facilitate this decoupling of lands from debt is to seek revenue from other sources. Other ways to generate value must be possible to decolonize and to stop leeching profits through violence, such as the brutality that Canada continues to enact on the Wet'suwet'en Nation and many other Indigenous nations. Activists who call for the abolition of the police note that the police do not work for the public, just as the public debt does not work in our benefit. Both, however, uphold "corporate sovereignty."[20] The public debt captures Indigenous territories as assets and directs profits squeezed from our dying ecosystems to future capital. To unmake this relationship between Canadian debt and Indigenous land is to let go of the relational binary of owner and property. In their discussion of visiting, Eve Tuck and her colleagues help us think about striving for a world beyond property:

> Visiting implies being in a relation that is by design impermanent; it is a passing-through of space and time. As an Indigenous feminist practice, visiting centers relationality and an ethic of care. Being a visitor is showing care and being responsible for our impact and presence. Visiting does not assume entitlement to space, or assert control, or ownership over land.[21]

Unpicking seams is tedious work: it demands that we centre ourselves in the mundane and embrace monotony. It needs us to work together at our differing capacities to undo the generational harm of colonialism, stitch by stitch. We can build futures on the foundations of respect and responsibility because we are all "the guest of our children and their children."[22] Like visiting and caring for an ailing loved one, the work of decolonization can be embraced as "a welcome responsibility."[23] How can we unpick the seams that bind Indigenous territories to the global market economy or that tie global anti-Blackness to economic exploitation? What would it mean to have no public debt? In 2008, Greece experienced a debt crisis of such magnitude that *Forbes* magazine wondered whether it were about to repudiate its debt. Unsurprisingly, the article remarked that "walking away from debts may be attractive to ethically-challenged debtors."[24] This sentiment echoes John Stuart Mill's attack on Washington for its attempt to change the terms of its loan contracts, as a heavy blow against morality and civilization. Both ignore the historical reality of the origin of such public debts. Was raising capital from stolen land and then violently maintaining control over that land (while decimating the environment in the process) not unethical? Does the debt belong to the public or to the people who made intergenerational profits from this particular system of colonialism? How might local economies that do not rely on global infrastructures survive, and how can we work toward an economics centred on degrowth?[25] Thus, we can start by consciously supporting local economies. In our local communities across Turtle Island, and in Wabanaki territory where I live now, what might we need to live so that we can dispense with the debt? How do we ensure that we do not saddle future generations with an unpayable debt? These are questions that I leave with the reader.

Notes

Prologue

1 *An Act to Declare Void an Alleged Marriage Between Ellen Turner, an Infant, and Edward Gibbon Wakefield,* June 14, 1827, Parliamentary Archives, HL/PO/PB/1/1827/7& 8G4n172.

2 For a fuller version of this harrowing story, see *The Trial of Edward Gibbon Wakefield,* 301.

3 *The Trial of Edward Gibbon Wakefield,* xii.

4 *The Trial of Edward Gibbon Wakefield,* 160.

5 *The Trial of Edward Gibbon Wakefield,* 164.

6 Piterberg and Veracini, "Wakefield, Marx," 461.

7 *The Trial of Edward Gibbon Wakefield,* 4.

8 *The Trial of Edward Gibbon Wakefield,* 164.

9 *An Act to Declare Void.*

10 *The Trial of Edward Gibbon Wakefield,* 36, 113, 115.

11 *The Trial of Edward Gibbon Wakefield,* 37.

12 *An Act to Declare Void.*

13 *An Act to repeal so much of the several Acts passed in the First and Second Years of the Reign of Philip and Mary, the Eighteenth of Charles the Second, the Ninth of George the First, and the Twelfth of George the Second, as inflicts Capital Punishment on certain Offences therein specified,* 1 Geo. IV, c. 115–17 (also known as Sir James Mackintosh's Act).

14 *The Trial of Edward Gibbon Wakefield,* xiv.

15 William Wakefield, "Petition," Lancaster Lent Assizes 1827, National Archives, HO/17/93/65.

16 For a few examples of the literature, see Kittrell, "Wakefield's Scheme," 87–112; Prichard, "Wakefield Changes His Mind," 251–69; and Pappe, "Wakefield and Marx," 88–97. For debates about emigration beyond Wakefield, see Grant, *Representations of British Emigration*.

17 Publishing *A Letter from Sydney* under a pseudonym, Wakefield posed as a wealthy landowner who had emigrated to Australia, only to find that his new property barely had market value, a problem that plagued many settlers. In *A Letter from Sydney,* he laid out a scheme to remedy it. See Ballantyne, "Remaking the Empire from Newgate."

18 Piterberg and Veracini, "Wakefield, Marx," 461. For more on Priscilla Wakefield, see Ballantyne, "The Theory and Practice," 92–93; Curtis, "Colonization, Education," 27–47; Graham, "Juvenile Travellers"; and Bridget Hill, "Priscilla Wakefield as an Author."

19 Audra Simpson, "The Ruse of Consent," 28.

20 Many scholarly works look at Wakefield and colonialism. For some in-depth studies, see Black, *Economic Thought;* Ghosh, "The Colonization Controversy"; Winch, *Classical Political Economy;* Manning, "E.G. Wakefield and the Beauharnois Canal"; de Silva, "The Third Earl Grey"; Pike, "Introduction of the Real Property"; Grant, "Edward Gibbon Wakefield."

21 Perelman, *The Invention of Capitalism,* 325.

22 Quoted in Perelman, *The Invention of Capitalism,* 332–33.

23 A massive thank you to the UBC Press Reader 3 for capturing the essence of this argument and distilling it into the clear terms of "conquest" and "mortgage."

24 Nichols, *Theft Is Property!,* 8.

25 The 2007–08 financial crisis prompted several popular studies that investigated debt and its genealogical roots in human societies. They generally see debt as something that is present in most cultures and do not discuss the public debt that was made possible with the formalization of the London Stock Exchange in 1801. For two examples of this approach, see Atwood, *Payback;* and Graeber, *Debt.*

Introduction

1 Karuka, *Empire's Tracks,* 159.

2 Mill, "The New Colony" (2), 737.

3 Miller et al., *Discovering Indigenous Lands,* 11–12.

4 Broadly, instead of the word "development," in the nineteenth century the term "improvement" was commonly used to signify a move toward progress and modernity. See Samson, *The Spirit of Industry.*

5 For a nuanced discussion of the differing meanings of sovereignty in Indigenous studies, see Kauanui, *Paradoxes of Hawaiian Sovereignty,* 25–30.

6 Ishiguro, "Histories of Settler Colonialism," 5–6. See also Bannister, "Settler Colonialism."

7 Bear Nicholas, "Settler Imperialism."

8 Stark, "Criminal Empire." See also Adam J. Barker, "The Contemporary Reality of Canadian Imperialism," 325. For more discussion on law and imperialism in the Canadian settler state, see Rück, *The Laws and the Land.*

9 Pasternak, *Grounded Authority.*

10 Seeley, *The Expansion of England,* 8. For select works on the "new" imperial history, see Bayly, *Imperial Meridian*; Darwin, *The Empire Project*; McClintock, *Imperial Leather*; Brantlinger, *Fictions of State*; Catherine Hall, *Civilising Subjects*; and Levine, *Prostitution, Race and Politics.*

11 Reynolds, *Canada and Colonialism,* 6.

12 Rachel Bryant, "Moses Perley's Legacy of Dishonorable Relations," paper presented at Atlantic Canada Studies Centre Conference, Fredericton, 2022.

13 See Audra Simpson's *Mohawk Interruptus* for ideas on the "politics of refusal" in settler states.

14 Brownlie and Kelm, "Desperately Seeking Absolution," 543–56.

15 Justice and Carleton, "Truth before Reconciliation." For an overview of settler colonial studies and how it intersects with studies of imperialism, see Veracini "Introducing"; and Veracini, *Settler Colonial Present.*

16 Tuck and Yang, "Decolonization Is Not a Metaphor," 1–40.

17 Marx, *Capital,* 1:919. For example, see Nerbas, *Dominion of Capital.*

18 As Stark puts it, "political authority of the United States and Canada paradoxically required the recognition of Indigenous sovereignty." Stark, "Criminal Empire," 2. See also Palmater, "Genocide, Indian Policy," 28.

19 Audra Simpson, *Mohawk Interruptus,* 12.

20 For a discussion on assimilation and eradication, see Palmater, "Genocide, Indian Policy," 31.

21 Damien Short has an excellent discussion about the complexities of reconciliation and the varied meanings of "internal colonialism." Short, "Reconciliation and the Problem of Internal Colonialism."

22 Pasternak and Dafnos, "How Does a Settler State Secure the Circuitry of Capital?"

23 See Hudson, "Imperial Designs"; and Gordon and Webber, "Imperialism and Resistance."

24 Marx, *Capital,* 1:919.

25 Brewer, *The Sinews of Power.*

26 Wilkins, *The History of Foreign Investment,* 54; Lester, "The Effect of Southern State," 420–21.

27 Dawson, *The First Latin American Debt Crisis,* 10–13.

28 According to Jeffrey McNairn, debt reform in 1820s and 1830s Upper Canada became "the colony's most prominent humanitarian cause." The push to abolish debtors' prison reached Upper Canada via Adam Smith's theories on debt. McNairn, "'The Common Sympathies,'" 51, 55. Examining debt in eighteenth-century Halifax, James Muir also concentrates on changes in the law. He shows that the vast

majority of civil cases between settlers that were heard at the Inferior Court of Common Pleas centred on debt collection. He notes that the large number of cases of "account debts" (as opposed to "debts by note") reveal that many Haligonians used credit and debt as an economic transaction. Muir, *Law, Debt,* 44. Markham Lester notes that imprisonment for non-payment of debt actually carried into the twentieth century despite the abolition of debtors' prisons in Britain and elsewhere, such as in Canada. See Lester, *Victorian Insolvency,* 12.

29 Poovey, *Genres of the Credit Economy,* 102.

30 Mulcaire, "Public Credit," 1033.

31 Wynter, "Unsettling the Coloniality," 322.

32 Davis and Huttenback, *Mammon and the Pursuit,* 75.

33 The Land-Grab Universities project shows that this broader practice of building settler societies *with* Indigenous lands occurred at a smaller scale, as, for example, with universities that derived their capital from Indigenous lands. Caitlin P.A. Harvey, "The Wealth of Knowledge."

34 Birla, *Stages of Capital,* 199–231. For an introduction to the vast literature on capital and India, see Metcalf, *Ideologies of the Raj*; Kennedy, *The Magic Mountains*; Bowen, *The Business of Empire*; and Chatterjee, "The Curious Career."

35 Belich, *Replenishing the Earth,* 133.

36 Harrington, "Edward Gibbon Wakefield," 336.

37 See Bell, "John Stuart Mill on Colonies," 37; and Weaver, *The Great Land Rush.*

38 Park, "Money, Mortgages." Park demonstrates how this "liquidity" of land via a credit/debt system could even be used as money for settlers as early as the seventeenth century.

39 I would like to thank Henry Yu for his insightful comments during a very crucial time in the development of this project. In May 2019, when we attended the "Realities of Canadian Democracy" symposium at the L.R. Wilson Institute, he generously discussed with me how the public debt system literally made land "real."

40 Miller et al., *Discovering Indigenous Lands,* 11–12.

41 Lauren Benton and Lisa Ford note that "empire played a central role in the emergence of international law" that managed orderly conduct between "'civilised' sovereignties." Benton and Ford, *Rage for Order,* 188.

42 Thomas Peace notes that the Treaty of Utrecht planted the "seeds of a settler conquest." Peace, *The Slow Rush,* 133.

43 Strachan, *The Clergy Reserves,* 12.

44 Miller et al., *Discovering Indigenous Lands,* 35; Borrows, "Wampum at Niagara." Thomas Peace shows how imperial "transitions" from French to British in the late seventeenth and the eighteenth centuries greatly shaped colonial power consolidation, especially after the Treaty of Utrecht (1713). For further reading on this period, see Peace, *The Slow Rush,* 125–47.

45 To look at usufructuary rights established in the Royal Proclamation as they pertain to Indigenous peoples in Canadian law, see Borrows, "With or Without You," 637*n*32. See also Borrows, "Wampum at Niagara."

46 Anishinaabe legal scholar John Borrows has written extensively on the Royal Proclamation; see, for example, Borrows, "Constitutional law." For a more specific discussion on the significance of pre-emption, see Blaakman, "'Haughty Republicans.'"

47 Mill, "The New Colony" (2), 737.

48 For select works on the institutions of finance capitalism, see Cain and Hopkins, "Gentlemanly Capitalism and British Expansion Overseas I"; Cain and Hopkins, *British Imperialism;* Neal, *The Rise of Financial Capitalism;* Michie, *The London Stock Exchange;* and North and Weingast, "Constitutions and Commitment." And for the rebuttal, see Sussman and Yafeh, "Institutional Reforms"; Bowen, *The Business of Empire;* Attard, "The London Stock Exchange"; Dickson, *The Financial Revolution;* and Vedoveli, "Information Brokers."

49 Walcott, *On Property.*

50 Moreton-Robinson notes, "As an attribute of patriarchal white sovereignty, virtue functions as a usable property to dispossess Indigenous peoples from the ground of moral value." Moreton-Robinson, *The White Possessive,* 176.

51 Unfortunately, the future of space exploration is embedded in our contemporary reality of capitalism and settler colonialism. For example, during a TED interview, Elon Musk outlined a colonization plan for Mars in which people could pay to emigrate by taking out a loan that they would work to pay off, something akin to indentured servitude. "Elon Musk: A Future Worth Getting Excited About | Tesla Texas Gigafactory Interview | TED," YouTube, https://www.youtube.com/watch?v=YRvf00NooN8&ab_channel=TED. See also Tim Levin, "Elon Musk, Once Again the World's Richest Person, Is Selling…" *Business Insider,* February 19, 2021, https://www.businessinsider.com/worlds-richest-person-elon-musk-dedicate-wealth-mars-colony-2021-1.

52 Byrd, *The Transit of Empire,* 221.

53 Tiffany Lethabo King, Jenell Navarro, and Andrea Smith, "Beyond Incommensurability: Toward an Otherwise Stance on Black and Indigenous Rationality," in King, Navarro, and Smith, *Otherwise Worlds,* 13.

54 Robinson, *Black Marxism;* and Wynter, "Unsettling the Coloniality"; for the Canadian context of racial capital, see Pasternak, "Assimilation and Partition," 303; Kelley, "What Did Cedric Robinson Mean." See also Bulushi, "Thinking Racial Capitalism"; Robinson and Gilmore, *Cedric J. Robinson*; McKittrick, ed., *Sylvia Wynter*; and Leroy and Jenkins, eds., *Histories of Racial Capitalism.*

55 Smallwood, "What Slavery Tells Us about Marx," 80–81.

56 For two works on capitalism and settler colonialism, see Adams, *Prison of Grass*; and Ward, ed., *Marxism and Native Americans.* The latter contains several deep critiques of capitalism and particularly Marxism, as dependent on capitalism and its social relations, rendering socialism incompatible with decolonization. See, for example, Frank Black Elk, "Observations on Marxism and Lakota Tradition," in Ward, *Marxism and Native Americans,* 141–42. See also Williams, *Capitalism and Slavery;* Fanon, *The Wretched of the Earth;* and Fanon, *Black Skin, White Masks.*

57 As Sylvia Wynter writes,

> the large-scale accumulation of unpaid land, unpaid labor, and overall wealth expropriated by Western Europe from non-European peoples, which was to lay the basis of its global expansion from the fifteenth century onwards, was carried out within the order of truth and the self-evident order of consciousness, of a creed-specific conception of what it was to be human – which, because a monotheistic conception, could not conceive of an Other to what it experienced as being human, and therefore an Other to its truth, its notion of freedom.

Wynter, "Unsettling the Coloniality," 291.

58 Wolfe, "Land, Labor, and Difference," 882.

59 Wolfe, "Land, Labor, and Difference," 876.

60 Day, *Alien Capital*, 23. This also tells us that the European "civilization" project from thinkers such as Kant and Hume cannot be separated from its exploitation of the peoples whom it racialized as labour and subhuman. To argue for "civilization" is to champion racism. Dupuy, *Haiti*, 24–26. For analysis of gender and race in the system of racialized chattel slavery, see Morgan, *Reckoning with Slavery;* Owens, *Medical Bondage;* and Morgan, *Laboring Women*.

61 Day, *Alien Capital*, 23.

62 See Walcott, *On Property*, 96: "Property sits at the nexus of our freedom," where the legal and cultural codes that developed to create and sustain the transatlantic slave trade attached property rights to whiteness – whiteness that only has meaning in opposition to Blackness. Walcott goes on to show that abolition of property would benefit all human and other than human beings.

63 For an interesting discussion of settler appropriation of the Haudenosaunee "Creator's Game," or lacrosse, as Canada's official sport, see Downey, *The Creator's Game*.

64 Joanne Barker, *Red Scare*, 5 (emphasis in original).

65 As Lorgia García Peña tells us, "complicity with whiteness will not save you," referring to non-Black racialized peoples replicating the power dynamics of white supremacy. Peña, *Community as Rebellion*, 32.

66 Day, *Alien Capital*, 45.

67 For example, the South Australia Act attempted to standardize settler colonialism across Empire; *An Act to provide for the better Government of the province of South Australia*, 5 & 6 Vic., c. 61. The 1842 South Australia Act repealed the 1834 statute when the colony could no longer extend its credit and therefore faced bankruptcy. However, the 1842 act made provisions for those who held South Australia government bonds and turned the colony into a Crown colony.

68 Audra Simpson, *Mohawk Interruptus*, 21.

69 Lowe, *The Intimacies*, 10.

70 Lowe, *The Intimacies*, 15–16 (emphasis in original).

71 John Rae to John Stuart Mill, December 5, 1853–January 9, 1854, with draft reply, London School of Economics Archives and Special Collections (LSEA), Mill-Taylor/1.

72 Yu, "Reckoning with the Realities of History," 414.
73 Brewer, *The Sinews of Power,* 73.
74 Willmott, "Taxes, Taxpayers, and Settler Colonialism," 14. See also the discussion on dispossession and the "public good" in Nichols, *Theft Is Property!* 18–22.
75 Bhambra and McClure, eds., *Imperial Inequalities.*
76 Two major recent works – *Give and Take,* by Shirley Tillotson, and Elsbeth Heaman's *Tax, Order, and Good Government* – provide much-needed insight into the complicated system of Canadian taxation. However, in analyzing Tillotson's work, Brian Gettler points out that though it does include Indigenous peoples, it does not discuss "the effects of colonial dispossession on Canada's fiscal system." Gettler, "Take and Take," 101.
77 Stasavage, *Public Debt,* 2.
78 Karuka, *Empire's Tracks,* 159.
79 Jenkins, *Bonds of Inequality,* 200–5.
80 Lowe, *The Intimacies,* 44, 102. Lowe suggests that China, specifically labour racialized as a form of "Chinese labour," became the core in British theories of a British world order. At the same time, "Chinese labour" would act as a buffer between newly freed Black labour and white society. In whiteness studies, scholars have long noted the many tropes, narratives, discourses, and ideologies where whiteness simply stands in for the normal; Baldwin, "Whiteness and Futurity," 174. For works on whiteness, and for race in Canada, see Dyer, *White*; Razack, "Introduction: When Place Becomes Race"; Sharma, *Home Economics*; Baldwin, Cameron, and Kobayashi, eds., *Rethinking the Great White North*; Meister, *The Racial Mosaic*; and Michele A. Johnson and Funké Aladejebi, eds., *Unsettling the Great White North.*
81 Chelsea Vowel shows that the idea of the "tax-paying citizen" is thrown around as rhetoric to disenfranchise Indigenous people, who are coded as "non-tax-paying" and therefore as not deserving of rights. This belief does not acknowledge that Indigenous peoples do, in fact, pay taxes. Vowel, *Indigenous Writes,* 137 42.
82 For the turn in political economy to include an examination of colonies, see Bell, *Reordering the World;* and Ince, *Colonial Capitalism.*
83 Carruthers and Babb, "The Color of Money," 1562.
84 Hammond, "The North's Empty Purse," 13–15.
85 Carruthers and Babb, "The Color of Money," 1563.
86 Timberlake, *Monetary Policy,* 89.
87 Carruthers and Babb, "The Color of Money," 1564.
88 J.S. Mill, Letter on national faith, written from Avignon, September 24, 1868, published in *The Nation,* October 15, 1868, 75, LSEA, Mill-Taylor/45.
89 Mill, Letter on national faith, 77.
90 Stasavage, *Public Debt,* 53.
91 Quoted in Prichard, "Wakefield Changes His Mind," 262–63.
92 As Allan Greer points out, Lower Canada's 1838 Declaration of Independence specifically mentioned that Indigenous peoples living "under the Free Government

of Lower Canada ... shall enjoy the same right as all other citizens in Lower Canada." See Greer, "Historical Roots," 16.

93 Girard, "Land Law," 121.

94 Girard, "Land Law," 129.

95 Maynard, "Police Abolition/Black Revolt," 71.

96 Charles Henry Darling to Lord R. Churchill, November 5, 1860, National Archives, CO 137/351/41, Charles Henry Darling Collection, vol. 156, Folios 249–216.

97 Battiste, "Narrating Mi'kmaw Treaties," 8.

98 Wolfe, "After the Frontier," 40.

99 "2020 R.W.B. Jackson Lecture: Dionne Brand and Rinaldo Walcott," posted December 17, 2020 by Ontario Institute for Studies in Education, YouTube, 53 min., 42 sec., https://www.youtube.com/watch?v=_wuBjTnWtiQ.

100 McKittrick, *Demonic Grounds,* 92.

101 Heaman, *Tax, Order, and Good Government,* 3.

Chapter 1: Colonial Reform

1 The attempted control of the reproductive capacity of the Black enslaved mother gestures toward the origins of the violent coercion behind such fantastical self-perpetuating systems in economic thought. See Hunt-Kennedy, *Between Fitness and Death,* 114.

2 For political economic assumptions about natural flow and equilibrium, see Morishima, *Ricardo's Economics*.

3 Perelman, *The Invention of Capitalism,* 230.

4 See, for example, Edward Said's *Culture and Imperialism*.

5 Wakefield, *A Letter from Sydney and Other Writings,* 7 (emphasis added.).

6 Polanyi, *The Great Transformation*. See Polanyi's concept of "fictitious commodities."

7 Quoted in Burroughs, "Parliamentary Radicals," 455.

8 Harrington, "Edward Gibbon Wakefield," 340.

9 Mill, "The New Colony" (2), 737.

10 Curtis, "Colonization, Education," 31–32.

11 Rae and Mill, "John Rae and John Stuart Mill: A Correspondence."

12 Perelman, *The Invention of Capitalism,* 341–42.

13 Bell, *Reordering the World,* 34. Political economists also believed that "closed" economies would experience "falling profits," and Wakefield proposed broadening the "field of employment" for capital via settler colonial investments for British capital. For a deeper discussion, see Ince, "Capitalism, Colonization."

14 *Poor Law Commissioners' Report of 1834*. See also Joshi, "Edwin Chadwick's Self-Fashioning."

15 Mill, "The Emigration Bill," 271.

16 Quoted in Ghosh, "The Colonization Controversy," 399.

17 Ghosh, "The Colonization Controversy," 399.

18 See Polanyi, *The Great Transformation*, 71–80; Meuret, "A Political Genealogy," 225–50; Klaver, *A/moral Economics;* and Schabas, *A World Ruled by Number.*

19 *Political Economy Club, Founded in London 1821: Centenary Volume* (London: MacMillan, 1921), 6:ix, LSEA, PEC box 15.

20 *Political Economy Club, Founded in London*, 6:viii.

21 *Political Economy Club, Founded in London*, 6:x.

22 London Political Economy Club Note Book, 5, 4, LSEA, PEC box 1.

23 Maria Edgeworth to Aunt Margaret Ruxton, March 9, 1822, in *Life and Letters of Maria Edgeworth*, vol. 2, ed. Augustus J.C. Hare (London: Edward Arnold, 1894), 65.

24 *Political Economy Club, Founded in London*, 6:xiii.

25 There is much to be said here about Edwin Chadwick, who worked on the New Poor Law and was deeply involved in the "modernization" of the police force. The New Poor Law's centralized system of workhouses essentially criminalized poverty. David Brion Davis points out the link between the New Poor Law and the Act for the Abolition of Slavery. Davis, *Slavery and Human Progress*, 340*n*26. This chapter broadens his assertion and includes the 1834 South Australia Act.

26 *Poor Law Commissioners' Report of 1834.*

27 Poovey, *Genres of the Credit Economy*, 131.

28 See, for example, Edward Gibbon Wakefield, *A View of the Art of Colonization*, which provides the clearest expression of his ideas on colonialism.

29 Wakefield, *A View of the Art of Colonization*, 463.

30 Churchman, *David Ricardo*, 23.

31 Mill, *Principles of Political Economy*, v.

32 Merivale, *Introduction to a Course*, 9.

33 Tennant, *Letters Forming Part*, 15.

34 Tennant, *Letters Forming Part*, 11.

35 Tennant, *Letters Forming Part*, 57.

36 Tennant, *Letters Forming Part*, 53.

37 Tennant, *Letters Forming Part*, 49.

38 *Political Economy Club, Founded in London*, 6:xvii.

39 *Political Economy Club, Founded in London*, 6:xix. At the end of the nineteenth century, this practice fell out of favour, and by the turn of the twentieth century, LPEC members such as Robert Giffen made efforts to preserve club discussions through printed texts. *Political Economy Club, Founded in London*, 6:xxvi.

40 London Political Economy Club, Roll of members and questions discussed 1821–1920, with documents bearing on the history of the club, 7–9, LSEA, PEC box 15.

41 London Political Economy Club, Roll of members, 9.

42 Mill asked the club, "Is not the exportation of British Capital a cause, and almost a necessary condition, of its continued increase at home?" London Political Economy Club, Roll of members, 54.

43 London Political Economy Club, Roll of members, 42.

44 London Political Economy Club, Roll of members, 49.
45 London Political Economy Club, Roll of members, 98.
46 London Political Economy Club, Roll of members, 18.
47 London Political Economy Club, Roll of members, 31.
48 London Political Economy Club, Roll of members, 33.
49 London Political Economy Club, Roll of members, 34.
50 London Political Economy Club, Roll of members, 24.
51 London Political Economy Club, Roll of members, 89.
52 "The Death of Mr. William Newmarch," *Journal of the Statistical Society of London* 45, 1 (March 1882): 117–19.
53 "The Death of Mr. William Newmarch," 120.
54 Merivale, *Introduction to a Course,* 18.
55 McNab, "Herman Merivale and Colonial Office," 100.
56 Linda Tuhiwai Smith, *Decolonizing Methodologies,* 90; McNab, "Herman Merivale and Colonial Office," 85.
57 McNab, "Herman Merivale and Colonial Office," 87.
58 McNab, "Herman Merivale and the Native Question," 365.
59 McNab, "Herman Merivale and Colonial Office," 89.
60 Merivale, *Introduction to a Course,* 26–27.
61 Merivale, *Introduction to a Course,* 20.
62 Quoted in Winch, "Science and the Legislator," 501.
63 *An Act to Empower His Majesty to Erect South Australia Into a British Province or Provinces, and to Provide for the Colonization and Government Thereof,* 4 &5 Will. IV, c. 95.
64 *An Act to provide for the better Government of the province of South Australia,* 5 & 6 Vic., c. 61.
65 Mill, "The New Colony" (1), 734.
66 "New Poor Law Bill in the Lords," *The Times,* July 4, 1834, Times Online Archive, https://link.gale.com/apps/doc/CS51274468/TTDA?u=fred46430&sid=bookmark-TTDA.
67 Scholars have attempted to show the causal tie between the rise of capitalism and the abolition of slavery since 1994, when Eric Williams published *Capitalism and Slavery.*
68 Mill, "The New Colony" (2), 735–36.
69 Mill, "The New Colony" (2), 737.
70 *The Course of the Exchange,* February 6, 1880.
71 See, for example, Trudel, *L'esclavage au Canada Français*; and Winks, *Blacks in Canada.*
72 Cooper, "Acts of Resistance."
73 Whitfield, *North to Bondage,* 7–8.
74 Whitfield, *North to Bondage,* 62.
75 Nelson, *Slavery, Geography and Empire,* 91–92.
76 Miller et al., *Discovering Indigenous Lands,* 11–12.

77 Nelson, *Slavery, Geography and Empire*, 59. For further discussion about diverse slavery practices, in particular with respect to Indigenous practices, see Rushforth, *Bonds of Alliance*.
78 Williams, *Capitalism and Slavery*, 7. For a rebuttal of Williams, see Drescher, *Econocide*.
79 See Brett Rushforth's account of the European difference making between Indigenous and Black slavery, in *Bonds of Alliance*, 135–92.
80 Lydon, "A Secret Longing," 190–91.
81 Caitlin Taylor, Pedersen, and Szeto, "Canada Halts Import of Goods."
82 Williams, *Capitalism and Slavery*, 105–7.
83 For example, the Navigation Acts played this role.
84 Ott, "Slaves."
85 Rosenthal, *Accounting for Slavery*, 127.
86 Bonnie Martin, "Slavery's Invisible Engine"; Bonnie Martin, "Neighbor-to-Neighbor Capitalism."
87 Marx, *Capital*, 1:931.
88 There is no need to go into much detail about the sufficient price concept, as scholars have already put great emphasis on that aspect of Wakefield's colonization plan.
89 Hart, "Denaturalizing Dispossession," 983; David Harvey, "From Globalization to the New Imperialism," 100.
90 Cited in House of Commons, *Report from the Select Committee on the Disposal of Lands*, 183.
91 Edward Gibbon Wakefield, *A Letter from Sydney*, 80.
92 Marx, *Capital*, 1:931*n*1.
93 Marx, *Capital*, 1:871–95. In his discussion of primitive accumulation, Marx used "so-called" to question the word "primitive." Michael Perelman points out that primitive accumulation did not happen in some mythical past, as Adam Smith imagined; Perelman, *The Invention of Capitalism*, 37.
94 Greer, *Property and Dispossession*.
95 Coulthard, *Red Skin, White Masks*, 7 (emphasis in original).
96 Wakefield, *England and America*, 43–44.
97 Lydon, "A Secret Longing," 204.
98 Guidi, "'My Own Utopia,'" 415.
99 Rosenthal, *Accounting for Slavery*, xiv.
100 Perelman, *The Invention of Capitalism*.
101 Edward Gibbon Wakefield, *England and America*, 215. He was referring to Buenos Aires.
102 Lydon, "A Secret Longing," 190–91.
103 Wakefield, *England and America*, 247–48.
104 Edward Gibbon Wakefield, *A View of the Art of Colonization*, 180.
105 Edward Gibbon Wakefield, *A View of the Art of Colonization*, 24.

106 Wakefield, *A View of the Art of Colonization*, 55–56 (asterisks added by author).
107 Robinson, *Black Marxism*.
108 Wynter, "Beyond the Categories of the Master Conception," 66.
109 Edward Gibbon Wakefield, *England and America*, 213.
110 Mill, "The New Colony" (2), 736 (emphasis in original).
111 Lydon, "A Secret Longing," 191.
112 Butler, *Kindred*.
113 da Silva, "Unpayable Debt: Reading Scenes," 86.
114 da Silva, *Unpayable Debt*, 45.
115 Joshua Whitehead, *Making Love with the Land*, 34.
116 da Silva, *Unpayable Debt*, 79.

Chapter 2: Wastelands

1 For a contemporary examination of the logics of wastelands and people-as-discard, see Hecht, *Residual Governance*.
2 Bhandar, *Colonial Lives of Property*, 77. See also de Soto, *The Mystery of Capital*.
3 Pasternak, "How Capitalism Will Save," 184.
4 Kristen Simmons, "Settler Atmospherics."
5 Moreton-Robinson, *The White Possessive*, 110.
6 Greer, "Commons and Enclosure," 374.
7 Girard, "Land Law," 132–34. See also Weaver, "While Equity Slumbered," 871.
8 For details on this process, see Harris, *Making Native Space;* and Keith D. Smith, *Liberalism, Surveillance, and Resistance*.
9 Woolford and Gacek, "Genocidal Carcerality."
10 Bhandar, *Colonial Lives*, 35.
11 Bhandar, *Colonial Lives*, 39.
12 An interesting literature worth investigating looks at the British cultural perception of the London Stock Exchange as gambling. Stockbrokers were seen as speculators engaging in gambling, and it took several decades with changes in the Gambling Acts to normalize stock exchange activity. See, for example, Attard, "Making a Market," 5–24; and Itzkowitz, "Fair Enterprise," 121–47.
13 Dickson, *The Financial Revolution*, 470.
14 For a clear picture of how the debt contributed to the development of the London Stock Exchange, see North and Weingast, "Constitutions and Commitment," 803–32. And for the rebuttal, see Sussman and Yafeh, "Institutional Reforms." For an interesting analysis of the overlap of the public debt, the LSE, and the rôle of anthropologists in colonization, see Flandreau, *Anthropologists in the Stock Exchange*, 102–23.
15 Brewer, *The Sinews of Power*, 74. See also Parkinson, "War, Peace and the Rise," 131–32.
16 Michie, *The London Stock Exchange*, 3.
17 Spufford, "From Antwerp and Amsterdam to London," 166.

18 Stasavage, *Public Debt*, 53.
19 Stasavage, *Public Debt*, 53.
20 Parkinson, "War, Peace and the Rise," 135.
21 Parkinson, "War, Peace and the Rise," 135.
22 Parkinson, "War, Peace and the Rise," 135.
23 Brewer, *The Sinews of Power*, 73.
24 Brewer, *The Sinews of Power*, 73–74.
25 Cain and Hopkins, "Gentlemanly Capitalism and British Expansion Overseas I," 504.
26 Bowen, *The Business of Empire*, 85.
27 Michie, *The London Stock Exchange*, 4.
28 Elsbeth Heaman's discussion of "tax revolts" in Canada reveals that liberals such as John Stuart Mill believed that a "good government" would tax as little as possible. Heaman, *Tax, Order, and Good Government*, 5. The history of taxes as revenue, as well as Heaman's work on the social history of taxes, paints a broad picture of the necessity of settler governments to claim Indigenous lands through law in order to tax in the first place. Chapter 5 returns to this subject. For older publications on taxes and Canada, see Harvey J. Perry, *Taxes, Tariffs, and Subsidies*; and Gillespie, *Tax, Borrow, and Spend*. For more recent scholarship on Canadian tax history, see Tillotson, *Give and Take*.
29 Greenfield, "Financing a New Order," 381.
30 Dawson, *The First Latin American Debt Crisis*, 17–20.
31 Dawson, *The First Latin American Debt Crisis*, 10–13.
32 Dawson, *The First Latin American Debt Crisis*, 22. For a nuanced and critical discussion about Bolívar and ideologies of debts in this specific historical context, see Corredera, *Odious Debt*, 121–37.
33 Belich, *Making Peoples*, 242. See also Attard, "The London Stock Exchange," 111; Cain and Hopkins, *British Imperialism*, particularly Chapters 1 and 21; and Hopkins, "Informal Empire," 469 84.
34 Foreign Stock Market Committee, Minute Book, November 1828 to May 1830, vol. 2, 43, GL, CLC/B/004/B/18/MS14617/2.
35 General Purpose Committee minutes, 1798–1946, GL, Ms 14600.
36 Foreign Stock Market Committee, November 1828 to May 1830, vol. 2, 43–46.
37 Michie, *The Global Securities Market*, 15.
38 *The Course of the Exchange*, January 1, 1813.
39 House of Commons, "Canada Waste-Lands Bill," 1034.
40 House of Commons, "Canada Waste-Lands Bill," 1037. For a detailed description of the land acquisition process in Upper Canada, see Clarke, *Land, Power, and Economics*, 94–154.
41 House of Commons, "Canada Waste-Lands Bill," 1037.
42 House of Commons, "Canada Waste Lands Bill," 1039.
43 House of Commons, *Report from the Select Committee on the Disposal of Lands*, 244.

44 Six Nations of the Grand River, "Land Rights," 44.
45 For example, Joseph Story, an associate justice of the Supreme Court of the United States, wrote in 1833 of an intent to "make land, to some degree, a substitute for money," where a system could be put in place to liquidate land and transform it into capital. Quoted in Clegg, "Credit Market Discipline," 349.
46 John Stuart Mill, "Conduct of the United States towards the Indian Tribes," *The Examiner*, January 9, 1831, in *Newspaper Writings*, ed. Robson and Robson, 236.
47 For further details on this process of "civilization" and in particular, see Donald B. Smith, *Sacred Feathers*. Unfortunately, misunderstanding the intent behind such civilizing missions, Smith defends Egerton Ryerson, who provided expert testimony for the Bagot Report in support of industrial schools (early residential schools) for Indigenous children that later informed the Indian Acts, noting that Ryerson had a close friendship with Chief Peter Jones. See Smith, "Egerton Ryerson Doesn't Deserve an Anti-Indigenous Label." For further reading on Francis Bond Head and the civilizing mission in British North American politics post-1818, see Binnema and Hutchings, "The Emigrant and the Noble Savage."
48 For a few examples in which the committee did consider North American colonization, see House of Commons, *Report from the Select Committee on the Disposal of Lands*, 32, 40, 108, 118, 121, 140, 182–85, 190.
49 House of Commons, *Report from the Select Committee on the Disposal of Lands*, iii.
50 House of Commons, *Report from the Select Committee on the Disposal of Lands*, iv.
51 House of Commons, *Report from the Select Committee on the Disposal of Lands*, 100.
52 House of Commons, *Report from the Select Committee on the Disposal of Lands*, iv.
53 House of Commons, *Report from the Select Committee on the Disposal of Lands*, 14.
54 House of Commons, *Report from the Select Committee on the Disposal of Lands*, 100.
55 House of Commons, *Report from the Select Committee on the Disposal of Lands*, 100.
56 House of Commons, *Report from the Select Committee on the Disposal of Lands*, 101.
57 House of Commons, *Report from the Select Committee on the Disposal of Lands*, 101.
58 Greg Taylor, *The Law of the Land*.
59 House of Commons, *Report from the Select Committee on the Disposal of Lands*, 123.
60 House of Commons, *Report from the Select Committee on the Disposal of Lands*, 123.
61 Mill, "The New Colony" (2), 737.
62 House of Commons, *Report from the Select Committee on the Disposal of Lands*, 135.
63 House of Commons, *Report from the Select Committee on the Disposal of Lands*, 244.
64 Attard, "The London Stock Exchange," 101.
65 Cain and Hopkins, *British Imperialism*, 262.
66 House of Commons, *Report from the Select Committee on the Disposal of Lands*, 135–36.
67 Hitchins, *The Colonial Land*, 20.
68 Cain and Hopkins, *British Imperialism*, 258.
69 For example, see Trotter, *Canadian Federation*; and, for a more recent study, Andrew Smith, *British Businessmen*.

70 Naylor's meaning as interpreted by Andrew Smith, *British Businessmen,* 11.
71 Attard, "The London Stock Exchange," 90.
72 As Chapter 3 details, the receiver general of Upper Canada, John Henry Dunn, was instrumental in pushing Upper Canada's once locally financed public debt to be issued on the LSE.
73 *British North America Act,* 1867, 30–31 Vic., c. 3.
74 Michael Piva's study on the union as a credit mechanism details such conflicts. See Piva, *The Borrowing Process.*
75 *In the Privy Council, in the Matter of Arbitration,* 2.
76 *In the Privy Council, in the Matter of Arbitration,* 45.
77 *In the Privy Council, in the Matter of Arbitration,* 52–53.
78 *Province of Ontario v The Dominion of Canada and Province of Quebec. In re Indian Claims* (1895), 25 S.C.R. 434 at 460–61.
79 *Province of Ontario v The Dominion* at 434–35.
80 General Purpose Committee minutes, vol. 9, 294, GL, CLC/B/004/B/01/MS14600/009.
81 General Purpose Committee, vol. 9, 301.
82 General Purpose Committee, vol. 10, 22, GL, CLC/B/004/B/01/MS14600/010.
83 Michie, *The Global Securities Market,* 67.
84 Vedoveli, "Information Brokers," 357.
85 Vedoveli, "Information Brokers," 361.
86 Poovey, *Genres of the Credit Economy,* 61–77.
87 Neal, *The Rise of Financial Capitalism,* 23.
88 Neal, *The Rise of Financial Capitalism,* 33.
89 Other major nineteenth-century periodicals, such as *The Investor's Monthly Manual, The Stock Exchange Year-Book,* and *Burdett's Official Intelligence,* also listed securities; see Dawson, *The First Latin American Debt Crisis,* 17. However, they have been omitted from the following analysis because their listings notoriously fail to align and because some, such as *The Investor's Monthly Manual,* excluded offerings, particularly in the foreign markets. They could provide conflicting information, and none of them boasted the lengthy pedigree of *The Course of the Exchange.* Any scholar who wishes to look at the total market capitalization or the flows of British capital will need to cross-reference all of them and will also need to consult the parliamentary papers to reach any accurate estimation of hard numbers. This would give a more specific idea of economic growth and flows of capital. However, the information in financial periodicals clearly shows the type of market and the breadth of specific markets. See Simon, "The Pattern of New British," 38.
90 Sussman and Yafeh, "Institutional Reforms," 920–23.
91 Quoted in Attard, "The London Stock Exchange," 99.
92 *The Course of the Exchange,* January 4, 1825.
93 Letters relating to the investments of David Ricardo, 1819–45, 4–5, LSEA, SR1124.
94 Michie, *The Global Securities Market,* 61.

95 *The Course of the Exchange*, March 6, 1857.
96 *The Course of the Exchange*, January 3, 1857.
97 *The Course of the Exchange*, March 6, 1857.
98 *The Course of the Exchange*, January 3, 1857.
99 See, for example, Samaraweera, *The Commission of Eastern Enquiry*.
100 Samaraweera, "Governor Sir Robert Wilmot," 211.
101 Samaraweera, "Governor Sir Robert Wilmot," 213*n*23; see also Kennedy, *The Magic Mountains*.
102 Drayton, *Nature's Government*, 208.
103 Meshnick and Dobson, "The History of Antimalarial Drugs," 18.
104 *The Course of the Exchange*, January 4, 1870.
105 Data calculated from *The Course of the Exchange*, 1801–80.
106 *Budget speech delivered by Sir S.L. Tilley, Minister of Finance in the House of Commons of Canada, on Friday March 30, 1883* (Ottawa: House of Commons, 1883), 7.
107 *Budget speech delivered by Sir S.L. Tilley, Minister of Finance in the House of Commons of Canada, on Friday March 30, 1883* (Ottawa: House of Commons, 1883), 8.
108 *The Course of the Exchange*, January 5, 1875.
109 Davis and Huttenback, *Mammon and the Pursuit*, 169.
110 *The Course of the Exchange*, March 6, 1857, March 13, 1857, January 5, 1875.
111 *Facts for the People*, Broadside [1885?], LAC, FC 02 0203, no. 08214, 1 microfiche. https://bac-lac.on.worldcat.org/oclc/77398978?lang=en&q=facts%20for%20the%20people%20debt%201885.
112 *Facts for the People*.
113 *Journals of the House of Commons*, 5th Sess., 7th Parl., May 7, 1895, 58–59.
114 Richard John Cartwright, *The Finances of Canada: Budget Speech Delivered in the House of Commons of Canada ... February 25, 1876* (Ottawa: Times Publishing Office, 1876), 23.
115 Cartwright, *The Finances of Canada*, 23.
116 Cartwright, *The Finances of Canada*, 21.
117 Charles Fenn, *A Compendium of the English and Foreign Funds*, vi.
118 James Mavor, "Preface," in Perry, *Public Debts in Canada*, 7.
119 James Mavor, "Preface," in Perry, *Public Debts in Canada*, 6.
120 As Brian Gettler notes, "The absence of Indigenous affairs from the Confederation debates and the inaction that followed the BNA Act requires us to revise modern Canada's origin story. We should understand the silence of 1867 as the colonial project at its most imperial"; he emphasizes that pre-Confederation Indigenous policy centred on dispossession that ultimately influenced Confederation. Gettler, "Indigenous Policy and Silence."

Chapter 3: Expansion Unbounded

1 *Province of Ontario v The Dominion of Canada and Province of Quebec. In re Indian Claims* (1895), 25 S.C.R. 434 at 449.

2 Receiver General's Office, Journal, January 31, 1849, LAC, RG19-D-2, vol. 2018.

3 Pasternak, "Jurisdiction and Settler Colonialism," 156–57; Borrows, "Wampum at Niagara."

4 Gates, *Land Policies in Upper Canada*, 9–13.

5 John G. Reid, "Empire, the Maritime Colonies," 84.

6 Quoted in Whetung, "(En)gendering Shoreline Law," 17.

7 For a more complete picture of the economic history of Upper Canada, which later became Ontario, see Craig, *Upper Canada;* McCalla, *Planting the Province;* Clarke, *Land, Power, and Economics;* and Baskerville, *Sites of Power.*

8 Officer and Smith, "The Canadian-American Reciprocity Treaty," 608. See also Saunders, "The Maritime Provinces."

9 Manoomin is the Anishinaabemowin word for "wild rice." Whetung, "(En)gendering Shoreline Law," 16. For a beautiful exegesis on the relationships between plants and humans, see Kimmerer, *Braiding Sweetgrass.*

10 Schrauwers, "'A Terrible Engine.'" Jeffrey McNairn, on the other hand, argues that the history of private interests backed by public money did not necessarily reflect an undemocratic society. McNairn, "Incorporating Contributory Democracy," 149.

11 *An Act to Incorporate, Certain Persons Therein Mentioned Under the Style of the Welland Canal Company,* 4 Geo. IV, c. 17, 2.

12 *An Act to Incorporate,* s. XIII, 6.

13 Pasternak, "How Capitalism Will Save," 182.

14 For example, in the 1820s John Brant sent petitions to receive compensation for the flooding damage caused by the Dunnville Dam on Six Nations of the Grand River lands. "The Petition of John Brant Esq. Superintendent of the Six Nation Indians Residing on the Grand River," February 4, 1829, Western Libraries Archives and Research Collections Centre, Reference AFC 406-F1, Box AFC 406-1/1. For more on the compensation for this flooding, see *Six Nations of the Grand River Band of Indians vs Attorney General of Canada and His Majesty the King in Right of Ontario,* Ontario Superior Court of Justice, CV-18-00594281-0000, https://sngrlitigation.com/wp-content/uploads/2023/11/1.-2023-02-03-Plaintiffs-Second-Fresh-as-Amended-Statement-of-Claim.pdf.

15 McKim, "Upper Canadian Thermidor," 257; Aitken, "The Family Compact," 63.

16 Karuka, *Empire's Tracks,* 150.

17 Aitken, "Financing the Welland Canal," 142.

18 Aitken, "Financing the Welland Canal," 138*n*6.

19 House of Commons, "Appendix B: Copies of Two Dispatches."

20 *An Act to Authorize the Government to Borrow A Certain Sum of Money, Upon Debenture, to be Loaned to the Welland Canal Company,* 7 Geo. IV, c. 20.

21 *An Act to Grant a Further Loan to the Welland Canal Company, and to Regulate Their Further Operations,* 11 Geo. IV, c. 11. Prior to the existence of the WCC, the government had passed a statute that allowed it to raise a £25,000 loan at a 6 percent

annual interest rate for the Government of Quebec, which referenced an earlier public debt. The legislation was *An Act For Making More Effectual Provision for the Government of the Province of Quebec, in North America, and to Make Further Provision for the Government of the Said Province,* 40 Geo. III, c. 1.

22 *An Act to Grant a Further Loan,* s. I.

23 *An Act to Grant a Further Loan,* s. I.

24 Dunn, John Henry, Archives of Ontario, RG 17–20, box 5, 1–2, https://aims.archives.gov.on.ca/SCRIPTS/MWIMAIN.DLL/IbLpQtJHNT2N8/2/1/1194877?RECORD&UNION=Y.

25 House of Commons, "Appendix B: Copies of Two Dispatches," 691.

26 Samuel Street to John Henry Dunn, Toronto, September 12, 1836, Archives of Ontario, Samuel Street fonds, file F 547-0-0-400, MS 500 reel 2.

27 House of Commons, "Copy of Dispatch from the Lieutenant Governor," 245.

28 Shortt, "The Financial Development," 378–79.

29 Borrows, "Wampum at Niagara," 161.

30 Lytwyn, "Waterworld," 15.

31 Hill, *The Clay We Are Made Of,* 170.

32 Six Nations of the Grand River, "Land Rights," 27.

33 Six Nations of the Grand River, "Land Rights," 44.

34 "The Petition of John Brant Esq.," February 4, 1829, Western Libraries Archives and Research Collections Centre.

35 For an elegant argument about the settler state's production of wastelands that are unfit for habitation and the devastating fallout for Indigenous peoples, see Kristen Simmons, "Settler Atmospherics."

36 James Givins, Chief Superintendent of Indian Affairs in Upper Canada, to the Claimant of Lands of the Six Nations Indians on the Grand River, January 1, 1835, Archives of Ontario, Samuel Street fonds, file F 547-0-0-400, microfilm MS 500 reel 2.

37 Whetung, "(En)gendering Shoreline Law," 22.

38 Leanne Betasamosake Simpson, "Looking after Gdoo-naaganinaa," 33.

39 Whetung, "(En)gendering Shoreline Law," 16–32.

40 Klein and Simpson, "Dancing the World into Being."

41 Angus, *Respectable Ditch,* 3.

42 Ransom, "Canals and Development," 373.

43 Davis and Huttenback, *Mammon and the Pursuit,* 183.

44 For a history of the Crown agents, see Sunderland, *Managing the British Empire*; and Abbott, *A Short History*.

45 Piva, "Financing the Union," 82–83.

46 Shortt, "The Financial Development," 375.

47 Piva, *The Borrowing Process,* 6–7.

48 Ireland, "John H. Dunn and the Bankers," 83–100.

49 *The Course of the Exchange,* July 13, 1838.

50 Longley, "Emigration and the Crisis," 33.

51 Quoted in Longley, "Emigration and the Crisis," 34.
52 Edward Gibbon Wakefield, *A Letter from Sydney*, 80.
53 Multiple avenues to access public loans proliferated in this period, with cities incorporating and taking out debts. Mechanisms such as the 1852 Municipal Loan Fund gave municipalities access to provincial credit. Rudin, "Boosting the French Canadian Town," 5.
54 *An Act to Repeal Certain Parts of an Act, Passed in the Fourteenth Year of His Majesty's Reign, intitled, An Act for Making More Effectual Provision For the Government of the Province of Quebec, in North America*, 31 Geo. III, c. 31, s. XXXV.
55 Wilson, "The Clergy Reserves," 283.
56 Wilson, "The Clergy Reserves," 284.
57 Macdonell, *Ghost Storeys*, 79.
58 Oosterhoff, "The Law of Mortmain."
59 Birla, *Stages of Capital*, 90–96.
60 "Copy of a Dispatch from the Right Hn. the Earl of Elgin and Kincardine to the Right Hon. the Earl Grey," July 19, 1850, in *Papers Relative to the Clergy Reserves in Canada* (London: Harrison and Son, 1851), 2.
61 The Rectories of Upper Canada, "Extract from a dispatch from Viscount Goderich to Sir J. Sir J. Colborne," November 21, 1831, in *Being a Return to an Address of the Honourable the House of Commons, Dated 11th March, 1839* (Toronto: Hugh Scobie, 1852), 47.
62 "Extract of a Dispatch from the Right Honourable C. Poulett Thomson to Lord John Russell," February 13, 1840, in House of Commons, *Copies or Extracts of Correspondence Respecting the Clergy Reserves in Canada, 1819–1840*, part 1 (London: HMSO, 1840), 184.
63 "Clergy Reserves Canada," House of Commons Debate, June 15, 1840, Hansard, vol. 54, cc 1175–202. Lord John Russell moved the Order of the Day for the second reading of the Canada Clergy Reserves Bill.
64 Strachan, *The Clergy Reserves*, 12.
65 *An act to provide for the disposal of the public lands in Upper Canada, and for other purposes therein mentioned* (London: House of Commons, 1840).
66 Strachan, *The Clergy Reserves*, 6–7.
67 Strachan, *The Clergy Reserves*, 8–9.
68 Strachan, *Remarks on Emigration from the United Kingdom*, 88–89.
69 Gates, *Land Policies in Upper Canada*, 198.
70 Karr, *The Canada Land Company*, 5–6.
71 Karr, *The Canada Land Company*, 78.
72 Schrauwers, "The Liberal Corporate Order," 534.
73 *The Course of the Exchange*, January 4, 1825.
74 Karr, *The Canada Land Company*, 9.
75 Land policy in the Province of Canada has an extensive literature. For studies on the Canada Company, Galt, and the Family Compact, see Norman MacDonald,

Canada, 1763–1841; Langman, *Patterns of Settlement*; Taylor, *The Law of the Land;* Little, *Nationalism, Capitalism, and Colonization*; Glynn, "'Exporting Outcast London'"; Clarke and Buffone, "Manifestations of Imperial Policy"; Clarke, *Land, Power, and Economics;* and Weaver, *The Great Land Rush.*

76 Karr, *The Canada Land Company,* 4.

77 Karr, *The Canada Land Company,* 40.

78 Brierley, "The Co-Existence," 286.

79 Brierley, "The Co-Existence," 279–80.

80 Brierley, "The Co-Existence," 281.

81 *An Act for rendering valid, conveyances of lands and other immoveable property held in free and common soccage within the Province of Lower Canada, and for other purposes therein mentioned,* 9 & 10 Geo. IV, c. 77; Brierley, "The Co-Existence," 285–86.

82 Greer, *The Patriots and the People,* 271.

83 Greer, *The Patriots and the People,* 273.

84 Département des terres de la Couronne, T. Bouthillier, "Plan of the Seigniory of Lauzon Showing a Certain Lot of Land Situate Near Quebec, to Be Granted in Free and Common Soccage to W. Price Esquire and Honorable P. McGill," September 17, 1847, Bibliothèque et Archives nationales du Québec, Fonds Ministère des Terres et Forêts.

85 The grant contained a "clause that is rarely seen in documents of this nature" and that "if Mr. Le Maître wants to give this piece of land a more honourable name and title, ... he can contact the king and Cardinal Richelieu" (author's translation).

86 Roy, *Histoire de la seigneurie de Lauzon,* 1:37.

87 Little, *Crofters and Habitants,* 33.

88 Little, *Crofters and Habitants,* 34.

89 Discussion focused on what debts Caldwell owed, where he took money from, how the colonial government would sort it out, and whether the imperial government or Caldwell himself should to pay back the money. Edmond J. Roy details that "l'action fut intentée devant les juges contre le Receveur Général, Sir John Caldwell, celui-ci déclara qu'il y avait 100,000 louis qu'il avait payés au gouverneur, qui devaient être déduits de sa dette, et pour lesquels il ne devait être condamné, et et [sic] qu'il ne reconnaissait que l'autre partie de la dette." ("The action was brought before the judges against the Receiver General, Sir John Caldwell, the latter declared that there were 100,000 louis which he had paid to the governor, which should be deducted from his debt, and for which he should not be condemned, and [sic] that he only recognized the other part of the debt." [author's translation]) Roy, *Histoire de la seigneurie,* 5:465.

90 "Appendix EEE: Report of the Select Committee to inquire into the manner in which the affairs of Seigniory of Lauzon, since its acquisition by the Province ..." in *Journal of the Legislative Assembly of the Province of Canada,* June 2–July 28, 1847, vol. 6, unpaginated.

91 For an in-depth discussion about the business of Price and McGill, particularly the debts incurred, see Dechêne, "Les affaires de William Price," 43–48.
92 Dechêne, "Les entreprises de William Price," 26.
93 Brierley, "The Co-Existence," 286.
94 New, "Lord Durham and the British Background," 135; Scrope, *Memoir of the Life,* 332; D.G. Hall, "Sir Charles Metcalfe," 100; Leacock, "Responsible Government."
95 Curthoys, "The Dog That Didn't Bark," 35.
96 Chester Martin, "Lord Durham's Report," 181.
97 Shaw, "British Attitudes to the Colonies," 71.
98 Quoted in Ged Martin, *The Durham Report,* 13.
99 Stuart Johnson Reid, *Life and Letters,* 2:368.
100 For an early work on Durham, see New, *Lord Durham.*
101 See Curthoys, "The Dog That Didn't Bark."
102 Trollope, *Australia and New Zealand,* 2:308.
103 Prichard, "Wakefield Changes His Mind," 253.
104 Felix Wakefield, *Colonial Surveying,* 2.
105 Edward Gibbon Wakefield to his mother, May 12, 1837, Family Correspondence, 28, British Library, ADD MS 35261.
106 *The Report and Dispatches of the Earl,* 242, 244.
107 *The Report and Dispatches of the Earl,* 155, 156; Dispatch from the Earl of Gosford, number 76, July 19, 1837, LAC, Papers of the 1st Earl of Durham, R2469-0-1-E, MG24-A27.
108 *The Report and Dispatches of the Earl,* 157–58, 156.
109 Ged Martin, *The Durham Report,* 18. Durham resigned in connection with eight Lower Canadian rebels whom he had exiled to Bermuda. Because they had never gone to trial, the imperial government eventually declared his actions illegal, after which his resignation was an inevitability. For a detailed discussion of the Bermuda issue, see Henderson, "Banishment to Bermuda," 321 48.
110 Wilson, "The Clergy Reserves," 298.
111 *The Report and Dispatches of the Earl,* 101.
112 House of Commons, "Copy of a Dispatch from the Right Hon.," 3.
113 Piva, "Financing the Union," 93. For a detailed discussion on the debates and history of the civil list, see La Forest, *Natural Resources.*
114 "A Cabinet Meeting Held at Lord Melbourne's on Wednesday the 21st Day of August 1839," 415, National Archives, Domestic Records of the Public Record Office, Gifts, Deposits, Notes and Transcripts, PRO/30/22/3C.
115 "A Cabinet Meeting," 415.
116 House of Commons, "Copy of a Dispatch from the Right Hon.," 2.
117 House of Commons, *Correspondence Relative to the Affairs,* 50.
118 House of Commons, *Correspondence Relative to the Affairs,* 54. In an unpublished paper titled "Moses Perley's Legacy," literary scholar Rachel Bryant shows that

the Puritan foundation in British colonization remained a formative colonial ideology throughout the centuries. See also Bryant, Peters, and Tozer, "In Wilderness."

119 Shortt, "The Financial Development," 375.

120 *An Act to facilitate the negotiation of a Loan in England, and for other purposes therein mentioned*, 4 & 5 Vic., c. 33.

121 *An Act for guaranteeing the Payment of the Interest on a Loan of One Million Five Hundred Thousand Pounds to be Raised by the Province of Canada*, 5 & 6 Vic., c. 118.

122 Shortt, "The Financial Development," 376.

123 Charles Edward Poulett Thomson, Baron Sydenham, to Earl John Russell, August 20, 1839, in Thomson, *Letters from Lord Sydenham*, 25.

124 *An Act to authorize the Legislature of the Province of Canada to make Provision concerning the Clergy Reserves in that Province, and the Proceeds thereof*, 16 Vic., c. 21, s. II.

125 Davis and Huttenback, *Mammon and the Pursuit*, 185.

126 Attard, "The London Stock Exchange," 107.

127 Davis and Huttenback, *Mammon and the Pursuit*, 185.

128 Attard, "The London Stock Exchange," 108.

129 Legislative Assembly of the Province of Canada, "Appendix NN: Report from the select committee appointed to enquire into the present method of disposing of the Crown, Clergy, and School Lands," in *Journals of the Legislative Assembly of the Province of Canada ... 28th Day of November, 1844, to the 29th Day of March, 1845* (Montreal: R. Campbell, 1845).

130 See Vosburgh, "The Crown Lands Department."

131 Innis, "The Penetrative Powers," 311.

132 House of Commons, "Copy of a Dispatch from the Right Hon.," 2.

133 Attard, "The London Stock Exchange," 101.

134 Officer and Smith, "The Canadian-American Reciprocity Treaty," 620–21.

135 Donald Masters points out that impetus for the treaty originated in the colonies. Masters, *The Reciprocity Treaty of 1854*, xi.

136 Ankli, "The Reciprocity Treaty of 1854," 2.

137 This parallel was significant to the United States. In seeking to retain the balance between slave-owning and non-slave-owning states, the Missouri Compromise of 1820 made slavery illegal above the thirty-sixth parallel.

138 Ankli, "The Reciprocity Treaty of 1854," 2.

139 "Fisheries and Reciprocity Treaty," 1854, Library and Archives Canada, R977-601-4-E, vol. 43, Article II, 1043. For more details about the three-mile limit see Kent, "The Historical Origins."

140 Haynes, *The Reciprocity Treaty with Canada*, 7:53.

141 Officer and Smith, "The Canadian-American Reciprocity Treaty," 619.

142 Saunders, "The Reciprocity Treaty of 1854," 43.

143 Luby, *Dammed*, 50.

Chapter 4: The Island's Gambit

1 Epekwitk Aqq Piktuk, which includes the island and part of Nova Scotia, is one of the seven (sometimes eight) districts of Mi'kma'ki, the Mi'kmaw homelands. I use the Francis-Smith orthography, as it is common on the island.

2 Edward Macdonald, "The Yankee Gale," 97.

3 "Appendix 13: Bannerman Lieut. Governor," *Journal of the Legislative Council of Prince Edward Island.*

4 "Appendix 13: Bannerman Lieut. Governor," *Journal of the Legislative Council of Prince Edward Island.*

5 "Appendix 13: Bannerman Lieut. Governor," *Journal of the Legislative Council of Prince Edward Island.*

6 Phillip Buckner convincingly argues that the island government had an eye to expand its economy with links to the mainland long before Confederation. Buckner, "Beware the Canadian Wolf," 180.

7 Price, "Fire Destroys Commercial Lobster Plant." See also Taryn Grant, "Vehicle Torched."

8 Bumsted, *Land, Settlement, and Politics,* 102.

9 The PEI land question has an extensive historiography. For key works, see Robertson, *The Tenant League;* Bumsted, "The Origins of the Land Question"; Bittermann, *Rural Protest;* Bittermann, *A Sailor's Hope;* and Bittermann and McCallum, *Lady Landlords.*

10 See Bhandar, *Colonial Lives.*

11 House of Commons, "Papers on the Subject of Affording," 20.

12 Quoted in *Hansard's Parliamentary Debates,* "Prince Edward Island Loan Committee," May 4, 1858 to June 17, 1858 (London: Cornelius Buck, 1858), 402. The two bills in question were *An Act to secure Compensation to Tenants in Prince Edward Island, and Thereby to Promote the Improvement of the Soil,* 18 Vic, c.11 1855; and *An Act to Impose a Rate or Duty on the Rent-rolls of the Proprietors of Certain Rented Township Lands in Prince Edward Island in Order to Defray the Expenses of Any Armed Force Which May Be Required on Account of the Withdrawal of the Troops, and for the Further Encouragement of Education,* 18 Vic., c. 9. Also note that the lieutenant governor, Charles Douglass Smith, set up a court of escheat in the early nineteenth century but with very little success. House of Commons, "Papers on the Subject of Affording." Bittermann's work on the Escheat Movement and its leader, William Cooper, is seminal in the land question literature. After the failure of the Escheat Movement, the Tenant League emerged, different from the Escheat Movement in that it wanted tenants to be able to purchase the lands they lived on from landlords, as opposed to lands to be escheated. For a detailed discussion on Escheat and William Cooper, see Bittermann, *Sailor's Hope,* 95–133.

13 MacNutt, "Political Advance and Social Reform."

14 Battiste, ed., *Living Treaties;* Peace, "Immigration and Sovereignty"; John G. Reid, "Empire, the Maritime Colonies," 78–97; Wicken, *Mi'kmaq Treaties on Trial.* These

scholars offer multifaceted discussions about Mi'kmaw sovereignty and the Peace and Friendship Treaties in the Maritimes.

15 Attard, "Making a Market," 5–24; Itzkowitz, "Fair Enterprise," 121–47.

16 Clarke, *Land, Power, and Economics*, 201. In 1818, Upper Canada instituted a "wild land tax" to penalize people who held land without improving it. Clarke, *Land, Power, Economics*, 177.

17 The island's public debt began in 1851, with an act to raise a £10,000 loan to pay for warrants.

18 Bear, Birla, and Puri, "Speculation," 387.

19 See the discussion of gambling and speculation in Birla, *Stages of Capital*, 143–98.

20 Bolger, *Prince Edward Island*, 170–71. Bolger has a pertinent discussion on the island's credit in London.

21 Buckner, "Beware the Canadian Wolf," 180; Bittermann and McCallum, "Upholding the Land Legislation." Buckner, Bittermann, and McCallum offer a nuanced history of PEI and Confederation.

22 Robertson, "Political Realignment"; MacKinnon, "Some Peculiarities." Robertson and MacKinnon offer concise narratives about mid-century PEI settler politics.

23 Peter J. Smith, "The Ideological Origins," 23.

24 Peter J. Smith, "The Ideological Origins," 9.

25 In Canadian law, Epekwitk comes under what is known as Aboriginal title. Currently, the Government of Prince Edward Island understands that "the Mi'kmaq of PEI assert Aboriginal and treaty rights on Prince Edward Island, including Aboriginal title to all of Prince Edward Island." Prince Edward Island Government, "Understanding Indigenous Matters," https://www.princeedwardisland.ca/en/information/executive-council-office/understanding-indigenous-matters. See also Battiste, "Narrating Mi'kmaw Treaties," 9. Battiste shows that the treaties are an "ongoing constitutional relationship."

26 Bear Nicholas, "Mascarene's Treaty of 1725," 11; Mercedes Peters, "Settler Forgetting in Saulnierville."

27 Paul, "Big Water Drowned," 4.

28 Paul, "Big Water Drowned," 4.

29 The Mi'kmawey Debert Cultural Centre, "An Ice-Age World," https://www.mikmaweydebert.ca/ancestors-live-here/debert/an-ice-age-world/.

30 Johnston and Francis, *Ni'n na L'nu*, 18.

31 Johnston and Francis, *Ni'n na L'nu*, 30.

32 A clear example of this was the 1845 "Report on the Affairs of the Indians in Canada," which greatly influenced Canadian Indigenous policy. Legislative Assembly of the Province of Canada, "Appendix EEE: Report on the Affairs."

33 Lelièvre, *Unsettling Mobility*, 53.

34 Augustine, "The Significance of Place," 46.

35 Lieutenant Governor Charles A. Fitzroy to Lord Glenelg, October 8, 1838, Public Archives and Records Office of Prince Edward Island (PA of PEI), CO 226 55/56.

36 Bumsted, *Land, Settlement, and Politics,* 3. Bumsted states that the Mi'kmaq "had at least summered there for centuries."

37 See Coulthard, *Red Skin, White Masks.* I use Coulthard's critique of "recognition" here.

38 Lennox Island interviews, November 2019, Angela Tozer. The names of all interviewees and Elders have been changed to maintain privacy.

39 Silas Tertius Rand's 1875 work on the Mi'kmaw language recorded that the word "Malpeque" came from "Makpaak," which he translated as "Big Bay." Rand, *A First Reading Book,* 93.

40 Paul, "Big Water Drowned," 4; Johnston and Francis, *Ni'n na L'nu,* 18.

41 Elder Maria Labobe, August 5, 2009, Morell, Prince Edward Island, transcript, L'nuey Archives.

42 Elder Cathy Sark, Judy, March 5, 2009, Lennox Island, transcript, L'nuey Archives.

43 George MacDonald, no date or location, transcript, L'nuey Archives.

44 Hornby, *Black Islanders,* 19–21.

45 The Elders gave several accounts of escaping Indian agents who attempted to take Mi'kmaw children to the Shubenacadie Residential School and also of living in various places on the island and returning to "wintering" locations. Jane Sark, no date or location, transcript, L'nuey Archives.

46 With the notable exception of Lieutenant Governor Charles Douglass Smith's small successes with escheat in the early nineteenth century.

47 Bittermann and McCallum, "The Pursuit of Gentility," 50.

48 Bittermann and McCallum, "The Pursuit of Gentility," 31, 38. Harvey Amani Whitfield reveals that the Prince Edward Island government had particular ties to slavery, with connections to the West Indies, and when it passed an act on the baptism of enslaved people it essentially legalized slavery until 1825. Baptism was important as from the Doctrine of Discovery onward, technically, a Christian could not be enslaved; this 1825 law made it clear that even baptized Black peoples could be enslaved. After slavery became illegal, anti-Black sentiment lived on. See Whitfield, *North to Bondage,* 85.

49 Chute, "Bound to Slavery." Fortunately, scholarship from Whitfield, Chute, and others examines these connections.

50 MacEachern, "Theophilus Stewart," 6–7.

51 Prince Edward Island, "Theophilus Stewart to Minister of the Interior: Report of Visiting Superintendent of Indians," in *Sessional Papers,* 8 (1875), 52.

52 Prince Edward Island, "Theophilus Stewart to Minister of the Interior: Report of Visiting Superintendent of Indians," in *Sessional Papers,* 8 (1875), 8.

53 Report by Theophilus Stewart, circa 1864, to the Aborigines Protection Society in London, PA of PEI, Theophilus Stewart fonds, CA PCA Acc4660, 1864(?).

54 *History of the New England Company,* 1.

55 Fingard, "The New England Company," 33.

56 Whetung, "(En)gendering Shoreline Law."

57 History of the New England Company, 224–25.
58 Upton, "Indians and Islanders," 39.
59 MacEachern, "Theophilus Stewart," 4.
60 Ryan, "'We're Going to Be Welcoming.'"
61 Lennox Island interviews, November 2019, Tozer.
62 See Fenn, "Biological Warfare"; Lux, "Care for the 'Racially Careless'"; and McCallum and Perry, *Structures of Indifference*.
63 Monique Roy, "Coastal Scourge."
64 Quoted in Campbell, *History of Prince Edward Island*, 89.
65 Livingston, *Responsible Government*, 11–15.
66 *Act to Authorise a Loan for the Use of this Island, and Also to Make Provisions Respecting the Payment of Treasury Bonds and Warrants and the Interest Thereon*, 14th Vic., c. 20, 727. Unless otherwise specified as pounds sterling, amounts are in legal island tender. During the 1850s and 1860s, £1.5 of island money amounted to approximately £1.0 sterling.
67 For example, George Washington issued many warrants during the American Revolutionary War. Library of Congress, George Washington Papers, series 5, Financial Papers: Revolutionary War Warrant Book 4, July 1779–January 1780, MSS 44693, reel 116.
68 *Act to Authorise a Loan for the Use of this Island*, 727.
69 Lester, "The Effect of Southern State," 415–40; Lester, *Victorian Insolvency*. Lester's scholarship enlightens us on the relationship between credit, debt, and bankruptcy.
70 Peter J. Smith, "The Ideological Origins," 23–24.
71 Pasternak, *Grounded Authority*, 22. Pasternak argues that assertions of jurisdiction have constituted a fundamental part of the settler state even in its early development, one where "the landscape was refitted to a new proprietary regime."
72 *An Act for the Purchase of Lands*, 16 Vic., c. 18, ss. IX.
73 *An Act for the Purchase of Lands*, 16 Vic., c. 18, ss. IX.
74 *An Act for the Purchase of Lands*, 16 Vic., c. 18, ss. XX.
75 *An Act for the Purchase of Lands*, 16 Vic., c. 18, ss. XXVI.
76 For example, see Henderson's reference to Durham's "wastelands" in Henderson, "Remember / Resist / Redraw #04: The 1837–1838 Rebellion."
77 Quoted in Bittermann, *A Sailor's Hope*, 203.
78 This means not that the government owed the entire £229,000, but that it could legally raise its public debt to this amount. The figure is based on a calculation that added together all the government's acts that raised its public debt.
79 Cited in *Parliamentary Reporter, or, Debates*, 20–21. It should be noted that schemes to raise land prices did exist, such as the notorious "Worrell Job." As Bittermann and McCallum note,

> The Island government, soon after, opened negotiations to acquire the Worrell estate, but members of the local elite used insider knowledge and connections to purchase the estate from the trustees and resell it to the

government at a price well above what Charles would have accepted for it. Although Charles did not share in the ill-gotten profits, the transaction became known as the "Worrell Job."

Bittermann and McCallum, *The Pursuit of Gentility*, 54.

80 Edward Gibbon Wakefield, *A Letter from Sydney*.

81 The petition was entitled "To the Queen's Most Excellent Majesty. The Humble Petition and Remonstrance of the Undersigned Proprietors and Agents of Land in Prince Edward Island," in House of Commons, "Papers on the Subject of Affording," 9–11. The quitrents were also a point of debate between the island and imperial governments.

82 PA of PEI, Commissioner of Public Lands, 1855-7-43 Executive Council fonds, RG 15, 1855–57 RG 15.

83 PA of PEI, Commissioner of Public Lands fonds, RG 15, series 12 Financial Records, sub-series 1 Bonds, vol. 1, 1855–57.

84 Cited in House of Commons, "Papers on the Subject of Affording," 9.

85 The government passed two bills in April 1855 to tax landowners, neither of which received Royal Assent. For the debates about the inability to tax, see House of Commons, "Papers on the Subject of Affording," 11–13.

86 House of Commons, "Papers on the Subject of Affording," 14–15.

87 House of Commons, "Papers on the Subject of Affording," 20.

88 House of Commons, "Papers on the Subject of Affording."

89 House of Commons, "Papers on the Subject of Affording," 16.

90 Receiver General's Office, November 1848, Journal, August 1848–December 1857, LAC, Reference 6: RG19-D-2, vol. 2018. For example, the accounts of the Province of Canada referenced the "olde debt" to the Barings Bank.

91 House of Commons, "Papers on the Subject of Affording," 20.

92 House of Commons, "Papers on the Subject of Affording," 11.

93 House of Commons, "Papers on the Subject of Affording," 15.

94 House of Commons, "Papers on the Subject of Affording," 11.

95 House of Commons, "Papers on the Subject of Affording," 20.

96 House of Commons, "Papers on the Subject of Affording," 21.

97 House of Commons, "Papers on the Subject of Affording," 21–22, 25–26.

98 House of Commons, *Parliamentary Debates*, 402.

99 Carruthers and Espeland, "Accounting for Rationality," 35; Peters and Emery, "The Role of Negative Numbers," 425–26.

100 Pasternak, *Grounded Authority*, 5. Pasternak helpfully defines jurisdiction as the "authority to have authority."

101 House of Commons, "Papers on the Subject of Affording," 24.

102 House of Commons, "Papers on the Subject of Affording," 24.

103 *An Act for the Purchase of Lands*, 16 Vic., c. 18; House of Commons, "Papers on the Subject of Affording," 25.

104 House of Commons, "Papers on the Subject of Affording," 31.

105 The act was titled *An Act for Raising Moneys to be Applied to the Purchase of Lands Under the Act 16 Vict. Ch 18. Intituled "An Act for the Purchase of Lands on behalf of the Government of Prince Edward Island, and to Regulate the Sale and Management Thereof, and for Other Purposes therein mentioned."* House of Commons, "Papers on the Subject of Affording," 25.

106 "Prince Edward Island Loan Committee," House of Commons, Parliamentary Debates, May 10, 1858, Hansard, 403.

107 House of Commons, *A Bill to Guarantee a Loan for the Service of Prince Edward Island*, 21 Vic., May 13, 1858.

108 *The Parliamentary Rememberancer* (London: Office of the Parliamentary Rememberancer, 1858), 146.

109 Robertson, *The Prince Edward Island Land Commission*, xxiii and 195.

110 Robertson, *The Prince Edward Island Land Commission*, xxi.

111 "Prince Edward Island Loan Committee," House of Commons, Parliamentary Debates, May 10, 1858, Hansard, 401.

112 House of Commons, "Papers on the Subject of Affording," 22.

113 *An Act to Provide for the Payment of Certain Debentures*, s. 50.

114 *An Act to Assist Leaseholders*, s. 90.

115 *An Act to Assist Leaseholders*, s. 4.

116 *An Act in Addition to and In Further Amendment of the Land Purchase Act*, ss. 1–3.

117 This amount does not include the 1851 act to raise a loan for £10,000 to pay for warrants, the separate 1864 act to raise money to pay for Land Purchase Act debentures of £19,000, or the act to raise money to assist tenants in buying land in 1865 of £50,000.

118 *An Act to Authorise the Construction of a Railroad through Prince Edward Island*, 34 Vic., c. 4, ss. 27–31.

119 Prince Edward Island – [Committee] of Council submit Minutes of [Conference] 8 March between [Committee] of Privy Council and Delegates from [Government of Prince Edward Island] as to terms and conditions of proposed Union with Canada of and [recommends], LAC, RG2, Privy Council Office, Series A-1-a, vol. 307.

120 "Debt Account: The Dominion of Canada in Account with the Province of Prince Edward Island," July 1, 1873, PA of PEI, RG8, Provincial Treasurer fonds, series 2, Accounting Records, sub-series 4, Ledgers, vol. 6, 1–2.

121 "Debt Account: The Dominion of Canada."

122 "Debt Account: The Dominion of Canada."

123 James Roy Perry, *Public Debts in Canada*, 57.

124 *The Stock Exchange Year-Book* (London: Thomas Skinner, 1875), 15.

125 Appadurai, "Afterword," 481.

126 White, *Railroaded*, 25.

127 See Bittermann, "Mi'kmaq Land Claims," 176; Jarvis, "Murder, Manslaughter, or Justified Retribution?" For further discussion on the use of petitions see De Costa, "Identity, Authority, and the Moral Worlds."

128 Walls, "Confederation and the Maritime First Nations," 159.

129 For settler encroachment on Wet'suwet'en land, see the documentary film Unist'ot'en Camp, dir., *Invasion*, https://unistoten.camp/media/invasion/.

130 White, *Railroaded*, 460–65.

Chapter 5: The New Canadian Empire

1 The literature on Confederation is vast. For a few major works, see Creighton, *The Road to Confederation*; Morton, *The Critical Years*; Waite, *The Life and Times of Confederation*; Ged Martin, *Britain and the Origins*; Ajzenstat, ed., *Canada's Founding Debates*; Peter J. Smith, ed., *Canada's Origins*; Andrew Smith, *British Businessmen*; and Brouillet, Gagnon, and Laforest, eds., *The Québec Conference of 1864*.

2 In *The Road to Confederation*, Donald Creighton refers to the loan guarantees, as does W.L. Morton in *The Critical Years*, but it should be noted that the guarantees were significant because they allowed the settler governments to access cheap loans. Minister of Finance – [Respecting] arrangements in England in [negotiating] the Intercolonial Railway Loan, Date approved: 1868-08-27, LAC, RG2, Privy Council Office, series A-1-a, vol. 260, reel C-3288, access code 90. The work of Ken Cruikshank is also significant here, particularly his discussions of the rhetoric of the "people's railway." See Cruikshank, "The People's Railway"; and Cruikshank, *Close Ties*.

3 Stark, "Criminal Empire."

4 Morton, *The Critical Years*, 232.

5 Bear Nicholas, "Mascarene's Treaty," 3–18.

6 Receiver General's Office, Cash Book, 1844–45, 106, 127, LAC, RG19-D-2, vol. 2062.

7 Receiver General's Office, Cash Book, 81–83.

8 Receiver General, Cash and Debenture Statement Book, April 1849–September 1849, 9–12, LAC, RG19-D-4, vol. 2412. The other six banks were the Quebec Bank, City Bank, Banque du Peuple, Commercial Bank, Bank of Upper Canada, and Gore Bank.

9 Receiver General, Cash and Debenture Statement Book, 17.

10 Receiver General, Cash and Debenture Statement Book, 37.

11 Receiver General, Cash and Debenture Statement Book, March 1851–August 1851, 27, LAC, RG19-D-4, vol. 2413.

12 Receiver General's Office, Journal, August 31, 1848, LAC, RG19-D-2, vol. 2018.

13 *Finances of the Dominion of Canada: Budget Speech Delivered by Sir Leonard Tilley, Minister of Finance, in the House of Commons of Canada, Friday, February 24, 1882* (n.p., [1882?]), 8–9.

14 Receiver General's Office, Journal, January 31, 1849, LAC, RG19-D-2, vol. 2018.

15 Den Otter, *Civilizing the West*, 53, 310.

16 Den Otter, *The Philosophy*, 97–98.

17 Den Otter, *The Philosophy*, 32.

18 House of Commons, *Copy of Correspondence between Any of the North American Provinces and the Imperial Government, Relating to Their Application for Assistance in Raising a Loan for an Intercolonial Railway* (London: HMSO, 1864), 22.

19 House of Commons, *Copy of Correspondence*, 18.
20 House of Commons, *Copy of Correspondence*, 19.
21 House of Commons, *Copy of Correspondence*, 20.
22 Hannay, *The Life and Times of Sir Leonard Tilley*, 233.
23 Hannay, *The Life and Times of Sir Leonard Tilley*, 233.
24 Hannay, *The Life and Times of Sir Leonard Tilley*, 237.
25 *British North America Act*, s. 145.
26 Debate on Canada (Rupert's Land) Loan Bill, House of Commons, Parliamentary Debates, Hansard, August 5, 1869, c. 1330.
27 Debate on Canada (Rupert's Land) Loan Bill, House of Commons, Parliamentary Debates, Hansard, August 5, 1869, c. 1330.
28 Achieving this particular loan guarantee was no easy feat; for example, see Morton, *The Critical Years*, 67–69. In 1867, Ottawa passed *An Act respecting the construction of the Intercolonial Railway*, 31 Vic., c. 13. It created a railway commission, which held its first meeting on December 17, 1868.
29 Charles Tupper, "Intercolonial Railway Loan," June 12, 1872, LAC, RG2, Privy Council Office, series A-1-a.
30 Charles Tupper, "Intercolonial Railway Loan," June 12, 1872.
31 *An Act for the Union of Canada, Nova Scotia, and New Brunswick, Together with the Act Authorising a Loan for the Halifax and Quebec Railway* (Halifax: Compton, 1867), 29–20, 45–46.
32 House of Commons, *Copy of Correspondence*, 27–29.
33 House of Commons, *Copy of Correspondence*, 16.
34 House of Commons, *Copy of Correspondence*, 22.
35 House of Commons, *Copy of Correspondence*, 23.
36 For the links between capitalism, settler colonialism, and fear of working-class rebellion, see Ince, *Colonial Capitalism*, especially 113–54.
37 House of Commons, *Copy of Correspondence*, 11.
38 House of Commons, *Copy of Correspondence*, 45.
39 Creighton, *Road to Confederation*, 24.
40 "Customs Claim of Mr Joseph Nelson, London, England – For services in securing Imperial Guarantee [Guarantee] to Loan of £3000000 [Sterling] for construction of Intercolonial [Railway]," December 28, 1867, LAC, RG2, Privy Council Office, series A-1-a.
41 Debate on Canada (Guarantee of Loan) Bill, House of Commons, Parliamentary Debates, July 29, 1870, Hansard, c. 1257.
42 Debate on Canada (Rupert's Land) Loan Bill, House of Commons, Parliamentary Debates, August 5, 1869, Hansard, columns 1324–34.
43 "Recommending that Interest due by Dominion of Canada in London on 1 January 1869 be paid by Agents out of moneys held by them on account of the Intercolonial Railway Loan," November 23, 1868, LAC, RG2, Privy Council Office, series A-1-a.

44 *Report of the Commissioners of the Intercolonial Railway.*
45 Appendix B in *Report of the Commissioners of the Intercolonial Railway.*
46 Appendix B in *Report of the Commissioners.* For a history of the New Brunswick timer industry, see Wynn, *Timber Colony.*
47 Appendix B in *Report of the Commissioners.*
48 "Intercolonial Railway – Imperial Guaranteed Loan," January 9, 1873, LAC, RG2, Privy Council Office, series A-1-a.
49 House of Commons, *Copy of Correspondence,* 28.
50 Frederic Rogers to the Secretary to the Treasury, March 23, 1867. Canada railway loan: copy of correspondence between the Colonial Office and the Treasury, respecting the proposed guarantee of the Intercolonial Railway loan (British North America). Treasury Chambers, March 27, 1867, George Ward Hunt, LAC Reserve HE2810 I6 C37 1867 fol., 1008.
51 Frederic Rogers to the Secretary to the Treasury, March 23, 1867.
52 Frederic Rogers to the Secretary to the Treasury, March 23, 1867.
53 *An Act Respecting the Provincial Debt guaranteed by the Imperial Government,* 22 Vic., c. 1.
54 New South Wales, Legislative Council and Legislative Assembly, Parliamentary Debates, August 27, 1895, 268.
55 New South Wales, Legislative Council and Legislative Assembly, Parliamentary Debates, August 27, 1895, 271.
56 Loan for Intercolonial Railway, LAC, RG2, Privy Council Office, series A-1-a.
57 *British North America Act,* s. 91.
58 Hansard, 1803–2005, June 10, 1870, Commons Sitting, Canada Railway Loan, Resolution, House of Commons, June 10, 1870, vol. 201, cols. 1844–53, 1844–48.
59 The Secretary of State to the Governor General, June 1, 1869, 33 Vic., Sessional Papers 13, 1870, in *Report of the Commissioners of the Intercolonial Railway.*
60 "The Law Officers of the Crown to Earl Granville," June 28, 1869, 33 Vic., Sessional Papers 13, 1870, in *Report of the Commissioners of the Intercolonial Railway.*
61 "A Report of a Committee of the Honourable the Privy Council Approved by his Excellency the Governor General in Council on the 29 March 1869," 33 Vic., Sessional Papers 13, 1870, in *Report of the Commissioners of the Intercolonial Railway.*
62 "A Report of a Committee of the Honourable the Privy Council Approved by his Excellency the Governor General in Council on the 29 March 1869," 33 Vic., Sessional Papers 13, 1870, in *Report of the Commissioners of the Intercolonial Railway.*
63 Cited in Debate on Canada Railway Loan, House of Commons, Parliamentary Debate, June 10, 1870, Hansard, column 1849.
64 Some of these complicated credit/debt mechanisms and processes were thrown into sharp relief by the Panic of 1866, a financial downturn triggered by the collapse of a major London bank. Leading to soaring interest rates, it also shaped British imperial financing. See Mills, *A Paper Read before the Economic Section;*

Bagehot, "What a Panic Is"; Schneider, "The Politics of Last Resort"; and Flandreau and Ugolini, "The Crisis of 1866," 89.

65 "Copy of a Minute of the Queen's Privy Council," June 18, 1869, 33 Vic., Sessional Papers 13, 1870, in *Report of the Commissioners of the Intercolonial Railway.*

66 "Canada, Minute of the Treasury Board, adopted August 11, 1869," 33 Vic., Sessional Papers 17–18, 1870, in *Report of the Commissioners of the Intercolonial Railway.*

67 "Recommending that Interest due by Dominion of Canada in London on 1 January 1869," LAC, RG2, Privy Council Office, series A-1-a.

68 Debate on the Canada Railway Loan, House of Commons, Parliamentary Debate, June 10, 1870, column 1849, https://hansard.parliament.uk/Commons/1870-06-10/debates/10c6d341-6e91-4105-80ca-32f7a1649bcc/CanadaRailwayLoan.

69 Canada, "No. 2, of the Canadian Debt Redeemed since 1st July, 1868, and of the Proceeds of Other Loans and Special Deposits Available for That Purpose," in *Sessional Papers,* no. 13 (1870), 24–26.

70 Canada, "Copy of a Report of a Committee of the Honorable the Privy Council, Approved by His Excellency the Governor General in Council on the 27th August, 1868," in *Sessional Papers,* no. 13 (1870), 28.

71 Much scholarship focuses on the Hudson's Bay Company, especially after the Hudson's Bay Archive moved to Manitoba in 1973 and subsequently opened to the public in 1975. For select works on the company, see Galbraith, *The Hudson's Bay Company*; Marsden and Galois, "The Tsimshian"; Henday and Belyea, *A Year Inland*; Deidre Simmons, *Keepers of the Record*; Cavanagh, "A Company with Sovereignty"; Binnema, *Enlightened Zeal*; and Adele Perry, "Designing Dispossession."

72 "William Land Credit and Debt Account," 1869, 27, Eagle Nest Indigenous debts, 1869–70, Archives of Manitoba, Eagle Nest accounts, B.58/d/8 microfilm 1M464.

73 Gettler, *Colonialism's Currency,* 99.

74 Watkins, "Taxes 1670–1960," 164.

75 Galbraith, "The Hudson's Bay Land Controversy," 469.

76 Mr. Thomas Baring and Others to the Duke of Newcastle, London, July 5, 1862, in *Correspondence between Her Majesty's Government and the Hudson's Bay Company* (London: Henry Kent Causton and Son, 1869), 5–6.

77 "Copy of a Report of a Committee of the Honourable the Executive Council, approved by His Excellency the Governor General in Council, on the 18th February, 1864," in 27 Vic., *Sessional Papers* 4, 2nd Sess., 8th Parl., Province of Canada, 1864; T. Fredk Elliot, Downing Street, to H.H. Berens, November 21, 1862, and C. Fortescue, Downing Street, to H.H. Berens, May 1, 1863, in *Correspondence between Her Majesty's,* 9–10.

78 H.H. Berens, Hudson's Bay House, London, to the Duke of Newcastle, August 11, 1862, in *Correspondence between Her Majesty's,* 7.

79 Galbraith, "The Hudson's Bay Land Controversy," 459.

80 W. Atherton and Roundell Palmer, Temple, to the Duke of Newcastle, July 9, 1863, in *Correspondence between Her Majesty's,* 19–20. See also Tough, "'A Great Inheritance.'"

81 Edmund Head, Hudson's Bay House, London, to Frederic Rogers November 11, 1863, in *Correspondence between Her Majesty's*, 28.
82 C. Fortescue, Downing Street, to Edmund Head, March 11, 1864, in *Correspondence between Her Majesty's*, 32.
83 Fortescue to Head, March 11, 1864, 33.
84 Fortescue to Head, March 11, 1864, 34.
85 Fortescue to Head, March 11, 1864, 36.
86 Luby, *Dammed*.
87 Edmund Head, Hudson's Bay House, London, to Chichester Fortescue, April 13, 1864, in *Correspondence between Her Majesty's*, 58, 55.
88 Kimberley, Hudson's Bay House, London, to C.B. Adderley, Colonial Office, October 27, 1868, in *Correspondence between Her Majesty's*, 154.
89 Kimberley to Adderley, October 27, 1868, 157.
90 *An Act for Enabling Her Majesty to Accept a Surrender Upon Terms of the Lands*.
91 *Rupert's Land and the North-Western Territory Order*, R.S.C. 1985, App II, no. 9, para. 6.
92 Col. Sec. no. 226, August 19, 1870, Rupert's Land Loan Act, LAC, RG2, Privy Council Office, series A-1-a.
93 *Journals of the House of Commons of Canada*, vol. 2 (May 28, 1869), 145.
94 Debate on Canada (Rupert's Land) Loan Bill, House of Commons, Parliamentary Debates, August 5, 1869, Hansard, c. 1329.
95 Debate on Canada (Rupert's Land) Loan Bill, August 5, 1869, c. 1332.
96 *Journals of the House of Commons of Canada* (May 28, 1869), 147.
97 Tough, "'A Great Inheritance,'" 30.
98 Debate on Canada (Rupert's Land) Loan Bill, August 5, 1869, c. 1328.
99 *An Act for Authorizing a Guarantee of a Loan to be Raised by Canada for a payment in respect of the Transfer of Rupert's Land*, 33 Vic., c. 101.
100 *An Act for Authorizing a Guarantee*, s. 4.
101 Debate on Canada (Rupert's Land) Loan Bill, August 5, 1869, c. 1330.
102 Hodgins and Edwards, "Federalism and the Politics of Ontario," 81.
103 Debate on Treaty of Washington – Canada, Guarantee Loan, £2,500,000, House of Commons, Parliamentary Debates, April 29, 1872, Hansard, c. 1934.
104 Debate on Treaty of Washington – Canada, Guarantee Loan, £2,500,000, House of Commons, Parliamentary Debates, April 29, 1872, Hansard, c. 1935.
105 Debate on Canada, Guarantee Loan, £2,500,000, House of Lords, Debates, July 8, 1873, Hansard, c. 6.
106 *A Bill to Authorise the Commissioners of Her Majesty's Treasury to Guarantee the Payment of Loan to be Raised by the Government of Canada for the Construction of Public Works in that Country, and to Repeal the Canada Defences Loan Act, 1870*, 36 Vic., c.45.
107 *Canada (Public Works) Loan Act of 1873*, 36 Vic., c. 45.
108 *Canada (Public Works) Loan Act of 1873*, 36 Vic., c. 45, s. 3.
109 Loans falling due prior to 1903/06/30 – currency loan 83 [1883] I.C.R. [Intercolonial Railway] loan guaranteed I.C.R. [Intercolonial Railway] guaranteed Ruperts Land

and loan of 1874, Min [Minister of] Finance authorized to make arrangements, 5, LAC, RG2, Privy Council Office, series A-1-a. For Order-in-Council see vol. 850, Access Code 90.

110 Loans falling due prior to 1903/06/30.

111 Loans falling due prior to 1903/06/30.

112 Notions of "whiteness" changed drastically during the late nineteenth century, when eastern Europeans began to settle the west. Now, "Britishness," as opposed to "whiteness," shaped discourses of supremacy. Carter, *Imperial Plots*, 310.

113 For westward expansion and genocide, see Daschuk, *Clearing the Plains*; Carter, *Lost Harvests;* Adele Perry, *On the Edge of Empire*; Wildcat, "Fearing Social and Cultural Death"; Mosby, "Administering Colonial Science"; Carleton, "'I Don't Need Any More Education'"; and Chester Martin, *Dominion Lands Policy.*

114 "From Scrip to Road Allowances: Canada's Complicated History with the Métis," *CBC Unreserved,* March 28, 2019, https://www.cbc.ca/radio/unreserved/from-scrip-to-road-allowances-canada-s-complicated-history-with-the-m%C3%A9tis-1.5100375. This is an interview with Métis historian Jesse Thistle. Thistle is working on much-needed research into the many historical legacies of the appropriation of Métis land.

115 Morrison, "The Background," 59.

116 A precursor to the Royal Canadian Mounted Police, these "red coats" highlighted the mixture of military population suppression and modern policing in settler colonies. The force was modelled on the paramilitary Irish Constabulary. For more details, see Marquis, "The 'Irish Model.'"

117 de Finney, "Rekinning," 475. Current Canadian discourses about the centrality of rural life commonly include "a surge of interest in homesteading" as a "response to the intersecting pressures of intensifying urbanization, a sweeping mental health crisis, anthropogenic climate devastation, and, most recently, the COVID-19 pandemic," but they can also echo the genocidal machinery of colonization. de Finney, "Rekinning," 478.

118 Dominion of Canada, House of Commons, Parliamentary Debates, April 27, 1882, 1186.

119 For an overview on the debates about the Indian Act and the implications of the act, see Kelm and Smith, *Talking Back*.

Conclusion

1 Rebecca Hall, *Wake,* 9.

2 For a discussion about the colonial archives, see Stoler, "Colonial Archives"; Stoler, *Along the Archival Grain*; and Gupta, "Writing Sex and Sexuality."

3 Countless examples of Western dystopian fiction simply apply the historical and contemporary circumstances of Black, Indigenous, and racialized people to white people. After the ghoulish decision to overturn *Roe v Wade,* Margaret Atwood weighed in that forced birth was, in fact, slavery. Her novel *The Handmaid's Tale,*

popularized recently in a successful television series, simply portrays white women as enduring what Black women endure, with limited access to prenatal care. Mahomes, "'You Should Have Said Something.'" See also Maynard and Simpson, *Rehearsals for Living*, 9.

4 See Rob Nixon's concept of "slow violence." Nixon, *Slow Violence*.

5 Ishiguro, "Growing Up," 16.

6 Indigenous and Black scholars, philosophers, and artists have done so much work on both what Grace Dillon describes as "Indigenous Futurism" and the movement of Afrofuturism. Dillon, "Indigenous Futurisms."

7 See Simmons, "Settler Atmospherics."

8 Unexpected though it may be, nothing is entirely unexpected to a historian. Labour reforms and a surge in unions followed in the wake of the 1918 H1N1 pandemic. Jones, *Influenza 1918*.

9 See Yazzie and Baldy, "Introduction."

10 Tuck and Yang, "Decolonization Is Not a Metaphor," 7.

11 Goeman, "Land as Life," 75, 87.

12 King, *The Inconvenient Indian*, 120.

13 Vowel, *Indigenous Writes*, 131.

14 A recent example of land rematriation is Quebec resident Grégoire Gollin's ecological gift of sixty hectares to Kanesatake. Deer, "Developer Offers."

15 *United Nations Declaration on the Rights of Indigenous Peoples Act*, S.C. 2021, c. 14, https://laws-lois.justice.gc.ca/eng/acts/U-2.2/.

16 Yarr, "Mill River Owner."

17 Ross, "Mill River Appeal."

18 "Supreme Court of Canada Will Not Hear."

19 Interview with Lennox Island members, Angela Tozer, November 27, 2019.

20 Pasternak, "Canada Is a Bad Company," 72.

21 Tuck et al., "Visiting as an Indigenous Feminist Practice," 144.

22 Tuck et al., "Visiting as an Indigenous Feminist Practicc," 153.

23 Tuck et al., "Visiting as an Indigenous Feminist Practice," 150.

24 Conerly, "Will Greece Default on Its Debt?" Defaulting on a public debt is a turn away from a global capitalist economy. When Alberta and Greece did it, mechanisms and policies reached out to bring them back into the capitalist fold. For the history of Alberta's default in 1936, see Ascah, *Politics and Public Debt*. For Greece, see Daniel and Nam, "The Greek Debt Crisis."

25 For an important discussion on degrowth economics and environment see Saito, *Marx in the Anthropocene*, 216–44.

Bibliography

Legislation

An Act for Authorizing a Guarantee of a Loan to be Raised by Canada for a payment in respect of the Transfer of Rupert's Land, 33 Vic., c. 101.

An Act for Enabling Her Majesty to Accept a Surrender Upon Terms of the Lands, Privileges, and Rights of 'The Governor and Company of Adventures of England Trading into Hudson's Bay,' and for Admitting the Same into the Dominion of Canada, 31 Vic., c. 105.

An Act for Guaranteeing the Payment of the Interest on a Loan of One Million Five Hundred Thousand Pounds to be Raised by the Province of Canada, 5 & 6 Vic., c.118, August 12, 1842.

An Act For Making More Effectual Provision for the Government of the Province of Quebec, in North America, and to Make Further Provision for the Government of the Said Province, 40 Geo. III, c. 1.

An Act for rendering valid, conveyances of lands and other immoveable property held in free and common soccage within the Province of Lower Canada, and for other purposes therein mentioned, 9 & 10 Geo. IV, c. 77.

An Act for the Purchase of Lands on Behalf of the Government of Prince Edward Island, and to Regulate the Sale and Management Thereof, and for Other Purposes Therein Mentioned, S.P.E.I. 1853, 16 Vic., c. 18, amended 20 Vic., c. 20, and 23 Vic., c. 21; amount of loan extended by 23 Vic., c. 25.

An Act for the Union of Canada, Nova Scotia, and New Brunswick, Together with the Act Authorising a Loan for the Halifax and Quebec Railway. Halifax: Compton, 1867.

An Act in Addition to and In Further Amendment of the Land Purchase Act, R.S.P.E.I 1866, 29 Vic., c.19.

An Act respecting the construction of the Intercolonial Railway, 31 Vic., c. 13.

An Act Respecting the Provincial Debt guaranteed by the Imperial Government, 22 Vic., c. 1.

An Act to Assist Leaseholders in the Purchase of the Fee-Simple of their Farms, R.S.P.E.I 1865, 28 Vic., c. 5.

An Act to Authorise a Loan for the Use of this Island, and Also to Make Provisions Respecting the Payment of Treasury Bonds and Warrants and the Interest Thereon, 14th Vic., c. 20.

An Act to Authorise the Construction of a Railroad through Prince Edward Island, 34 Vic., c. 4.

An Act to Authorize the Government to Borrow A Certain Sum of Money, Upon Debenture, to be Loaned to the Welland Canal Company, 7 Geo. IV, c. 20.

An Act to authorize the Legislature of the Province of Canada to make Provision concerning the Clergy Reserves in that Province, and the Proceeds thereof, 16 Vic., c. 21.

An Act to Empower His Majesty to Erect South Australia Into a British Province or Provinces, and to Provide for the Colonization and Government Thereof, 4 & 5 William, c. 95.

An Act to facilitate the negotiation of a Loan in England, and for other purposes therein mentioned, 4 & 5 Vic., c. 33.

An Act to Grant a Further Loan to the Welland Canal Company, and to Regulate Their Further Operations, 11 Geo. IV, c. 11.

An Act to Incorporate, Certain Persons Therein Mentioned Under the Style of the Welland Canal Company, 4 Geo. IV, c. 17.

An Act to provide for the better Government of the province of South Australia, 5 & 6 Vic., c. 61.

An act to provide for the disposal of the public lands in Upper Canada, and for other purposes therein mentioned. London: House of Commons, 1840.

An Act to Provide for the Payment of Certain Debentures, 27 Vic., c. 33.

An Act to Repeal Certain Parts of an Act, Passed in the Fourteenth Year of His Majesty's Reign, intitled, An Act for Making More Effectual Provision For the Government of the Province of Quebec, in North America, 31 Geo. III, c. 31, s. XXXV.

British North America Act, 1867, 30–31 Vic., c. 3. http://www.legislation.gov.uk/ukpga/1867/3/pdfs/ukpga_18670003_en.pdf.

Canada (Public Works) Loan Act of 1873, 36 Vic., c. 45.

Rupert's Land and the North-Western Territory Order, R.S.C. 1985, App II, no. 9.

South Australia Colonization Act, 4 & 5 Will. IV, c. 95.

United Nations Declaration on the Rights of Indigenous Peoples Act, S.C. 2021, c. 14, https://laws-lois.justice.gc.ca/eng/acts/U-2.2/.

Government Documents

"Appendix 13: Bannerman Lieut. Governor, Government House P.E. Island, to the Right Honourable Earl Grey Etc., Etc., November 15, 1851." In *Journal of the Legislative Council of Prince Edward Island.* Charlottetown: John Ings, 1853.

"Bannerman, Government House, P.E. Island, to Grey, February 12, 1852." In *Journal of the Legislative Council of Prince Edward Island.* Charlottetown: John Ings, 1853, Appendix 13.

Canada. *A Bill Intitled an Act for Authorizing a Guarantee of Interest on a Loan to be by Canada Towards the Construction of a Railway Connecting Quebec and Halifax.* London: HMSO, 1867.

"Dispatch to Right Hon Lord Grey, from Lt Gov Bannerman, Government House P.E. Island, November 15, 1851." In *Journal of the Legislative Council of Prince Edward Island.* Charlottetown: John Ings, 1853, Appendix 13.

House of Commons. "Appendix B: Copies of Two Dispatches, Dated 12 March 1827, and 18 February 1828 From the Lieutenant Governor of Upper Canada to the Secretary of State for the Colonies, Upon the Subject of the Welland Canal." In *Journals of the House of Commons*, vol. 83 (June 17, 1828), 660–714.

–. *A Bill to Guarantee a Loan for the Service of Prince Edward Island.* 21 Vic. May 13, 1858.

–. "Canada Waste Lands Bill." March 15, 1825. In *Parliamentary Debates:* Official Report: Session of February 3–April 18, 1825. Vol. 12. London: Hansard, 1825.

–. *Copies of the Regulations Lately Adopted in the Canadas for Granting Waste Lands in These Provinces, and Respecting the Clergy Reserved Lands in Canada.* London: House of Commons, 1837.

–. "Copy of a Dispatch from the Right Hon. C. Poulett Thomson to Lord John Russell, Government House, Montreal, June 27, 1840." In *Correspondence Relative to the Affairs of Canada, 1841,* 1–4. London: William Clowes and Sons, 1841.

–. *Correspondence Relative to the Affairs of Canada, 1841.* London: William Clowes and Sons, 1841.

–. "Papers on the Subject of Affording the Imperial Guarantee to a Loan for the Service of Prince Edward Island." In *Accounts and Papers,* Vol. 9, December 3, 1857–August 2, 1858, iii–31.

–. *Report from the Select Committee on the Disposal of Lands in the British Colonies Together with Minutes of Evidence and Appendix.* London: House of Lords, 1836.

In the Privy Council, in the Matter of Arbitration and Award under the 142nd Section of the British North America Act, 1867. Between the Province of Ontario, in the Dominion of Canada, and the Province of Quebec, in the Dominion of Canada. Toronto: Hunter Rose, 1877. https://www.canadiana.ca/view/oocihm.58934/1.

Legislative Assembly of the Province of Canada. "Appendix EEE: Report on the Affairs of the Indians in Canada." In *Journals of the Legislative Assembly of the Province of Canada ... 28th Day of November, 1844, to the 29th Day of March, 1845.* Montreal: R. Campbell, 1845.

The Parliamentary Remembrancer. London: Office of the Parliamentary Rememberancer, 1858.

Parliamentary Reporter, or, Debates and Proceedings of the House of Assembly of Prince Edward Island, for the Year 1867, Being the First Session of the Twenty-Third General Assembly. Charlottetown: J. Ings, 1867.

Poor Law Commissioners' Report of 1834. London: HMSO, 1905.

The Report and Dispatches of the Earl of Durham, Her Majesty's High Commissioner and Governor-General of British North America. London: Ridgways, 1839.

Report of the Commissioners of the Intercolonial Railway. Ottawa: L.B. Taylor, 1870.

Other Sources

Abbott, Arthur William. *A Short History of the Crown Agents and Their Office*. London: Eyre and Spottiswoode, 1959.

Adams, Howard. *Prison of Grass: Canada from the Native Point of View*. Toronto: New Press, 1975.

Aitken, Hugh G.J. "The Family Compact and the Welland Canal Company." *Canadian Journal of Economics and Political Science/Revue canadienne d'économique et science politique* 18, 1 (1952): 63–76.

–. "Financing the Welland Canal: An Episode in the History of the St. Lawrence Waterway." *Business History Review* 26, 3 (1952): 135–64.

Ajzenstat, Janet, ed. *Canada's Founding Debates*. Toronto: University of Toronto Press, 2003.

Angus, James T. *Respectable Ditch: A History of the Trent-Severn Waterway, 1833–1920*. Montreal and Kingston: McGill-Queen's University Press, 1988.

Ankli, Robert E. "The Reciprocity Treaty of 1854." *Canadian Journal of Economics/Revue canadienne d'economique* 4, 1 (1971): 1–20.

Appadurai, Arjun. "Afterword: The Dreamwork of Capitalism." *Comparative Studies of South Asia, Africa and the Middle East* 35, 3 (2015): 481–85.

Ascah, Robert. *Politics and Public Debt: The Dominion, the Banks and Alberta's Social Credit*. Edmonton: University of Alberta Press, 1999.

Attard, Bernard. "The London Stock Exchange and the Colonial Market: The City, Internationalisation, and Power." In *The Foundations of Worldwide Economic Integration: Power, Institutions, and Global Markets, 1850–1930*, ed. Christof Dejung and Niels P. Petersson, 89–111. Cambridge: Cambridge University Press, 2013.

–. "Making a Market: The Jobbers of the London Stock Exchange, 1800–1986." *Financial History Review* 7, 1 (2000): 5–24.

Atwood, Margaret. *Payback: Debt and the Shadow Side of Wealth*. CBC Massey Lectures Series. Toronto: Anansi, 2008.

Augustine, Patrick J. "The Significance of Place in Textual and Geographical Representation: The Mi'kmaq on Lennox Island, Prince Edward Island, and the Penobscot on Indian Island." Master's thesis, University of Prince Edward Island, 2009.

Bagehot, Walter. "What a Panic Is and How It Might Be Mitigated." *Economist*, May 12, 1866.

Baldwin, Andrew. "Whiteness and Futurity: Towards a Research Agenda." *Progress in Human Geography* 36, 2 (2012): 172–87.

Baldwin, Andrew, Laura Cameron, and Audrey Kobayashi, eds. *Rethinking the Great White North: Race, Nature and the Historical Geographies of Whiteness in Canada*. Vancouver: UBC Press, 2011.

Ballantyne, Tony. "Remaking the Empire from Newgate: Wakefield's A Letter from Sydney." In *Ten Books That Shaped the British Empire: Creating an Imperial Commons*, ed. Isabel Hofmeyr and Antoinette Burton, 29–49. Durham, NC: Duke University Press, 2014.

–. "The Theory and Practice of Empire Building: Edward Gibbon Wakefield and 'Systematic Colonization.'" In *The Routledge History of Western Empires*, ed. Robert Aldrich and Kirsten McKenzie, 89–101. London: Routledge, 2014.

Bannister, Jerry. "Settler Colonialism and the Future of Canadian History." *Acadiensis Blog*, August 30, 2017. https://acadiensis.wordpress.com/2017/08/30/settler-colonialism-and-the-future-of-canadian-history-2/.

Barker, Adam J. "The Contemporary Reality of Canadian Imperialism: Settler Colonialism and the Hybrid Colonial State." *American Indian Quarterly* 33, 3 (2009): 325–51.

Barker, Joanne. *Red Scare: The State's Indigenous Terrorist*. Oakland: University of California Press, 2021.

Baskerville, Peter A. *Sites of Power: A Concise History of Ontario*. Oxford: Oxford University Press, 2005.

Battiste, Marie, ed. *Living Treaties: Narrating Mi'kmaw Treaty Relations.* Sydney, NS: Cape Breton University Press, 2016.

–. "Narrating Mi'kmaw Treaties: Linking the Past to the Future." In *Living Treaties: Narrating Mi'kmaw Treaty Relations*, ed. Marie Battiste, 1–15. Sydney, NS: Cape Breton University Press, 2016.

Bayly, C.A. *Imperial Meridian: The British Empire and the World, 1780–1830*. London: Longman, 1989.

Bear, Laura, Ritu Birla, and Stine Simonsen Puri. "Speculation: Futures and Capitalism in India." *Comparative Studies of South Asia, Africa and the Middle East* 35, 3 (2015): 387–91.

Bear Nicholas, Andrea. "Mascarene's Treaty of 1725." *University of New Brunswick Law Journal* 43 (1994): 3–18.

–. "Settler Imperialism and the Dispossession of the Maliseet." In *Shaping an Agenda for Atlantic Canada*, ed. John Reid and Donald Savoie, 21–57 (Halifax: Fernwood, 2011).

Belich, James. *Making Peoples: A History of the New Zealanders, from Polynesian Settlement to the End of the Nineteenth Century*. Honolulu: University of Hawai'i Press, 1996.

–. *Replenishing the Earth: The Settler Revolution and the Rise of the Anglo-World, 1783–1939.* Oxford: Oxford University Press, 2009.

Bell, Duncan. "John Stuart Mill on Colonies." *Political Theory* 38, 1 (2010): 34–64.

–. *Reordering the World: Essays on Liberalism and Empire*. Princeton, NJ: Princeton University Press, 2016.

Benton, Lauren A., and Lisa Ford. *Rage for Order: The British Empire and the Origins of International Law, 1800–1850*. Cambridge, MA: Harvard University Press, 2016.

Bhambra, Gurminder, and Julia McClure, eds. *Imperial Inequalities: The Politics of Economic Governance across European Empires*. Manchester: Manchester University Press, 2022.

Bhandar, Brenna. *Colonial Lives of Property: Law, Land, and Racial Regimes of Ownership*. Durham, NC: Duke University Press, 2018.

Binnema, Ted. *Enlightened Zeal: The Hudson's Bay Company and Scientific Networks, 1670–1870.* Toronto: University of Toronto Press, 2014.

Binnema, Theodore, and Kevin Hutchings. "The Emigrant and the Noble Savage: Sir Francis Bond Head's Romantic Approach to Aboriginal Policy in Upper Canada, 1836–1838." *Journal of Canadian Studies* 39, 1 (2004): 115–38.

Birla, Ritu. *Stages of Capital: Law, Culture, and Market Governance in Late Colonial India.* Durham, NC: Duke University Press, 2009.

Bittermann, Rusty. "Mi'kmaq Land Claims and the Escheat Movement in Prince Edward Island." *University of New Brunswick Law Journal* 55 (2006): 172–76.

–. *Rural Protest on Prince Edward Island: From British Colonization to the Escheat Movement*. Toronto: University of Toronto Press, 2006.

–. *A Sailor's Hope: The Life and Times of William Cooper Agrarian Radical in an Age of Revolutions*. Montreal and Kingston: McGill-Queen's University Press, 2010.

Bittermann, Rusty, and Margaret McCallum. *Lady Landlords of Prince Edward Island: Imperial Dreams and the Defence of Property*. Montreal and Kingston: McGill-Queen's University Press, 2014.

–. "The Pursuit of Gentility in an Age of Revolution: The Family of Jonathan Worrell." *Acadiensis* 43, 2 (2014): 31–56.

–. "Upholding the Land Legislation of a Communistic and Socialist Assembly: The Benefits of Confederation for Prince Edward Island." *Canadian Historical Review* 87, 1 (2006): 1–28.

Blaakman, Michael A. "'Haughty Republicans,' Native Land, and the Promise of Preemption." *William and Mary Quarterly* 78, 2 (2021): 243–50.

Black, R.D. Collison. *Economic Thought and the Irish Question, 1817–1870.* Cambridge: Cambridge University Press, 1960.

Bolger, Francis W.P. *Prince Edward Island and Confederation, 1863–1873.* Charlottetown: St. Dunstan's University Press, 1964.

Borrows, John. "Constitutional Law from a First Nation Perspective: Self-Government and the Royal Proclamation." *UBC Law Review* 28 (1994): 1–47.

–. "Wampum at Niagara: The Royal Proclamation, Canadian Legal History, and Self-Government." In *Aboriginal and Treaty Rights in Canada: Essays on Law, Equity, and Respect for Difference,* ed. Michael Asch, 155–72. Vancouver: UBC Press, 1997.

–. "With or Without You: First Nations Law (in Canada)." *McGill Law Journal* 41, 3 (1995): 629–65.

Bowen, H.V. *The Business of Empire: The East India Company and Imperial Britain, 1756–1833*. Cambridge: Cambridge University Press, 2006.

Brantlinger, Patrick. *Fictions of State: Culture and Credit in Britain, 1694–1994*. Ithaca, NY: Cornell University Press, 1996.

Brewer, John. *The Sinews of Power: War, Money and the English State, 1688–1783*. London: Unwin Hyman, 1989.

Brierley, J.E.C. "The Co-Existence of Legal Systems in Quebec: 'Free and Common Socage' in Canada's 'pays de droit civil.'" *Les Cahiers de droit* 20, 1–2 (1979): 277–87.

Brouillet, Eugénie, Alain-G. Gagnon, and Guy Laforest, eds. *The Québec Conference of 1864: Understanding the Emergence of the Canadian Federation*. Montreal and Kingston: McGill-Queen's University Press, 2018.

Brownlie, Robin, and Mary-Ellen Kelm. "Desperately Seeking Absolution: Native Agency as Colonialist Alibi?" *Canadian Historical Review* 75, 4 (1994): 543–56.

Bryant, Rachel, Mercedes Peters, and Angela Tozer. "In Wilderness, in Community: Mentorship, Academia, and 'Emerging' as a Scholar in Settler Colonial Institutions." *Settler Colonial Studies* (2024). https://doi.org/10.1080/2201473X.2024.2430081.

Buckner, Phillip. "Beware the Canadian Wolf: The Maritimes and Confederation." *Acadiensis* 46, 2 (2017): 177–95.

Bulushi, Yousuf Al-. "Thinking Racial Capitalism and Black Radicalism From Africa: An Intellectual Geography of Cedric Robinson's World-System." *Geoforum* 132 (2022): 252–62.

Bumsted, J.M. *Land, Settlement, and Politics on Eighteenth-Century Prince Edward Island.* Montreal and Kingston: McGill-Queen's University Press, 1987.

–. "The Origins of the Land Question on Prince Edward Island, 1767–1805." *Acadiensis* 11, 1 (1981): 43–56.

Burroughs, Peter. "Parliamentary Radicals and the Reduction of Imperial Expenditure in British North America, 1827–1834." *Historical Journal* 11, 3 (1968): 446–61.

Butler, Octavia E. *Kindred*. New York: Pocket Books, 1981.

Byrd, Jodi A. *The Transit of Empire: Indigenous Critiques of Colonialism*. Minneapolis: University of Minnesota Press, 2011.

Cain, P.J., and A.G. Hopkins. *British Imperialism: Innovation and Expansion, 1688–1914*. London: Longman, 1993.

–. "Gentlemanly Capitalism and British Expansion Overseas I: The Old Colonial System, 1688–1850." *Economic History Review* 39, 4 (1986): 501–25.

Campbell, Duncan. *History of Prince Edward Island*. Charlottetown: Bremner Brothers, 1875.

Carleton, Sean. "'I Don't Need Any More Education': Senator Lynn Beyak, Residential School Denialism, and Attacks on Truth and Reconciliation in Canada." *Settler Colonial Studies* 11, 4 (2021): 466–86.

Carruthers, Bruce, and Sarah Babb. "The Color of Money and the Nature of Value: Greenbacks and Gold in Postbellum America." *American Journal of Sociology* 101, 6 (1996): 1556–91.

Carruthers, Bruce, and Bruce G. Espeland. "Accounting for Rationality: Double-Entry Bookkeeping and the Rhetoric of Economic Rationality." *American Journal of Sociology* 97, 1 (1991): 31–69.

Carter, Sarah. *Imperial Plots: Women, Land, and the Spadework of British Colonialism on the Canadian Prairies*. Winnipeg: University of Manitoba Press, 2016.

–. *Lost Harvests: Prairie Indian Reserve Farmers and Government Policy*. Montreal and Kingston: McGill-Queen's University Press, 2019.

Cavanagh, Edward. "A Company with Sovereignty and Subjects of Its Own? The Case of the Hudson's Bay Company, 1670–1763." *Canadian Journal of Law and Society/La Revue Canadienne Droit et Société* 26, 1 (2011): 25–50.

Chatterjee, Partha. "The Curious Career of Liberalism in India." *Modern Intellectual History* 8, 3 (2011): 687–96.

Churchman, Nancy. *David Ricardo on Public Debt*. Basingstoke, UK: Palgrave Macmillan, 2001.

Chute, Sarah Elizabeth. "Bound to Slavery: Economic and Biographical Connections to Atlantic Slavery between the Maritimes and West Indies after 1783." Master's thesis, University of Vermont and State Agricultural College, 2021.

Clarke, John C. *Land, Power, and Economics on the Frontier of Upper Canada*. Montreal and Kingston: McGill-Queen's University Press, 2001.

Clarke, John, and John Buffone. "Manifestations of Imperial Policy: The New South Wales System and Land Prices in Upper Canada in 1825." *Canadian Geographer/Le Géographe canadien* 40, 2 (1996): 121–36.

Clegg, John J. "Credit Market Discipline and Capitalist Slavery in Antebellum South Carolina." *Social Science History* 42, 2 (2018): 343–76.

Conerly, Bill. "Will Greece Default on Its Debt?" *Forbes*, updated February 2, 2015. https://www.forbes.com/sites/billconerly/2015/02/02/will-greece-default-on-its-debt/.

Cooper, Afua. "Acts of Resistance: Black Men and Women Engage Slavery in Upper Canada, 1793–1803." *Ontario History* 99, 1 (2007): 9–12.

Corredera, Edward Jones. *Odious Debt: Bankruptcy, International Law, and the Making of Latin America.* Oxford: Oxford University Press, 2025.

Coulthard, Glen. *Red Skin, White Masks: Rejecting the Colonial Politics of Recognition.* Minneapolis: University of Minnesota Press, 2014.

Craig, Gerald M. *Upper Canada: The Formative Years, 1784–1841*. Toronto: McClelland and Stewart, 1963.

Creighton, Donald. *The Road to Confederation: The Emergence of Canada, 1863–1867.* Westport, CT : Greenwood Press, 1976.

Cruikshank, Ken. *Close Ties: Railways, Government and the Board of Railway Commissioners, 1851–1933*. Montreal and Kingston: McGill-Queen's University Press, 1991.

–. "The People's Railway: The Intercolonial Railway and the Canadian Public Enterprise Experience," *Acadiensis* 16, 1 (1986): 78–100.

Curthoys, Ann. "The Dog That Didn't Bark: The Durham Report, Indigenous Dispossession, and Self-Government for Britain's Settler Colonies." In *Within and without the Nation: Canadian History as Transnational History,* ed. Karen Dubinsky, Adele Perry, and Henry Yu, 25–48. Toronto: University of Toronto Press, 2015.

Curtis, Bruce. "Colonization, Education, and the Formation of Moral Character: Edward Gibbon Wakefield's *A Letter from Sydney*." *Historical Studies in Education/Revue d'histoire de l'éducation* 31, 2 (Fall 2019): 27–47.

da Silva, Denise Ferreira. *Unpayable Debt*. London: Sternberg Press, 2022.

–. "Unpayable Debt: Reading Scenes of Value Against the Arrow of Time." In *The Documenta 14 Reader,* ed. Quinn Latimer and Adam Szymczyk, 84–112. London: Prestel Publishing, 2017.

Daniel, Betty C., and Jinwook Nam. "The Greek Debt Crisis: Excusable vs. Strategic Default." *Journal of International Economics* 138 (2022): 103632. https://doi.org/10.1016/j.jinteco.2022.103632.

Darwin, John. *The Empire Project: The Rise and Fall of the British World-System, 1830–1970*. Cambridge: Cambridge University Press, 2009.

Daschuk, James William. *Clearing the Plains: Disease, Politics of Starvation, and the Loss of Aboriginal Life*. Regina: University of Regina Press, 2013.

Davis, David Brion. *Slavery and Human Progress*. New York: Oxford University Press, 1984.

Davis, Lance, and Robert Huttenback. *Mammon and the Pursuit of Empire: The British Political Economy of British Imperialism, 1860–1912*. Cambridge: Cambridge University Press, 1986.

Dawson, Frank G. *The First Latin American Debt Crisis: The City of London and the 1822–25 Loan Bubble.* New Haven: Yale University Press, 1990.

Day, Iyko. *Alien Capital: Asian Racialization and the Logic of Settler Colonial Capitalism.* Durham, NC: Duke University Press, 2016.

De Costa, Ravi. "Identity, Authority, and the Moral Worlds of Indigenous Petitions." *Comparative Studies in Society and History* 48, 3 (2006): 669–98.

de Finney, Sandrina. "Rekinning the Homeland: Rurality, Gender-Based Genocide, and Indigenous Sovereignty in Colonial Canada." *Journal of Rural Studies* 95 (2022): 475–81.

de Silva, K.M. "The Third Earl Grey and the Maintenance of an Imperial Policy on the Sale of Crown Lands in Ceylon, c. 1832–1852: Some Influences of Edward Gibbon Wakefield's Doctrines in a Tropical Colony." *Journal of Asian Studies* 27, 1 (1967): 5–20.

de Soto, Hernando. *The Mystery of Capital: Why Capitalism Triumphs in the West and Fails Everywhere Else*. New York: Bantam Press, 2000.

Dechêne, Louise. "Les entreprises de William Price, 1810–1850." *Histoire Sociale/Social History* 1, 1 (1968): 16–52.

Deer, Ka'nhehsí:io. "Developer Offers to Give Land Back to First Nation Where Oka Crisis Happened." *CBC News,* July 11, 2019. https://www.cbc.ca/news/indigenous/kanesatake-pines-gregoire-gollin-1.5204242.

Den Otter, A.A. *Civilizing the West: The Galts and the Development of Western Canada*. Edmonton: University of Alberta Press, 1982.

–. *The Philosophy of Railways: The Transcontinental Railway Idea in British North America.* Toronto: University of Toronto Press, 1997.

Dickson, P.G.M. *The Financial Revolution in England: A Study in the Development of Public Credit, 1688–1756*. London: Routledge, 2016.

Dillon, Grace L. "Indigenous Futurisms, Bimaashi Biidaas Mose, Flying and Walking towards You." *Extrapolation* 57, 1–2 (2016): 1–6.

Downey, Allan. *The Creator's Game: Lacrosse, Identity, and Indigenous Nationhood*. Vancouver: UBC Press, 2018.

Drayton, Richard. *Nature's Government: Science, Imperial Britain, and the "Improvement" of the World*. New Haven: Yale University Press, 2000.

Drescher, Seymour. *Econocide: British Slavery in the Era of Abolition*. Chapel Hill: University of North Carolina Press, 2010.

Dupuy, Alex. *Haiti: From Revolutionary Slaves to Powerless Citizens: Essays on the Politics and Economics of Underdevelopment, 1804–2013*. New York: Routledge, 2014.

Dyer, Richard. *White*. New York: Routledge, 1997.

Fanon, Frantz. *Black Skin, White Masks.* Translated by Richard Philcox. New York: Grove Press, 2008.

–. *The Wretched of the Earth*. Translated by Richard Philcox. New York: Grove Press, 2004.

Fenn, Charles. *A Compendium of the English and Foreign Funds, and the Principal Joint Stock Companies*. London: Effingham Wilson, Royal Exchange, 1874.

Fenn, Elizabeth A. "Biological Warfare in Eighteenth-Century North America: Beyond Jeffery Amherst." *Journal of American History* 86, 4 (2000): 1552–80.

Fingard, Judith. "The New England Company and the New Brunswick Indians, 1786–1826: A Comment on the Colonial Perversion of British Benevolence." *Acadiensis* 1, 2 (1972): 29–42.

Flandreau, Marc. *Anthropologists in the Stock Exchange: A Financial History of Victorian Science*. Chicago: University of Chicago Press, 2016.

Flandreau, Marc, and Stefano Ugolini. "The Crisis of 1866." In *British Financial Crises since 1825,* ed. Nicholas Dimsdale and Anthony Hotson, 76–92. Oxford: Oxford University Press, 2014.

Galbraith, John S. *The Hudson's Bay Company as an Imperial Factor, 1821–1869*. Berkeley: University of California Press, 1957.

–. "The Hudson's Bay Land Controversy, 1863–1869." *Mississippi Valley Historical Review* 36, 3 (1949): 457–78.

Gates, Lillian F. *Land Policies in Upper Canada*. Toronto: University of Toronto Press, 1968.

Gettler, Brian. *Colonialism's Currency: Money, State, and First Nations in Canada, 1820–1950*. Montreal and Kingston: McGill-Queen's University Press, 2020.

–. "Indigenous Policy and Silence at Confederation." Early Canadian History, June 26, 2017. https://earlycanadianhistory.ca/2017/06/26/indigenous-policy-and-silence-at-confederation/.

–. "Take and Take: The Citizen-Taxpayer and the Rise of Democratic Colonialism in Canada." *Journal of the Canadian Historical Association/Revue de la Société historique du Canada* 31, 1 (2021): 97–103.

Ghosh, R.N. "The Colonization Controversy: R.J. Wilmot-Horton and the Classical Economists." *Economica* 31, 124 (1964): 385–400.

Gidwani, V.K. "'Waste' and the Permanent Settlement in Bengal." *Economic and Political Weekly* 25 (1992): 31–46.

Gillespie, W. Irwin. *Tax, Borrow, and Spend: Financing Federal Spending in Canada, 1867–1990.* Ottawa: Carleton University Press, 1991.

Girard, Philip. "Land Law, Liberalism, and the Agrarian Ideal: British North America, 1750–1920." In *Despotic Dominion: Property Rights in British Settler Societies,* ed. John McLaren, A.R. Buck, and Nancy E. Wright, 120–43. Vancouver: UBC Press, 2005.

Glynn, Desmond. "'Exporting Outcast London': Assisted Emigration to Canada, 1886–1914." *Histoire Sociale/Social History* 15, 29 (1982): 209–38.

Goeman, Mishuana. "Land as Life: Unsettling the Logics of Containment." In *Native Studies Keywords,* ed. Stephanie Nohelani Teves, Andrea Smith, and Michelle Raheja, 71–89. Tuscon: University of Arizona Press, 2015.

Gordon, Todd, and Jeffery R. Webber. "Imperialism and Resistance: Canadian Mining Companies in Latin America," *Third World Quarterly* 29, 1 (2008): 63–87.

Graeber, David. *Debt: The First 5,000 Years*. Brooklyn: Melville House, 2014.

Graham, Ruth. "Juvenile Travellers: Priscilla Wakefield's Excursions in Empire." *Journal of Imperial and Commonwealth History* 38, 3 (2010): 373–93.

Grant, Robert. "Edward Gibbon Wakefield, England and 'Ignorant, Dirty, Unsocial ... Restless, More than Half-Savage' America." *Comparative American Studies* 1, 4 (2003): 471–87.

–. *Representations of British Emigration, Colonisation and Settlement: Imagining Empire, 1800–1860*. Hampshire: Palgrave Macmillan, 2005.

Grant, Taryn. "Vehicle Torched, Lobster Pounds Storing Mi'kmaw Catches Trashed During Night of Unrest in N.S." *CBC,* October 14, 2020. https://www.cbc.ca/news/canada/nova-scotia/mi-kmaw-lobster-fishery-unrest-1.5761468.

Greenfield, Jerome. "Financing a New Order: The Payment of Reparations by Restoration France, 1817–18." *French History* 30, 3 (2016): 376–400.

Greer, Allan. "Commons and Enclosure in the Colonization of North America." *American Historical Review* 117, 2 (2012): 365–86.

–. "Historical Roots of Canadian Democracy." *Journal of Canadian Studies* 34, 1 (1999): 7–26.

–. *The Patriots and the People: The Rebellion of 1837 in Rural Lower Canada.* Toronto: University of Toronto Press, 1993.

–. *Property and Dispossession: Natives, Empire, and Land in Early Modern North America*. Cambridge: Cambridge University Press, 2018.

Guha, Ranajit. *A Rule of Property for Bengal: An Essay on the Idea of Permanent Settlement*. New Delhi: Orient Longman, 1984.

Guidi, Marco E.L. "'My Own Utopia': The Economics of Bentham's Panopticon." *European Journal of the History of Economic Thought* 11, 3 (2004): 405–31.

Gupta, Charu. "Writing Sex and Sexuality: Archives of Colonial North India." *Journal of Women's History* 23, 4 (2011): 12–35.

Hall, Catherine. *Civilising Subjects: Metropole and Colony in the English Imagination, 1830–1867*. Chicago: University of Chicago Press, 2002.

Hall, D.G. "Sir Charles Metcalfe: Governor of Jamaica, Sept., 1839 to May, 1842." *Caribbean Quarterly* 3, 2 (1953): 90–100.

Hall, Rebecca. *Wake: The Hidden History of Women-Led Slave Revolts*. New York: Simon and Schuster, 2022.

Hammond, Bray. "The North's Empty Purse, 1861–1862." *American Historical Review* 67, 1 (1961): 1–18.

–. *Sovereignty and an Empty Purse*. Princeton: Princeton University Press, 2014.

Hannay, James. *The Life and Times of Sir Leonard Tilley: Being a Political History of New Brunswick for the Past Seventy Years.* Saint John, NB: n.p., 1897.

Harring, Sidney L. *White Man's Law: Native People in Nineteenth-Century Canadian Jurisprudence.* Toronto: University of Toronto Press, 1998.

Harrington, Jack. "Edward Gibbon Wakefield, the Liberal Political Subject and the Settler State." *Journal of Political Ideologies* 20, 3 (2015): 333–51.

Harris, Cole. *Making Native Space: Colonialism, Resistance and Reserves in British Columbia*. Vancouver: UBC Press, 2007.

Hart, Gillian. "Denaturalizing Dispossession: Critical Ethnography in the Age of Resurgent Imperialism." *Antipode* 38, 5 (2006): 977–1004.

Harvey, Caitlin P.A. "The Wealth of Knowledge: Land-Grab Universities in a British Imperial and Global Context." *Native American and Indigenous Studies* 8, 1 (2021): 97–105.

Harvey, David. "From Globalization to the New Imperialism." In *Critical Globalization Studies,* ed. Richard P. Appelbaum and William I. Robinson, 91–100. New York: Routledge, 2005.

Haynes, Frederick E. *The Reciprocity Treaty with Canada of 1854, Vol. 7, No. 6.* Baltimore: American Economic Association, 1892.

Heaman, Elsbeth. *Tax, Order, and Good Government: A New Political History of Canada, 1867–1917*. Montreal and Kingston: McGill-Queen's University Press, 2017.

Hecht, Gabrielle. *Residual Governance: How South Africa Foretells Planetary Futures.* Durham, NC: Duke University Press, 2023.

Henday, Anthony, and Barbara Belyea. *A Year Inland: The Journal of a Hudson's Bay Company Winterer.* Waterloo: Wilfrid Laurier University Press, 2000.

Henderson, Jarett. "Banishment to Bermuda: Gender, Race, Empire, Independence and the Struggle to Abolish Irresponsible Government in Lower Canada." *Histoire Sociale/Social History* 46, 92 (2013): 321–48.

–. "Remember / Resist / Redraw #04: The 1837–1838 Rebellion." *Active History*, April 28, 2017. http://activehistory.ca/2017/04/remember-resist-redraw-04-the-1837-1838-rebellion/.

Hill, Bridget. "Priscilla Wakefield as an Author of Children's Educational Books." *Women's Writing* 4, 1 (1997): 1–13.

Hill, Susan M. *The Clay We Are Made Of: Haudenosaunee Land Tenure on the Grand River*. Winnipeg: University of Manitoba Press, 2017.

History of the New England Company, from Its Incorporation in the Seventeenth Century to the Present Time. Including a Detailed Report of the Company's Proceedings for the Civilization and Conversion of Indians, Blacks, and Pagans in the Dominion of Canada, British Columbia, the West Indies, and S. Africa during the Two Years 1869–1870. London: Taylor, 1871.

Hitchins, Fred. *The Colonial Land and Emigration Commission, 1840–78.* Philadelphia: University of Pennsylvania Press, 1931.

Hodgins, Bruce W., and Robert C. Edwards. "Federalism and the Politics of Ontario, 1867–80." In *Federalism in Canada and Australia: The Early Years*, ed. Bruce W. Hodgins, Don Wright, and W.H. Heick, 61–96. Waterloo: Wilfrid Laurier University Press, 1978.

Hopkins, A.G. "Informal Empire in Argentina: An Alternative View." *Journal of Latin American Studies* 26, 2 (1994): 469–84.

Hornby, Jim. *Black Islanders: Prince Edward Island's Historical Black Community*. Charlottetown: Institute of Island Studies, 1991.

Hudson, Peter James. "Imperial Designs: The Royal Bank of Canada in the Caribbean." *Race and Class* 52, 1 (2010): 33–48.

Hunt-Kennedy, Stefanie. *Between Fitness and Death: Disability and Slavery in the Caribbean*. Urbana: University of Illinois Press, 2020.

Ince, Onur Ulas. "Capitalism, Colonization, and Contractual Dispossession: Wakefield's Letters from Sydney." APSA 2012 Annual Meeting Paper, July 13, 2012. https://papers.ssrn.com/sol3/papers.cfm?abstract_id=2105112.

–. *Colonial Capitalism and the Dilemmas of Liberalism*. Oxford: Oxford University Press, 2018.

Innis, Harold. "The Penetrative Powers of the Price System." *Canadian Journal of Economics and Political Science* 4, 3 (1938): 299–319.

Ireland, John. "John H. Dunn and the Bankers." *Ontario History* 62 (1970): 83–100.

Ishiguro, Laura. "Growing Up and Grown Up … in Our Future City: Discourses of Childhood and Settler Futurity in Colonial British Columbia." *BC Studies* 190 (2016): 15–37.

–. "Histories of Settler Colonialism: Considering New Currents." *BC Studies* 190 (2016): 5–14.

Itzkowitz, David C. "Fair Enterprise or Extravagant Speculation: Investment, Speculation, and Gambling in Victorian England." *Victorian Studies* 45, 1 (2002): 121–47.

Jarvis, Anna K.G. "Murder, Manslaughter, or Justified Retribution? Tom Williams, Mi'kmaw Law, and Colonial Justice on Prince Edward Island, 1839." *Acadiensis* 51, 1 (2022): 39–65.

Jenkins, Destin. *Bonds of Inequality: Debt and the Making of the American City*. Chicago: University of Chicago Press, 2021.

Johnson, Michele A., and Funké Aladejebi, eds. *Unsettling the Great White North: Black Canadian History*. Toronto: University of Toronto Press, 2022.

Johnston, A.B.J., and Jesse Francis. *Ni'n na L'nu: The Mi'kmaq of Prince Edward Island*. Charlottetown: Acorn Press, 2013.

Jones, Esyllt. *Influenza 1918: Disease, Death and Struggle in Winnipeg*. Toronto: University of Toronto Press, 2007.

Joshi, Priti. "Edwin Chadwick's Self-Fashioning: Professionalism, Masculinity, and the Victorian Poor." *Victorian Literature and Culture* 32, 2 (2004): 353–70.

Justice, Daniel Heath, and Sean Carleton. "Truth before Reconciliation: 8 Ways to Identify and Confront Residential School Denialism." *The Conversation*, August 5, 2021, https://theconversation.com/truth-before-reconciliation-8-ways-to-identify-and-confront-residential-school-denialism-164692.

Karr, Clarence. *The Canada Land Company: The Early Years. An Experiment in Colonization, 1823–1843*. Ottawa: Love Printing Services, 1974.

Karuka, Manu. *Empire's Tracks: Indigenous Nations, Chinese Workers, and the Transcontinental Railway*. Oakland: University of California Press, 2019.

Kauanui, J. Kēhaulani. *Paradoxes of Hawaiian Sovereignty: Land, Sex, and the Colonial Politics of State Nationalism*. Durham, NC: Duke University Press, 2018.

Kelley, Robin D.G. "What Did Cedric Robinson Mean by Racial Capitalism?" *Boston Review*, January 12, 2017. https://www.bostonreview.net/articles/robin-d-g-kelley-introduction-race-capitalism-justice/.

Kelm, Mary-Ellen, and Keith D. Smith. *Talking Back to the Indian Act: Critical Readings in Settler Colonial Histories*. Toronto: University of Toronto Press, 2018.

Kennedy, Dane. *The Magic Mountains: Hill Stations and the British Raj*. Berkeley: University of California Press, 1996.

Kent, Heinz Sigfrid Koplowitz. "The Historical Origins of the Three-Mile Limit." *American Journal of International Law* 48, 4 (1954): 537–53.

Kimmerer, Robin Wall. *Braiding Sweetgrass: Indigenous Wisdom, Scientific Knowledge, and the Teaching of Plants.* Minneapolis: Milkweed, 2013.

King, Thomas. *The Inconvenient Indian: A Curious Account of Native People in North America*. Minneapolis: University of Minnesota Press, 2013.

King, Tiffany Lethabo, Jenell Navarro, and Andrea Smith, eds. *Otherwise Worlds: Against Settler Colonialism and Anti-Blackness*. Durham, NC: Duke University Press, 2020.

Kittrell, Edward. "Wakefield's Scheme of Systematic Colonization and Classical Economics." *American Journal of Economics and Sociology* 32, 1 (1973): 87–112.

Klaver, Claudia C. *A/moral Economics: Classical Political Economy and Cultural Authority in Nineteenth-Century England.* Columbus: Ohio State University Press, 2003.

Klein, Naomi, and Leanne Simpson. "Dancing the World into Being: A Conversation with Idle No More's Leanne Simpson." *Common Dreams*, March 6, 2013. http://www.commondreams.org/views/2013/03/06/dancing-world-being.

La Forest, G.V. *Natural Resources and Public Property under the Canadian Constitution*. Toronto: University of Toronto Press, 1969, reprinted 2017.

Langman, R.G. *Patterns of Settlement in Southern Ontario*. Toronto: McClelland and Stewart, 1971.

Leacock, Stephen. "Responsible Government in the British Colonial System." *American Political Science Review* 1, 3 (1907): 355–92.

Lee, Erica Violet. "In Defence of the Wastelands: A Survival Guide." *Guts*, November 30, 2016. http://gutsmagazine.ca/wastelands/.

Lelièvre, Michelle A. *Unsettling Mobility: Mediating Mi'kmaw Sovereignty in Post-Contact Nova Scotia: The Archaeology of Colonialism in Native North America.* Tucson: University of Arizona Press, 2017.

Leroy, Justin, and Destin Jenkins, eds., *Histories of Racial Capitalism*. New York: Columbia University Press, 2021.

Lester, V. Markham. "The Effect of Southern State Bond Repudiation and British Debt Collection Efforts on Anglo-American Relations, 1840–1940." *Journal of British Studies* 52, 2 (2013): 415–40.

–. *Victorian Insolvency: Bankruptcy, Imprisonment for Debt, and Company Winding-Up in Nineteenth-Century England*. Oxford: Clarendon Press, 1995.

Levine, Philippa. *Prostitution, Race and Politics: Policing Venereal Disease in the British Empire*. Hoboken: Taylor and Francis, 2013.

Little, J.I. *Crofters and Habitants: Settler Society, Economy, and Culture in a Quebec Township, 1848–1881*. Montreal and Kingston: McGill-Queen's University Press, 1991.

–. *Nationalism, Capitalism, and Colonization in Nineteenth-Century Quebec: The Upper St Francis District*. Montreal and Kingston: McGill-Queen's University Press, 1989.

Livingston, Walter Ross. *Responsible Government in Prince Edward Island: A Triumph of Self-Government under the Crown*. Iowa City: University of Iowa Press, 1931.

Longley, Ronald Stewart. "Emigration and the Crisis of 1837 in Upper Canada." *Canadian Historical Review* 17, 1 (1936): 29–40.

Lowe, Lisa. *The Intimacies of Four Continents*. Durham, NC: Duke University Press, 2015.

Luby, Brittany. *Dammed: The Politics of Loss and Survival in Anishinaabe Territory*. Winnipeg: University of Manitoba Press, 2020.

Lux, Maureen K. "Care for the 'Racially Careless': Indian Hospitals in the Canadian West, 1920–1950s." *Canadian Historical Review* 91, 3 (2010): 407–34.

Lydon, Jane. "A Secret Longing for a Trade in Human Flesh: The Decline of British Slavery and the Making of the Settler Colonies." *History Workshop Journal* 90 (2020): 189–210.

Lytwyn, Victor. "Waterworld: The Aquatic Territory of the Great Lakes First Nations." *Gin Das Winan: Documenting Aboriginal History in Ontario* 14 (1996): 14–28.

Macdonald, Edward. "The Yankee Gale, the August Gale and Popular Culture on Prince Edward Island: A Meditation on Memory." *Dalhousie Review* 90, 1 (2010): 95–110.

MacDonald, Norman. *Canada, 1763–1841: Immigration and Settlement: The Administration of the Imperial Land Regulations.* London: Longmans, Green, 1939.

Macdonell, Cameron. *Ghost Storeys: Ralph Adams Cram, Modern Gothic Media, and Deconstructive Microhistory at a Canadian Church.* Montreal and Kingston: McGill-Queen's University Press, 2017.

MacEachern, Alan Andrew. "Theophilus Stewart and the Plight of the Micmac." *Island Magazine* 28 (Fall-Winter 1990): 3–11.

MacKinnon, Frank. "Some Peculiarities of Cabinet Government in Prince Edward Island." *Canadian Journal of Economics and Political Science/Revue canadienne d'économique et de science politique* 15, 3 (1949): 310–21.

MacNutt, William Stewart. "Political Advance and Social Reform, 1842–1861." In *Canada's Smallest Province: A History of Prince Edward Island,* ed. Francis W. Bolger, 115–34. Charlottetown: Prince Edward Island Centennial Commission, 1973.

Mahomes, Ambria D. "'You Should Have Said Something': Exploring the Ways That History, Implicit Bias, and Stereotypes Inform the Current Trends of Black Women Dying in Childbirth." *University of San Francisco Law Review* 55 (2020): 17–30.

Manning, Helen Taft. "E.G. Wakefield and the Beauharnois Canal." *Canadian Historical Review* 48, 1 (1967): 1–25.

Marquis, Greg. "The 'Irish Model' and Nineteenth-Century Canadian Policing." *Journal of Imperial and Commonwealth History* 25, 2 (1997): 193–218.

Marsden, Susan, and Robert Galois. "The Tsimshian, the Hudson's Bay Company, and the Geopolitics of the Northwest Coast Fur Trade, 1787–1840." *Canadian Geographer/Le Géographe canadien* 39, 2 (1995): 169–83.

Martin, Bonnie. "Neighbor-to-Neighbor Capitalism: Local Credit Networks and the Mortgaging of Slaves." In *Slavery's Capitalism: A New History of American*

Economic Development, ed. Sven Beckert and Seth Rockman, 107–21. Philadelphia: University of Pennsylvania Press, 2016.

–. "Slavery's Invisible Engine: Mortgaging Human Property." *Journal of Southern History* 76, 4 (2010): 817–66.

Martin, Chester. *Dominion Lands Policy*, ed. Lewis H. Thomas. Toronto: McClelland and Stewart, 1973.

Martin, Ged. *Britain and the Origins of Canadian Confederation, 1837–67*. Vancouver: UBC Press, 1995.

–. *The Durham Report and British Policy: A Critical Essay*. Cambridge: Cambridge University Press, 1972.

Marx, Karl. *Capital*. Vol. 1. Translated by Ben Fowkes. New York: Penguin Classics, 1990.

Masters, Donald C. *The Reciprocity Treaty of 1854: Its History, Its Relation to British Colonial and Foreign Policy and to the Development of Canadian Fiscal Autonomy*. Toronto: McClelland and Stewart, 2014. Originally published London: Longmans, Green, 1937.

Maynard, Robyn. "Police Abolition/Black Revolt." *TOPIA: Canadian Journal of Cultural Studies* 41 (2020): 70–78.

Maynard, Robyn, and Leanne Betasamosake Simpson. *Rehearsals for Living*. Toronto: Vintage Canada, 2022.

Mbembe, Achille. *Necropolitics*. Translated by Steve Corcoran. Durham, NC: Duke University Press, 2019.

McCalla, Douglas. *Planting the Province: The Economic History of Upper Canada, 1784–1870*. Toronto: University of Toronto Press, 1993.

McCallum, Mary Jane Logan, and Adele Perry. *Structures of Indifference: An Indigenous Life and Death in a Canadian City*. Winnipeg: University of Manitoba Press, 2018.

McClintock, Anne. *Imperial Leather: Race, Gender, and Sexuality in the Colonial Contest*. New York: Routledge, 1995.

McKim, Denis. "Upper Canadian Thermidor: The Family Compact and the Counter Revolutionary Atlantic." *Ontario History* 106, 2 (2014): 235–62.

McKittrick, Katherine. *Demonic Grounds: Black Women and the Cartographies of Struggle*. Minneapolis: University of Minnesota Press, 2006.

–., ed. *Sylvia Wynter: On Being Human as Praxis*. Durham, NC: Duke University Press, 2015.

McNab, David T. "Herman Merivale and Colonial Office Indian Policy in the Mid-Nineteenth Century." In *As Long as the Sun Shines and Water Flows: A Reader in Canadian Native Studies*, ed. Ian A.L. Getty and Antoine S. Lussier, 85–103. Vancouver: UBC Press, 1983.

–. "Herman Merivale and the Native Question, 1837–1861." *Albion* 9, 4 (1977): 359–84.

McNairn, Jeffrey L. "'The Common Sympathies of Our Nature': Moral Sentiments, Emotional Economies, and Imprisonment for Debt in Upper Canada." *Histoire Sociale/Social History* 49, 98 (2016): 49–71.

–. "Incorporating Contributory Democracy: Self-Taxation and Self-Government in Upper Canada." In *Constant Struggle: Histories of Canadian Democratization*, ed. Julien Mauduit and Jennifer Tunnicliffe, 148–71. Montreal and Kingston: McGill-Queen's University Press, 2021.

Meister, Daniel R. *The Racial Mosaic: A Pre-History of Canadian Multiculturalism.* Montreal and Kingston: McGill-Queen's University Press, 2021.

Merivale, Herman. *Introduction to a Course of Lectures on Colonization and Colonies, Begun in March 1839.* London: Longman, Orme, Brown, Green, and Longmans, 1839.

Meshnick, Steven, and Mary Dobson. "The History of Antimalarial Drugs." In *Antimalarial Chemotherapy*, ed. Philip J. Rosenthal, 15–25. Totowa, NJ: Humana Press, 2001.

Metcalf, Thomas R. *Ideologies of the Raj*. Cambridge: Cambridge University Press, 1995.

Meuret, Denis. "A Political Genealogy of Political Economy." *Economy and Society* 17, 2 (1988): 225–50.

Michie, Ranald. *The Global Securities Market: A History.* Oxford: Oxford University Press, 2006.

–. *The London Stock Exchange: A History.* Oxford: Oxford University Press, 2001.

Mill, John Stuart. "The Emigration Bill." *Examiner*, February 27, 1831. In *Collected Works of John Stuart Mill*. Vols. 22–25, *Newspaper Writings*, ed. John M. Robson and Ann P. Robson, 270–73. Toronto: University of Toronto Press, 1986.

–. "The New Colony" (1). *Examiner*, June 29, 1834. In *Collected Works of John Stuart Mill*. Vols. 22–25, *Newspaper Writings*, ed. John M. Robson and Ann P. Robson, 733–34. Toronto: University of Toronto Press, 1986.

–. "The New Colony" (2). *Examiner*, July 6, 1834. In *Collected Works of John Stuart Mill*. Vols. 22–25, *Newspaper Writings*, ed. John M. Robson and Ann P. Robson, 735–37. Toronto: University of Toronto Press, 1986.

–. *Principles of Political Economy with Some of Their Application to Social Philosophy.* London: Longmans, Green, Reader, and Dyer, 1871.

Miller, J.R. "Compact, Contract, Covenant: Canada's Treaty-Making Tradition." The Michael Keenan Memorial Lecture 2003, St. Thomas More College. Library and Archives Canada. https://www.collectionscanada.gc.ca/obj/g4/11/780973431612_13244st.pdf.

Miller, Robert J., Jacinta Ruru, Larissa Behrendt, and Tracey Lindberg. *Discovering Indigenous Lands: The Doctrine of Discovery in the English Colonies.* Oxford: Oxford University Press, 2010.

Mills, John. *A Paper Read before the Economic Section of the National Social Science Association at Manchester*. London: Simpkin, Marshall, 1866.

Moreton-Robinson, Aileen. *The White Possessive: Property, Power, and Indigenous Sovereignty*. Minneapolis: University of Minnesota Press, 2015.

Morgan, Jennifer L. *Laboring Women: Reproduction and Gender in New World Slavery*. Philadelphia: University of Pennsylvania Press, 2011.

–. *Reckoning with Slavery: Gender, Kinship, and Capitalism in the Early Black Atlantic*. Durham, NC: Duke University Press, 2021.

Morishima, Michio. *Ricardo's Economics: A General Equilibrium Theory of Distribution and Growth*. Cambridge: Cambridge University Press, 1989.

Morrison, Hugh M. "The Background of the Free Land Homestead Law of 1872." *Rapports annuels de la Société historique du Canada* 14, 1 (1935): 58–66.

Morton, W.L. *The Critical Years: The Union of British North America, 1857–1873*. Toronto: McClelland and Stewart, 1964.

Mosby, Ian. "Administering Colonial Science: Nutrition Research and Human Biomedical Experimentation in Aboriginal Communities and Residential Schools, 1942–1952." *Histoire Sociale/Social History* 46, 1 (2013): 145–72.

Muir, James. *Law, Debt, and Merchant Power: The Civil Courts of Eighteenth-Century Halifax*. Toronto: University of Toronto Press, 2016.

Mulcaire, Terry. "Public Credit; or, the Feminization of Virtue in the Marketplace." *Publications of the Modern Language Association of America* 114, 5 (1999): 1029–42.

Naylor, R.T. *The History of Canadian Business, 1867–1914*. Toronto: Lorimer, 1975.

Neal, Larry. *The Rise of Financial Capitalism: International Capital Markets in the Age of Reason*. Cambridge: Cambridge University Press, 1990.

Nelson, Charmaine. *Slavery, Geography and Empire in Nineteenth-Century Marine Landscapes of Montreal and Jamaica*. London: Routledge, 2016.

Nerbas, Don. *Dominion of Capital: The Politics of Big Business and the Crisis of the Canadian Bourgeoisie, 1914–1947*. Toronto: University of Toronto Press, 2013.

New, Chester. *Lord Durham, a Biography of John George Lambton, First Earl of Durham*. Oxford: Clarendon Press, 1929.

–. "Lord Durham and the British Background of His Report." *Canadian Historical Review* 20, 2 (1939): 119–35.

Nichols, Robert. *Theft Is Property! Dispossession and Critical Theory*. Durham, NC: Duke University Press, 2020.

Nixon, Rob. *Slow Violence and the Environmentalism of the Poor*. Cambridge: Harvard University Press, 2011.

North, D.C., and B.R. Weingast. "Constitutions and Commitment: The Evolution of Institutions Governing Public Choice in Seventeenth-Century England." *Journal of Economic History* 49, 4 (1989): 803–32.

Officer, Lawrence H., and Lawrence B. Smith. "The Canadian-American Reciprocity Treaty of 1855 to 1866." *Journal of Economic History* 28, 4 (1968): 598–623.

Oosterhoff, A.H. "The Law of Mortmain: An Historical and Comparative Review." *University of Toronto Law Journal* 27, 3 (1977): 258–61.

Ott, Julia. "Slaves: The Capital That Made Capitalism." Robert L. Heilbroner Center for Capitalism Studies, August 20, 2015. https://capitalismstudies.org/julia-ott-slaves-the-capital-that-made-capitalism/.

Owens, Deirdre Cooper. *Medical Bondage: Race, Gender, and the Origins of American Gynecology*. Athens: University of Georgia Press, 2017.

Palmater, Pamela. "Genocide, Indian Policy, and Legislated Elimination of Indians in Canada." *Aboriginal Policy Studies* 3, 3 (2014): 27–54.

Pappe, O. "Wakefield and Marx." *Economic History Review* 4, 1 (1951): 88–97.

Park, K-Sue. "Money, Mortgages, and the Conquest of America." *Law and Social Inquiry* 41, 4 (2016): 1006–35.

Parkinson, Giles. "War, Peace and the Rise of the London Stock Market." In *The Political Economy of Empire in the Early Modern World*, ed. Sophus Reinert and Røge Pernille, 131–46. London: Palgrave Macmillan, 2013.

Pasternak, Shiri. "Assimilation and Partition: How Settler Colonialism and Racial Capitalism Co-produce the Borders of Indigenous Economies." *South Atlantic Quarterly* 119, 2 (2020): 301–24.

–. "Canada Is a Bad Company: Police as Colonial Mercenaries for State and Capital." In *Disarm, Defund, Dismantle: Police Abolition in Canada*, ed. Shiri Pasternak, Kevin Walby, and Abby Stadnyk, 66–73. Toronto: Between the Lines, 2022.

–. *Grounded Authority: The Algonquins of Barriere Lake against the State.* Minneapolis: University of Minnesota Press, 2017.

–. "How Capitalism Will Save Colonialism: The Privatization of Reserve Lands in Canada." *Antipode* 47, 1 (2015): 179–96.

–. "Jurisdiction and Settler Colonialism: Where Do Laws Meet?" *Canadian Journal of Law and Society/La Revue Canadienne Droit et Société* 29, 2 (2014): 145–61.

Pasternak, Shiri, and Tia Dafnos. "How Does a Settler State Secure the Circuitry of Capital?" *Environment and Planning D: Society and Space* 36, 4 (2018): 739–57.

Paul, William Benoit. "Big Water Drowned the World." In *Mi'kmaq and the Crown: Understanding Treaties in Maritime Canadian History*, ed. Keptin John Joe Sark, 4–5. 2000.

Peace, Thomas. "Immigration and Sovereignty: Lessons from the Distant Past." *Journal of the Royal Nova Scotia Historical Society* 19 (2016): 54–66.

–. *The Slow Rush of Colonization: Spaces of Power in the Maritime Peninsula, 1680–1790*. Vancouver: UBC Press, 2023.

Peña, Lorgia García. *Community as Rebellion: A Syllabus for Surviving Academia as a Woman of Color*. Chicago: Haymarket Books, 2022.

Perelman, Michael. *The Invention of Capitalism: Classical Political Economy and the Secret History of Primitive Accumulation*. Durham, NC: Duke University Press, 2000.

Perry, Adele. "Designing Dispossession: The Select Committee on the Hudson's Bay Company, Fur-Trade Governance, Indigenous Peoples and Settler Possibility." In *Indigenous Communities and Settler Colonialism: Land Holding, Loss and Survival in an Interconnected World*, ed. Laidlaw Zoë and Alan Lester, 158–72. London: Palgrave Macmillan, 2015.

–. *On the Edge of Empire: Gender, Race, and the Making of British Columbia, 1849–1871*. Toronto: University of Toronto Press, 2001.

Perry, Harvey J. *Taxes, Tariffs, and Subsidies: A History of Canadian Fiscal Development*. Toronto: University of Toronto Press, 1955.

Perry, James Roy. *Public Debts in Canada*. Toronto: University of Toronto, University Library, 1898. https://www.canadiana.ca/view/oocihm.11834/1.

Peters, Mercedes. "Settler Forgetting in Saulnierville: The Sipekne'katik Mi'kmaw Fishery as Reminder." Network in Canadian History and Environment, October 19, 2020. https://niche-canada.org/2020/10/19/settler-forgetting-in-saulnierville-the-sipeknekatik-mikmaw-fishery-as-reminder/.

Peters, Richard, and Douglas R. Emery. "The Role of Negative Numbers in the Development of Double Entry Bookkeeping." *Journal of Accounting Research* 16, 2 (1978): 424–26.

Pike, Douglas. "Introduction of the Real Property Act in South Australia." *Adelaide Law Review* 1 (1960): 169–89.

Piterberg, Gabriel, and Lorenzo Veracini. "Wakefield, Marx, and the World Turned Inside Out." *Journal of Global History* 10, 3 (2015): 457–78.

Piva, Michael J. *The Borrowing Process: Public Finance in the Province of Canada, 1840–1867*. Ottawa: University of Ottawa Press, 1992.

–. "Financing the Union: The Upper Canadian Debt and Financial Administration in the Canadas, 1837–1845." *Journal of Canadian Studies* 25, 4 (1991): 82–98.

Polanyi, Karl. *The Great Transformation: The Political and Economic Origins of Our Time*. Boston: Beacon Press, 2001.

Poovey, Mary. *Genres of the Credit Economy: Mediating Value in Eighteenth- and Nineteenth-Century Britain*. Chicago: University of Chicago Press, 2008.

Price, Melanie. "Fire Destroys Commercial Lobster Plant in New Edinburgh, N.S." *CTV News*, November 26, 2021. https://atlantic.ctvnews.ca/fire-destroys-commercial-lobster-plant-in-new-edinburgh-n-s-1.5682623.

Prichard, M.F. Lloyd. "Wakefield Changes His Mind about the 'Sufficient Price.'" *International Review of Social History* 8, 2 (1963): 251–69.

Rae, John, and John Stuart Mill. "John Rae and John Stuart Mill: A Correspondence." *Economica* 10, 39 (1943): 253–55.

Rand, Silas Tertius. *A First Reading Book in the Micmac Language: Comprising the Micmac Numerals, and the Names of the Different Kinds of Beasts, Birds, Fishes, Trees etc*. Halifax: Nova Scotia Printing, 1875.

Ransom, Roger L. "Canals and Development: A Discussion of the Issues." *American Economic Review* 54, 3 (1964): 365–76.

Razack, Sherene. "Introduction: When Place Becomes Race." In *Race, Space and the Law: Unmapping a White Settler Society*, ed. Sherene Razack, 1–20. Toronto: Between the Lines Press, 2002.

Reid, John G. "Empire, the Maritime Colonies, and the Supplanting of Mi'kma'ki/ Wulstukwik, 1780–1820." *Acadiensis* 38, 2 (Summer-Autumn 2009): 78–97.

Reid, Stuart Johnson. *Life and Letters of the First Earl of Durham, 1792–1840*. 2 vols. London: Longmans, Green, 1906.

Reynolds, Jim. *Canada and Colonialism: An Unfinished History.* Vancouver: UBC Press, 2024.

Robertson, Ian Ross. "Political Realignment in Pre-Confederation Prince Edward Island, 1863–1870." *Acadiensis* 15, 1 (1985): 35–58.

–. *The Prince Edward Island Land Commission of 1860*. Fredericton, NB: Acadiensis Press, 1988.

–. *The Tenant League of Prince Edward Island, 1864–1867: Leasehold Tenure in the New World.* Toronto: University of Toronto Press, 1996.

Robinson, Cedric J. *Black Marxism: The Making of the Black Radical Tradition*. Chapel Hill: University of North Carolina Press, 2000.

Robinson, Cedric J., and Ruth Wilson Gilmore. *Cedric J. Robinson: On Racial Capitalism, Black Internationalism, and Cultures of Resistance*. London: Pluto Press, 2019.

Rosenthal, Caitlin. *Accounting for Slavery: Masters and Management*. Cambridge, MA: Harvard University Press, 2018.

Ross, Shane. "Mill River Appeal Raises Wider Issue of Aboriginal Rights over Private Land, Lawyer Says." *CBC News,* May 13, 2019. https://www.cbc.ca/news/canada/prince-edward-island/pei-mill-river-aboriginal-land-claim-1.5129457.

Roy, Edmond J. *Histoire de la seigneurie de Lauzon,* 5 vols. Lévis: Mercier et cie, 1897–1904. https://collections.banq.qc.ca/ark:/52327/2022757.

Roy, Monique. "Coastal Scourge." Canada Foundation for Innovation, March 13, 2024. https://www.innovation.ca/projects-results/research-stories/coastal-scourge.

Rück, Daniel. *The Laws and the Land: The Settler Colonial Invasion of Kahnawà:ke in Nineteenth-Century Canada*. Vancouver: UBC Press, 2021.

Rudin, Ronald. "Boosting the French Canadian Town: Municipal Government and Urban Growth in Quebec, 1850-1900." *Urban History Review* 11, 1 (1982): 1–10.

Rushforth, Brett. *Bonds of Alliance: Indigenous and Atlantic Slaveries in New France*. Chapel Hill: University of North Carolina Press, 2012.

Ryan, Carolyn. "'We're Going to Be Welcoming the World Here,' Lennox Island Chief Says of New Park Funding." *CBC,* April 17, 2024. https://www.cbc.ca/news/canada/prince-edward-island/pei-indigenous-economic-funding-budget-1.7176455.

Said, Edward. *Culture and Imperialism*. New York: Vintage, 1993.

Saito, Kohei. *Marx in the Anthropocene: Towards the Idea of Degrowth Communism*. Cambridge: Cambridge University Press, 2022.

Samaraweera, Vijaya. *The Commission of Eastern Enquiry in Ceylon, 1822–1837: A Study of a Royal Commission of Colonial Enquiry*. Oxford: University of Oxford Press, 1969.

–. "Governor Sir Robert Wilmot Horton and the Reforms of 1833 in Ceylon." *Historical Journal* 15, 2 (1972): 209–28.

Samson, Daniel. *The Spirit of Industry and Improvement: Liberal Government and Rural-Industrial Society, Nova Scotia, 1790–1862*. Montreal and Kingston: McGill-Queen's University Press, 2014.

Saunders, Stanley A. "The Maritime Provinces and the Reciprocity Treaty." In *Historical Essays on the Atlantic Provinces*, ed. George A. Rawlyk, 161–78. Toronto: McClelland and Stewart, 2014.

–. "The Reciprocity Treaty of 1854: A Regional Study." *Canadian Journal of Economics and Political Science/Revue canadienne d'économique et science politique* 2, 1 (1936): 41–53.

Schabas, Margaret. *A World Ruled by Number: William Stanley Jevons and the Rise of Mathematical Economics*. Princeton: Princeton University Press, 1990.

Schneider, Sabine. "The Politics of Last Resort: Lending and the Overend and Gurney Crisis of 1866." *Economic History Review* 75 (2022): 579–600.

Schrauwers, Albert. "The Liberal Corporate Order and the Market Transition in Colonial Upper Canada, 1825–1841." *Settler Colonial Studies* 11, 4 (2021): 533–52.

–. "'A Terrible Engine in the Hands of the Provincial Administration': The Corporate Franchise State and Joint-Stock Democracy in the Last of the Atlantic Revolutions." In *Constant Struggle: Histories of Canadian Democratization*, ed. Julien Mauduit and Jennifer Tunnicliffe, 116–47. Montreal and Kingston: McGill-Queen's University Press, 2021.

Scrope, George Poulett, ed. *Memoir of the Life of the Right Honourable Charles Lord Sydenham, G.C.B. with a Narrative of His Administration in Canada*. London: John Murray, 1843.

Seeley, John Robert. *The Expansion of England*. London: Macmillan and Co., 1890.

Sharma, Nandita Rani. *Home Economics: Nationalism and the Making of 'Migrant Workers' in Canada*. Toronto: University of Toronto Press, 2006.

Shaw, Alan George Lewers. "British Attitudes to the Colonies, ca. 1820–1850." *Journal of British Studies* 9, 1 (1969): 71–95.

Short, Damien. "Reconciliation and the Problem of Internal Colonialism." *Journal of Intercultural Studies* 26, 3 (2005): 267–82.

Shortt, Adam. "The Financial Development of British North America, 1840–1867." In *The Cambridge History of the British Empire*. Vol. 6, *Canada and Newfoundland*, ed. J. Holland Rose, A.P. Newton, and E.A. Benians, 369–95. Cambridge: Cambridge University Press, 1930.

Simmons, Deidre. *Keepers of the Record: The History of the Hudson's Bay Company Archives*. Montreal and Kingston: McGill-Queen's University Press, 2007.

Simmons, Kristen. "Settler Atmospherics." Society for Cultural Anthropology, November 20, 2017. https://culanth.org/fieldsights/settler-atmospherics.

Simon, Matthew. "The Pattern of New British Portfolio Foreign Investment, 1865–1914." In *Capital Movements and Economic Development,* ed. John Adler and Paul Kuznets, 33–70. London: Stockton Press, 1967.

Simpson, Audra. *Mohawk Interruptus: Political Life across the Borders of Settler States*. Durham, NC: Duke University Press, 2014.

–. "The Ruse of Consent and the Anatomy of 'Refusal': Cases from Indigenous North America and Australia." *Postcolonial Studies* 20, 1 (2017): 18–33.

Simpson, Leanne Betasamosake. "Looking after Gdoo-naaganinaa: Precolonial Nishnaabeg Diplomatic and Treaty Relationships." *Wicazo Sa Review* 23, 2 (2008): 29–42.

Six Nations of the Grand River. "Land Rights: A Global Solution for the Six Nations of the Grand River." 2019. https://iaac-aeic.gc.ca/050/documents/p80100/130877E.pdf.

Smallwood, Stephanie. "What Slavery Tells Us about Marx." In *Race Capitalism Justice,* ed. Walter Johnson and Robin D.G. Kelley, 78–82. Cambridge, MA: Boston Review, 2017.

Smith, Andrew. *British Businessmen and Canadian Confederation: Constitution Making in an Era of Anglo Globalization*. Montreal and Kingston: McGill-Queen's University Press, 2008.

Smith, Donald. "Egerton Ryerson Doesn't Deserve an Anti-Indigenous Label." *Globe and Mail,* July 5, 2017, https://www.theglobeandmail.com/opinion/egerton-ryerson-doesnt-deserve-an-anti-indigenous-label/article35558895/.

–. *Sacred Feathers: The Reverend Peter Jones (Kahkewaquonaby) and the Mississauga Indians*. Toronto: University of Toronto Press, 1987.

Smith, Keith D. *Liberalism, Surveillance, and Resistance: Indigenous Communities in Western Canada, 1877–1927*. Edmonton: Athabasca University Press, 2009.

Smith, Linda Tuhiwai. *Decolonizing Methodologies: Research and Indigenous Peoples.* 2nd ed. London: Zed Books, 2012.

Smith, Peter J., ed. *Canada's Origins: Liberal, Tory, or Republican?* Montreal and Kingston: McGill-Queen's University Press, 1995.

–. "The Ideological Origins of Canadian Confederation." *Canadian Journal of Political Science/Revue Canadienne de Science politique* 20, 1 (1987): 3–30.

Spufford, Peter. "From Antwerp and Amsterdam to London: The Decline of Financial Centres in Europe." *De economist* 154 (2006): 143–75.

Stark, Heidi Kiiwetinepinesiik. "Criminal Empire: The Making of the Savage in a Lawless Land." *Theory and Event* 19, 4 (2016).

Stasavage, David. *Public Debt and the Birth of the Democratic State: France and Great Britain, 1688–1789*. Cambridge: Cambridge University Press, 2003.

Stein, Burton. *Thomas Munro: The Origins of the Colonial State and His Vision of Empire*. Oxford: Oxford University Press, 1989.

Stoler, Ann Laura. *Along the Archival Grain: Epistemic Anxieties and Colonial Common Sense*. Princeton: Princeton University Press, 2010.

–. "Colonial Archives and the Arts of Governance." *Archival Science* 2 (2002): 87–109.

Strachan, John. *The Clergy Reserves: Letter from the Lord Bishop of Toronto to the Duke of Newcastle, Her Majesty's Secretary for the Colonies*. Toronto: Churchman Office, 1853.

–. *Remarks on Emigration from the United Kingdom: Addressed to Robert Wilmot Horton, Esq., M.P., Chairman of the Select Committee of Emigration in the Last Parliament*. London: John Murray, 1827.

Sunderland, David. *Managing the British Empire: The Crown Agents, 1833–1914*. London: Royal Historical Society, 2004.

"Supreme Court of Canada Will Not Hear Mi'kmaq Appeal of Mill River Sale." *CBC News,* Prince Edward Island, April 23, 2020. https://www.cbc.ca/news/canadaprince-edward-island/pei-mill-river-resort-crown-land-indigenous-rights-1.5542249.

Sussman, Nathan, and Yishay Yafeh. "Institutional Reforms, Financial Development and Sovereign Debt: Britain, 1690–1790." *Journal of Economic History* 66, 4 (2006): 906–35.

Taylor, Caitlin, Katie Pedersen, and Eric Szeto. "Canada Halts Import of Goods Linked to Forced Labour from China, Malaysia." *CBC News,* November 17, 2021, https://www.cbc.ca/news/canada/canada-stop-forced-labour-imports-1.6252283.

Taylor, Greg. *The Law of the Land: The Advent of the Torrens System in Canada*. Toronto: University of Toronto Press, 2008.

Tennant, Charles. *Letters Forming Part of a Correspondence with Nassau William Senior, Esq: Concerning Systematic Colonization, and the Bill Now before Parliament for Promoting Emigration: Also, a Letter to the Canada Land Company, and a Series of Questions, in Elucidation of the Principles of Colonization*. London: Ridgway, Piccadilly, 1831.

Thomson, Charles Edward Poulett. *Letters from Lord Sydenham, Governor-General of Canada, 1839–1841*. Edited by Paul Knaplund. New York: A.M. Kelley, 1973.

Tillotson, Shirley. *Give and Take: The Citizen-Taxpayer and the Rise of Canadian Democracy*. Vancouver: UBC Press, 2017.

Timberlake, Richard H. *Monetary Policy in the United States: An Intellectual and Institutional History.* Chicago: University of Chicago Press, 1993.

Tough, Frank J. "'A Great Inheritance and a Great Property': The Hudson's Bay Company, English Finance Capital and the Fertile Belt 1." *Canadian Issues* (Spring 2021): 24–31.

The Trial of Edward Gibbon Wakefield, William Wakefield, and Frances Wakefield, Indicted with One Edward Thevenot, a Servant, for a Conspiracy, and for the Abduction of Miss Ellen Turner, the Only Child and Heiress of William Turner, Esq, of Shrigley Park, in the County of Chester. London: John Murray, 1827.

Trollope, Anthony. *Australia and New Zealand.* 2 vols. London: Chapman and Hall, 1873.

Trotter, Reginald. *Canadian Federation: Its Origins and Achievement, a Study in Nation Building*. Toronto: Dent, 1924.

Trudel, Marcel. *L'esclavage au Canada Français: Histoire et conditions de l'esclavage*. Quebec City: Les presses universitaires Laval, 1960.

Tuck, Eve, Haliehana Stepetin, Rebecca Beaulne-Stuebing, and Jo Billows. "Visiting as an Indigenous Feminist Practice." *Gender and Education* 34, 5 (2022): 144–55.

Tuck, Eve, and K. Wayne Yang. "Decolonization Is Not a Metaphor." *Decolonization: Indigeneity, Education and Society* 1, 1 (2012): 1–40.

Upton, L.S.F. "Indians and Islanders: The Micmacs in Colonial Prince Edward Island." *Acadiensis* 6, 1 (1976): 21–42.

Vedoveli, Paula. "Information Brokers and the Making of the Baring Crisis, 1857–1890." *Financial History Review* 25, 3 (2018): 357–86.

Veracini, Lorenzo. "Introducing: Settler Colonial Studies." *Settler Colonial Studies* 1, 1 (2011): 1–12.

–. *The Settler Colonial Present*. Basingstoke, UK: Palgrave Macmillan, 2015.

Vosburgh, Michelle. "The Crown Lands Department, the Government, and the Settlers of McNab Township, Canada West." *Ontario History* 100, 1 (2008): 80–99.

Vowel, Chelsea. *Indigenous Writes: A Guide to First Nations, Métis, and Inuit Issues in Canada*. Winnipeg: HighWater Press, 2016.

Waite, Peter B. *The Life and Times of Confederation, 1864–1867: Politics, Newspapers, and the Union of British North America*. 3rd ed. Toronto: Robin Brass Studio, 2001.

Wakefield, Edward Gibbon. *England and America: A Comparison of the Social and Political State of Both Nations in Two Volumes*. London: Richard Bentley, 1833.

–. *A Letter from Sydney, the Principal Town of Australia: Together with the Outline of a System of Colonization*. Edited by Robert Gouger. London: Joseph Cross, 1829.

–. *A Letter from Sydney and Other Writings*. London: J.M. Dent and Sons, 1929.

–. *A View of the Art of Colonization: With Present Reference to the British Empire in Letters between a Statesman and a Colonist*. London: John W. Parker, 1849.

Wakefield, Felix. *Colonial Surveying with a View to the Disposal of Waste Land in a Report to the New-Zealand Company*. London: John W. Parker, 1849.

Walcott, Rinaldo. *On Property: Policing, Prisons, and the Call for Abolition*. Toronto: Biblioasis, 2021.

Walls, Martha. "Confederation and the Maritime First Nations." *Acadiensis* 46, 2 (2017): 155–76.

Ward, Churchill, ed. *Marxism and Native Americans*. Boston: South End Press, 1983.

Watkins, F.W. "Taxes 1670–1960." *Canadian Tax Journal* 8 (1960): 162–70.

Weaver, John C. *The Great Land Rush and the Making of the Modern World, 1650–1900*. Montreal and Kingston: McGill-Queen's University Press, 2003.

–. "While Equity Slumbered: Creditor Advantage, a Capitalist Land Market, and Upper Canada's Missing Court." *Osgoode Hall Law Journal* 28 (1990): 871–914.

Whetung, Madeline. "(En)gendering Shoreline Law: Nishnaabeg Relational Politics along the Trent Severn Waterway." *Global Environmental Politics* 19, 3 (2019): 16–32.

White, Richard. *Railroaded: The Transcontinentals and the Making of Modern America*. New York: W.W. Norton, 2011.

Whitehead, Joshua. *Making Love with the Land*. Toronto: Knopf Canada, 2022.

Whitehead, Judy. "John Locke and the Governance of India's Landscape: The Category of Wasteland in Colonial Revenue and Forest Legislation." *Economic and Political Weekly* 45, 50 (2010): 83–93.

Whitfield, Harvey Amani. *North to Bondage: Loyalist Slavery in the Maritimes*. Vancouver: UBC Press, 2016.

Wicken, William C. *Mi'kmaq Treaties on Trial: History, Land and Donald Marshall Junior*. Toronto: University of Toronto Press, 2002.

Wildcat, Matthew. "Fearing Social and Cultural Death: Genocide and Elimination in Settler Colonial Canada – An Indigenous Perspective." *Journal of Genocide Research* 17, 4 (2015): 391–409.

Wilkins, Mira. *The History of Foreign Investment in the United States to 1914*. Cambridge: Cambridge University Press, 1989.

Williams, Eric Eustace. *Capitalism and Slavery*. Chapel Hill: University of North Carolina Press, 1994.

Willmott, Kyle. "Taxes, Taxpayers, and Settler Colonialism: Toward a Critical Fiscal Sociology of Tax as White Property." *Law and Society Review* 56, 1 (2022): 6–27.

Wilson, Alan. "The Clergy Reserves: 'Economical Mischiefs' or Sectarian Issue?" *Canadian Historical Review* 42, 4 (1961): 281–99.

Winch, Donald. *Classical Political Economy and Colonies*. Cambridge, MA: Harvard University Press, 1965.

–. "Science and the Legislator: Adam Smith and After." *Economic Journal* 93, 371 (1983): 501–20.

Winks, Robin. *Blacks in Canada*. Montreal and Kingston: McGill-Queen's University Press, 1997.

Wolfe, Patrick. "After the Frontier: Separation and Absorption in US Indian Policy." *Settler Colonial Studies* 1, 1 (2011): 13–51.

–. "Land, Labor, and Difference: Elementary Structures of Race." *American Historical Review* 106, 3 (2001): 866–905.

Woolford, Andrew, and James Gacek. "Genocidal Carcerality and Indian Residential Schools in Canada." *Punishment and Society* 18, 4 (2016): 400–19.

Wynn, Graeme. *Timber Colony: A Historical Geography of Early Nineteenth Century New Brunswick*. Toronto: University of Toronto Press, 1980.

Wynter, Sylvia. "Beyond the Categories of the Master Conception: The Counterdoctrine of the Jamesian Poiesis." In *CLR James's Caribbean*, ed. Paget Henry and Paul Buhle, 63–91. Durham, NC: Duke University Press, 1992.

–. "Unsettling the Coloniality of Being/Power/Truth/Freedom: Towards the Human, after Man, Its Overrepresentation – An Argument." *CR: The New Centennial Review* 3, 3 (2003): 257–337.

Yarr, Kevin. "Mill River Owner Testifies He Trusted Province to Clear Title with Mi'kmaq." *CBC News*, January 16, 2018. https://www.cbc.ca/news/canada/prince-edward-island/pei-mill-river-court-challenge-mi-kmaq-don-macdougall-1.4489229.

Yazzie, Melanie K., and Cutcha Risling Baldy. "Introduction: Indigenous Peoples and the Politics of Water." *Decolonization: Indigeneity, Education and Society* 7, 1 (2018): 25–39.

Yu, Henry. "Reckoning with the Realities of History: The Politics of White Supremacy and the Expansion of Settler Democracy in the Nineteenth and Early Twentieth Centuries." In *Constant Struggle: Histories of Canadian Democratization*, ed. Julien Mauduit and Jennifer Tunnicliffe, 390–421. Montreal and Kingston: McGill-Queen's University Press, 2021.

Index

Note: "(f)" after a page number indicates a figure or map. LPEC stands for London Political Economy Club; LSE, for London Stock Exchange. All statutes are Canadian unless otherwise indicated. The entry "Glyn's Bank" covers the various iterations of this bank under its different names.

Printed and bound in Canada
Set in Sabon next LT Pro and Myriad Pro by Apex CoVantage, LLC
Copyeditor: Deborah Kerr
Proofreader: Kristy Lynn Hankewitz
Indexer: Cheryl Lemmens
Cartographer: Eric Leinberger
Cover designer: John van der Woude
Authorized Representative: Easy Access System Europe – Mustamäe tee 50, 10621 Tallinn, Estonia, gpsr.requests@easproject.com